THE STUDENT'S OXFORD ARISTOTLE

THE
STUDENT'S OXFORD
ARISTOTLE

TRANSLATED INTO ENGLISH UNDER THE EDITORSHIP

OF

W. D. ROSS, M.A., Hon. LL.D. (Edin.)

PROVOST OF ORIEL COLLEGE
HONORARY FELLOW OF MERTON COLLEGE
FELLOW OF THE BRITISH ACADEMY

VOLUME V · ETHICS

ETHICA NICOMACHEA

OXFORD UNIVERSITY PRESS
LONDON   NEW YORK   TORONTO
1942

PREFACE

THE works which have come down to posterity under the name of Aristotle include several which, however important as preserving the Aristotelian tradition, can no longer be supposed to have been written by the master himself. Further, of those which he did write, several are not of decisive importance for the understanding of his philosophy. The present series (which is a selection from *The Works of Aristotle translated into English* under the auspices of the Clarendon Press, Oxford) contains the works which are of central importance for this purpose; though a student who is interested in logic, or biology, or oratory, might be well advised to read also the whole or part of works not included—the *Topics,* the biological works, or the *Rhetoric.* The works that are included are included in their entirety.

Indexes, which (it is hoped) will be of considerable assistance to the student, will be found in the following places: vol. 1, end; vol. 2, after the *Physics,* after the *De Caelo,* after the *De Generatione et Corruptione;* vol. 3, after the *De Anima,* after the *Parva Naturalia;* vol. 4, end; vol. 5, end; vol. 6, after the *Politics,* after the *Poetics.* Readers who know Greek should be informed on what text the translation is based; it is based on Bekker's quarto text (1831), with the following exceptions: *De Caelo* (Prantl, 1881), *Parva Naturalia* (Biehl), *Metaphysics* (Christ, 1895), *Ethics* (Bywater), *Politics* (Immisch), *Poetics* (Bywater, 1909).

W. D. ROSS

ETHICA NICOMACHEA

CONTENTS

BOOK I. THE GOOD FOR MAN

A. *Subject of our inquiry.*

I. 1. All human activities aim at some good : some goods subordinate to others.

2. The science of *the* good for man is politics.

B. *Nature of the science.*

3. We must not expect more precision than the subject-matter admits. The student should have reached years of discretion.

C. *What is the good for man?*

4. It is generally agreed to be happiness, but there are various views as to what happiness is. What is required at the start is an unreasoned conviction about the facts, such as is produced by a good upbringing.

5. Discussion of the popular views that the good is pleasure, honour, wealth ; a fourth kind of life, that of contemplation, deferred for future discussion.

6. Discussion of the philosophical view that there is an Idea of good.

7. The good must be something final and self-sufficient. Definition of happiness reached by considering the characteristic function of man.

8. This definition is confirmed by current beliefs about happiness.

9. Is happiness acquired by learning or habituation, or sent by God or by chance?

10. Should no man be called happy while he lives?

11. Do the fortunes of the living affect the dead?

12. Virtue is praiseworthy, but happiness is above praise.

D. *Kinds of virtue.*

13. Division of the faculties, and resultant division of virtue into intellectual and moral.

BOOKS II-V. MORAL VIRTUE

II. 1—III. 5. GENERAL ACCOUNT

A. *Moral virtue, how produced, in what materials and in what manner exhibited.*

II. 1. It, like the arts, is acquired by repetition of the corresponding acts.

2. These acts cannot be prescribed exactly, but must avoid excess and defect.

3. Pleasure in doing virtuous acts is a sign that the virtuous disposition has been acquired: a variety of considerations show the essential connexion of moral virtue with pleasure and pain.

4. The actions that produce moral virtue are not good in the same sense as those that flow from it: the latter must fulfil certain conditions not necessary in the case of the arts.

B.   *Definition of moral virtue.*

5. Its genus: it is a state of character, not a passion nor a faculty.

6. Its differentia: it is a disposition to choose the mean.

7. This proposition illustrated by reference to the particular virtues.

C.   *Characteristics of the extreme and mean states: practical corollaries.*

8. The extremes are opposed to each other and to the mean.

9. The mean is hard to attain, and is grasped by perception, not by reasoning.

D.   *Inner side of moral virtue: conditions of responsibility for action.*

III. 1. Praise and blame attach to voluntary actions, i.e. actions done (1) not under compulsion, and (2) with knowledge of the circumstances.

2. Moral virtue implies that the action is done (3) by choice ; the object of choice is the result of previous deliberation.

3. The nature of deliberation and its objects: choice is deliberate desire of things in our own power.

4. The object of rational wish is the end, i.e. the good or the apparent good.

5. We are responsible for bad as well as for good actions.

III. 6—V. 11.   THE VIRTUES AND VICES

A.   *Courage.*

6. Courage concerned with the feelings of fear and confidence—strictly speaking, with the fear of death in battle.

7. The motive of courage is the sense of honour: characteristics of the opposite vices, cowardice and rashness.

8. Five kinds of courage improperly so called.

9. Relation of courage to pain and pleasure.

B.   *Temperance.*

10. Temperance is limited to certain pleasures of touch.

11. Characteristics of temperance and its opposites, self-indulgence and 'insensibility'.

12. Self-indulgence more voluntary than cowardice: comparison of the self-indulgent man to the spoilt child.

CONTENTS

C. *Virtues concerned with money.*

IV. 1. Liberality, prodigality, meanness.
2. Magnificence, vulgarity, niggardliness.

D. *Virtues concerned with honour.*

3. Pride, vanity, humility.
4. Ambition, unambitiousness, and the mean between them.

E. *The virtue concerned with anger.*

5. Good temper, irascibility, inirascibility.

F. *Virtues of social intercourse.*

6. Friendliness, obsequiousness, churlishness.
7. Truthfulness, boastfulness, mock-modesty.
8. Ready wit, buffoonery, boorishness.

G. *A quasi-virtue.*

9. Shame, bashfulness, shamelessness.

H. *Justice.*

I. Its sphere and outer nature: in what sense it is a mean.

V. 1. The just as the lawful (universal justice) and the just as the fair and equal (particular justice): the former considered.
2. The latter considered: divided into distributive and rectificatory justice.
3. Distributive justice, in accordance with geometrical proportion.
4. Rectificatory justice, in accordance with arithmetical progression.
5. Justice in exchange, reciprocity in accordance with proportion.
6. Political justice and analogous kinds of justice.
7. Natural and legal justice.

II. Its inner nature as involving choice.

8. The scale of degrees of wrongdoing.
9. Can a man be voluntarily treated unjustly? Is it the distributor or the recipient that is guilty of injustice in distribution? Justice not so easy as it might seem, because it is not a way of acting but an inner disposition.
10. Equity, a corrective of legal justice.
11. Can a man treat himself unjustly?

BOOK VI. INTELLECTUAL VIRTUE

A. *Introduction.*

VI. 1. Reasons for studying intellectual virtue: intellect divided into the contemplative and the calculative.
2. The object of the former is truth, that of the latter truth corresponding with right desire.

B. *The chief intellectual virtues.*

3. Science—demonstrative knowledge of the necessary and eternal.

4. Art—knowledge of how to make things.

5. Practical wisdom—knowledge of how to secure the ends of human life.

6. Intuitive reason—knowledge of the principles from which science proceeds.

7. Philosophic wisdom—the union of intuitive reason and science.

8. Relations between practical wisdom and political science.

C. *Minor intellectual virtues concerned with conduct.*

9. Goodness in deliberation, how related to practical wisdom.

10. Understanding—the critical quality answering to the imperative quality practical wisdom.

11. Judgement—right discrimination of the equitable: the place of intuition in morals.

D. *Relation of philosophic to practical wisdom.*

12. What is the use of philosophic and of practical wisdom? Philosophic wisdom is the formal cause of happiness; practical wisdom is what ensures the taking of proper means to the proper ends desired by moral virtue.

13. Relation of practical wisdom to natural virtue, moral virtue, and the right rule.

BOOK VII. CONTINENCE AND INCONTINENCE. PLEASURE

A. *Continence and incontinence.*

VII. 1. Six varieties of character: method of treatment: current opinions.

2. Contradictions involved in these opinions.

3. Solution of the problem, in what sense the incontinent man acts against knowledge.

4. Solution of the problem, what is the sphere of incontinence: its proper and its extended sense distinguished.

5. Incontinence in its extended sense includes a brutish and a morbid form.

6. Incontinence in respect of anger less disgraceful than incontinence proper.

7. Softness and endurance: two forms of incontinence—weakness and impetuosity.

8. Self-indulgence worse than incontinence.

9. Relation of continence to obstinacy, incontinence, 'insensibility', temperance.

CONTENTS

10. Practical wisdom is not compatible with incontinence, but cleverness is.

B. *Pleasure.*

11. Three views hostile to pleasure, and the arguments for them.
12. Discussion of the view that pleasure is not a good.
13. Discussion of the view that pleasure is not the chief good.
14. Discussion of the view that most pleasures are bad, and of the tendency to identify bodily pleasures with pleasure in general.

BOOKS VIII, IX. FRIENDSHIP

A. *Kinds of friendship.*

VIII. 1. Friendship both necessary and noble: main questions about it.
2. Three objects of love: implications of friendship.
3. Three corresponding kinds of friendship: superiority of friendship whose motive is the good.
4. Contrast between the best and the inferior kinds.
5. The state of friendship distinguished from the activity of friendship and from the feeling of friendliness.
6. Various relations between the three kinds.

B. *Reciprocity of friendship.*

7. In unequal friendships a proportion must be maintained.
8. Loving is more of the essence of friendship than being loved.

C. *Relation of reciprocity in friendship to that involved in other forms of community.*

9. Parallelism of friendship and justice: the state comprehends all lesser communities.
10. Classification of constitutions: analogies with family relations.
11. Corresponding forms of friendship, and of justice.
12. Various forms of friendship between relations.

D. *Casuistry of friendship.*

13. Principles of interchange of services (*a*) in friendship between equals.
14. (*b*) In friendship between unequals.
IX. 1. (*c*) In friendship in which the motives on the two sides are different.
2. Conflict of obligations.
3. Occasions of breaking off friendship.

E. *Internal nature of friendship.*

4. Friendship is based on self-love.
5. Relation of friendship to goodwill.

6. Relation of friendship to unanimity.

7. The pleasure of beneficence.

8. The nature of true self-love.

F.   *The need of friendship.*

9. Why does the happy man need friends?

10. The limit to the number of friends.

11. Are friends more needed in good or in bad fortune?

12. The essence of friendship is living together.

BOOK X. PLEASURE. HAPPINESS

A.   *Pleasure.*

X. 1. Two opposed views about pleasure.

2. Discussion of the view that pleasure is the good.

3. Discussion of the view that pleasure is wholly bad.

4. Definition of pleasure.

5. Pleasures differ with the activities which they accompany and complete: criterion of the value of pleasures.

B.   *Happiness.*

6. Happiness is good activity, not amusement.

7. Happiness in the highest sense is the contemplative life.

8. Superiority of the contemplative life further considered.

9. Legislation is needed if the end is to be attained: transition to *Politics.*

I. 1094^a 1, 2 = *M. M.* 1182^a 32-5   3-5 = *E. E.* 1219^a 13-17, *M. M.*
1184^b 9-11, 1197^a 3-10   22-4 = *E. E.* 1214^b 6-11   24-8 = *E. E.*
1218^b 10-14 ^{b} 22-1095^a 2 = *E. E.* 1216^b 35-1217^a 10 1095^a 14-19
= *E. E.* 1217^a 18-22   22, 23 = *E. E.* 1214^b 6-9   26-8 = *E. E.* 1217^b
2-16, *M. M.* 1182^b 9   28-30 = *E. E.* 1214^b 28-1215^a 7 ^{b} 17-19 = *E. E.*
1215^a 32-^{b} 1, 1216^a 27-9   19, 20 = *E. E.* 1215^b 30-5   22, cf. *E. E.*
1216^a 16   26-30 = *E. E.* 1216^a 19-22 1096^a 5-7 = *E. E.* 1215^a 25-32
17-19 = *E. E.* 1218^a 1-10   19-22, 23-9 = *E. E.* 1217^b 25-34, *M. M.*
1183^a 9-12, 1205^a 8-14   29-34 = *E. E.* 1217^b 34-1218^a 1   34-^{b} 5 = *E. E.*
1218^a 10-15 ^{b} 30, 31 = *E. E.* 1217^b 16-23   32-5 = *E. E.* 1217^b 23-5,
1218^b 1-4 1097^a 22-4 = *E. E.* 1218^b 10-12 ^{b} 16-20 = *M. M.* 1184^a
14-38   23-33 = *E. E.* 1219^a 2-8 1098^a 5-7 = *E. E.* 1219^a 9-18
7-12 = *E. E.* 1219^a 18-23   12-18 = *E. E.* 1219^a 23-35   18-20 = *E. E.*
1219^a 35-9   33-^{b} 3 = *E. E.* 1218^b 22-4 ^{b} 9-12 = *E. E.* 1216^b 26-35
12-16 = *E. E.* 1218^b 32-4, *M. M.* 1184^a 2-5   20-2 = *E. E.* 1219^a 39-^{b} 3
23-5 = *E. E.* 1214^a 30-^{b} 6   31-1099^a 3 = *E. E.* 1215^a 20-5, 1219^a 23-5,
M. M. 1185^a 9-13 1099^a 3-7 = *E. E.* 1219^b 9, 10   24-31 = *E. E.*
1214^a 1-8 ^{b} 7, 8 = *E. E.* 1214^a 25, 26   9-11 = *E. E.* 1214^a 14-24
14-20 = *E. E.* 1215^a 12-19   32-1100^a 1 = *E. E.* 1217^a 24-9 1100^a
1-5 = *E. E.* 1219^a 35-9, ^{b} 4-6, *M. M.* 1185^a 3-9   10, 11 = *E. E.* 1219^b
6-8, *M. M.* 1185^a 6-9 1101^a 14-16 = *E. E.* 1219^a 38, 39 ^{b} 10-14, 21-7
= *E. E.* 1219^b 11-16, *M. M.* 1183^b 20-30   31-4 = *E. E.* 1219^b 8, ·9
1102^a 28-32 = *E. E.* 1219^b 32-6   32-^{b} 3 = *E. E.* 1219^b 36-1220^a 2 ^{b} 3-
11 = *E. E.* 1219^b 16-26   7 = *E. E.* 1219^a 25   13, 14 = *E. E.* 1219^b
27-32 1103^a 3-10 = *E. E.* 1220^a 4-13

II. 1103^a 17-23 = *E. E.* 1220^a 39-^{b} 5, *M. M.* 1185^b 38-1186^a 8 ^{b} 26-
30 = *E. E.* 1216^b 21-5 1104^a 11-27 = *M. M.* 1185^b 13-32   27-^{b} 3 =
E. E. 1220^a 22-34 ^{b} 16-18 = *E. E.* 1220^a 34-7   18-25 = *E. E.* 1221^b
39-1222^a 5 1105^a 7, 8 = *E. E.* 1223^b 22-4 ^{b} 19-28 = *E. E.* 1220^b
6-20, *M. M.* 1186^a 9-19 1106^a 26-^{b} 16 = *E. E.* 1220^b 21-35 ^{b} 36-
1107^a 2 = *E. E.* 1227^b 5-9 1107^a 8-17 = *E. E.* 1221^b 18-26,
M. M. 1186^a 36-^{b} 1   28-1108^b 6 = *E. E.* 1220^b 35-1221^b 3 1108^a
35-^{b} 6 = *E. E.* 1233^b 16-26, *M. M.* 1192^b 18-29 ^{b} 11-15 = *E. E.*
1222^a 17-22   15-19 = *M. M.* 1186^b 11-13   23-6 = *M. M.* 1186^b 13-17
35-1109^a 19 = *E. E.* 1222^a 22-^{b} 4, 1234^b 6-13, *M. M.* 1186^b 4-11, 17-32
1109^a 20-30 = *M. M.* 1186^b 32-1187^a 4

III. 1109^b 30-5 = *E. E.* 1223^a 9-23, *M. M.* 1187^b 31-4   35, 1110^a 1
= *E. E.* 1224^a 9-11 1110^a 4-^{b} 7 = *E. E.* 1225^a 2-27 ^{b} 9-17 = *M. M.*
1188^b 16-23   24-1111^a 15 = *E. E.* 1225^a 36-^{b} 16   30-1111 ^{a} 15 =

$M.M.$ 1188^b 25–38   1111^a 24 = $E.E.$ 1223^a 28–36, ^{b} 18–24, $M.M.$ 1187^b 37–1188^a 5, 1188^a 23–5 ^{b} 4–34 = $E.E.$ 1225^b 16–1226^a 17, $M.M.$ 1189^a 1–22 ^{b} 5, 6 = $E.E.$ 1228^a 11–14   1112^a 13–^{b} 8 = $E.E.$ 1226^a 20–^{b} 9   13–17 = $M.M.$ 1189^a 22–^{b} 3   14, 15 = $E.E.$ 1226^b 30–6   21–3 = $E.E.$ 1226^a 2–4   30, 31 = $M.M.$ 1189^b 6–8   34–^{b} 9 = $M.M.$ 1189^b 9–25 ^{b} 11–20, 1113^a 5–7 = $E.E.$ 1226^b 9–13, 1227^a 5–18, ^{b} 25–33   1113^a 9–12 = $E.E.$ 1226^b 13–17, 1227^a 3–5   15–31 = $E.E.$ 1227^a 18–31   33–^{b} 2 = $E.E.$ 1227^a 38–^{b} 1 ^{b} 11–14 = $E.E.$ 1223^a 4–9   14–17 = $M.M.$ 1187^a 5–13   17–21 = $E.E.$ 1222^b 15–20, $M.M.$ 1187^b 4–9   21–30 = $M.M.$ 1187^a 13–19   1114^a 13–21 = $M.M.$ 1187^b 20–30   21–31 = $M.M.$ 1187^a 23–9 ^{b} 26, 27, 1115^a 4–6 = $E.E.$ 1228^a 23–6   1115^a 6–9 = $E.E.$ 1228^a 26–^{b} 4   10–^{b} 6 = $E.E.$ 1229^a 32–^{b} 21, $M.M.$ 1190^b 9–21 ^{b} 7–17 = $E.E.$ 1228^b 18–1229^a 11, $M.M.$ 1191^a 17–36   17–24 = $E.E.$ 1230^a 26–33   26–28 = $E.E.$ 1229^b 28, 29   1116^a 12–15 = $E.E.$ 1229^b 32–1230^a 4   16–^{b} 3 = $E.E.$ 1229^a 11–13, $M.M.$ 1191^a 5–13 ^{b} 3–23 = $E.E.$ 1229^a 14–16, 1230^a 4–21, $M.M.$ 1190^b 22–32   23–1117^a 9 = $E.E.$ 1129^a 20–29, $M.M.$ 1190^b 35–1191^a 4   1117^a 9–22 = $E.E.$ 1229^a 18–20, $M.M.$ 1191^a 13–17   22–7 = $E.E.$ 1229^a 16–18, $M.M.$ 1190^b 32–5 ^{b} 20–3 = $E.E.$ 1230^a 33–8, $M.M.$ 1191^a 36–8   27–1118^b 8 = $E.E.$ 1230^a 21–1231^a 26, $M.M.$ 1191^a 5–10   1118^b 16–21 = $E.E.$ 1221^b 15–17   1119^a 5–11 = $E.E.$ 1230^b 13–18, 1231^a 26–34   33–^{b} 1 = $E.E.$ 1230^b 3–7

IV.   1119^b 22–32 = $E.E.$ 1231^b 27–38, $M.M.$ 1191^b 39–1192^a 8   1121^b 21–34 = $E.E.$ 1232^a 10–15, $M.M.$ 1192^a 8–10   1122^a 18–1123^a 33 = $E.E.$ 1233^a 31–^{b} 15, $M.M.$ 1192^a 37–^{b} 17   1123^a 34–1125^a 35 = $M.M.$ 1192^a 21–36 ^{b} 5–15 = $E.E.$ 1232^b 31–1233^a 9   1124^a 4–12 = $E.E.$ 1232^b 14–21 ^{b} 6–9 = $E.E.$ 1232^b 10–12   1125^a 17–34 = $E.E.$ 1233^a 9–30 ^{b} 26–1126^b 10 = $E.E.$ 1231^b 5–26, $M.M.$ 1191^b 23–38   1126^a 8–28 = $E.E.$ 1221^b 9–15 ^{b} 11–1127^a 12 = $E.E.$ 1233^b 29–38, $M.M.$ 1193^a 20–7   1127^a 13–^{b} 32 = $E.E.$ 1233^b 38–1234^a 3, $M.M.$ 1193^a 28–38 ^{b} 33–1128^b 9 = $E.E.$ 1234^a 4–23, $M.M.$ 1193^a 11–19   1128^b 10–33 = $E.E.$ 1233^b 26–9, $M.M.$ 1193^a 1–10

V.   1129^a 3–1130^a 13 = $M.M.$ 1193^a 39–^{b} 19   1131^a 10–^{b} 24, 1132^b 21–1133^b 28 = $M.M.$ 1193^b 19–1194^b 3   1134^a 24–1135^a 5 = $M.M.$ 1194^b 3–1195^a 8   1135^a 8–1136^a 9 = $M.M.$ 1195^a 8–^{b} 4   1136^a 10–^{b} 14 = $M.M.$ 1195^b 4–34 ^{b} 15–1137^a 4 = $M.M.$ 1196^a 33–^{b} 3   1137^a 31–1138^a 3 = $M.M.$ 1198^b 24–33   1138^a 4–^{b} 13 = $M.M.$ 1195^b 35–1196^a 33

VI.   1138^b 18–34 = $E.E.$ 1249^a 21–^{b} 6, $M.M.$ 1196^b 4–11   35–1139^b 13 = $M.M.$ 1196^b 11–34   1139^b 14–18 = $M.M.$ 1196^b 34–7   18–36 = $M.M.$ 1196^b 37–1197^a 1   1140^a 1–23 = $M.M.$ 1197^a 3–13   24–^{b} 30 = $M.M.$ 1197^a 13–20 ^{b} 31–1141^a 8 = $M.M.$ 1197^a 20–3   1141^a 9–20 = $M.M.$ 1197^a 23–30   20–^{b} 3 = $M.M.$ 1197^a 32–^{b} 11   21, 33–^{b} 2 = $E.E.$ 1217^a 33   1142^a 31–^{b} 33 = $M.M.$ 1199^a 4–14 ^{b} 34–1143^a 18 = $M.M.$ 1197^b 11–17   1143^a 19–24 = $M.M.$ 1198^b 34–1199^a 3   1144^a 6–22 = $E.E.$ 1227^b 19–1228^a 2   23–^{b} 1 = $M.M.$ 1197^b 17–27 ^{b} 1–1145^a

$6 = M. M.$ 1197^b 36–1198^b 8 ^{b} 18–20 $= E. E.$ 1216^b 6   1145^a 6–11
$= M. M.$ 1198^b 8–20

VII. 1145^a 15–^{b} 2 $= M. M.$ 1200^b 4–19 ^{b} 21–1146^a 4 $= M. M.$ 1200^b
20–1201^a 6   1146^a 9–^{b} 5 $= M. M.$ 1201^a 9–39 ^{b} 6–1147^b 19 $= M. M.$
1201^a 39–1202^a 8   1147^b 20–1148^b 14 $= M. M.$ 1202^a 29–^{b} 9   1148^b
15–1149^a 20 $= M. M.$ 1202^a 19–29   1149^a 24–^{b} 26 $= M. M.$ 1202^b
9–29 ^{b} 8–13 $= M. M.$ 1202^b 23–6   26–1150^a 8 $= M. M.$ 1203^a 18–
25 1150^a 9–^{b} 19 $= M. M.$ 1202^b 29–38 ^{b} 19–28 $= M. M.$ 1203^a 29–^{b} 11
29–36 $= M. M.$ 1203^a 11–18, 25–9   1151^a 1–28 $= M. M.$ 1203^a 29–
^{b} 11   15–19 $= E. E.$ 1227^a 7–9, ^{b} 22–30   29–^{b} 22 $= M. M.$ 1202^a 8–19
^{b} 32–1152^a 33 $= M. M.$ 1203^b 11–1204^a 18   1152^b 1–8 $= M. M.$ 1204^a
19–31   10, 11 $= M. M.$ 1205^a 7, 8   11, 12 $= M. M.$ 1206^a 31   12–20
$= M. M.$ 1204^a 31–^{b} 4   33–1153^a 7 $= M. M.$ 1204^b 4–20   1153^a 7–15
$= M. M.$ 1204^b 20–1205^a 7   20–3 $= M. M.$ 1205^b 37–1206^a 25   23–7 $=$
$M. M.$ 1206^a 25–30 ^{b} 7–9 $= M. M.$ 1205^a 25–^{b} 2   25–8 $= M. M.$ 1205^b
33–7   29–31 $= M. M.$ 1205^a 16–25, ^{b} 2–13

VIII. 1155^a 3–31 $= E. E.$ 1234^b 18–1235^a 4, $M. M.$ 1208^b 3–7   32–^{b}
8 $= E. E.$ 1235^a 4–28, $M. M.$ 1208^b 7–20 ^{b} 8–13 $= E. E.$ 1235^a 29–33,
$M. M.$ 1208^b 22–6   17–27 $= E. E.$ 1235^b 13–1236^a 7, $M. M.$ 1208^b 36–
1209^a 3   27–1156^a 5 $= E. E.$ 1236^a 7–15; $M. M.$ 1208^b 27–36   1156^a
6–^{b} 6 $= E. E.$ 1236^a 15–^{b} 26 ^{b} 7–17 $= E. E.$ 1236^b 26–32, $M. M.$ 1209^a
3–7   17–1157^a 25 $= E. E.$ 1237^b 8–30, $M. M.$ 1209^b 11–17   1158^b
1–3 $= E. E.$ 1238^b 15–17, $M. M.$ 1211^b 4–8   11–28 $= E. E.$ 1238^b 18–
30, 1239^a 6–12, $M. M.$ 1211^b 8–17   1159^a 12–^{b} 1 $= E. E.$ 1239^a 21–^{b}
2, $M. M.$ 1210^b 2–20 ^{b} 1–24 $= E. E.$ 1239^b 6–1240^a 4   25–1160^a 8 $=$
$E. E.$ 1241^b 12–17, $M. M.$ 1211^a 6–12   1160^a 8–30 $= E. E.$ 1241^b 24–6
35 $= E. E.$ 1241^b 36 ^{b} 22–1161^a 9 $= E. E.$ 1241^b 27–32, 38–40   1161^a
30–^{b} 10 $= E. E.$ 1241^b 17–24, 1242^a 13–19 ^{b} 11–33 $= E. E.$ 1242^a 1–13
34, cf. $E. E.$ 1238^a 34   1162^a 29–33 $= E. E.$ 1242^a 19–32   34–^{b} 4 $=$
$E. E.$ 1242^b 2–21 ^{b} 21–1163^a 23 $= E. E.$ 1242^b 31–1243^b 14   1163^a
24–^{b} 27 $= E. E.$ 1242^b 2–21

IX. 1163^b 32–1164^b 21 $= E. E.$ 1243^b 14–38, $M. M.$ 1210^a 24–^{b} 2 1164^b
22–1165^a 35 $= E. E.$ 1244^a 1–36   1166^a 1–^{b} 29 $= E. E.$ 1240^a 8–^{b} 39,
$M. M.$ 1210^b 32–1211^a 6, 1211^a 15–36 ^{b} 30–1167^a 21 $= E. E.$ 1241^a
1–15, $M. M.$ 1211^b 39–1212^a 13   1167^a 22–^{b} 16 $= E. E.$ 1241^a 15–34,
$M. M.$ 1212^a 14–27 ^{b} 17–1168^a 27 $= E. E.$ 1241^a 35–^{b} 9, $M. M.$ 1211^b
20–39   1168^a 28–35 $= M. M.$ 1212^a 28–^{b} 3   35–^{b} 10 $= M. M.$ 1211^a 36–
^{b} 3 ^{b} 6–10 $= E. E.$ 1240^b 1–4   10–1169^b 2 $= M. M.$ 1212^b 8–23   1169^b
3–1170^b 19 $= E. E.$ 1244^b 1–1245^b 19, $M. M.$ 1212^b 24–1213^b 2   1170^b
20–1171^a 20 $= E. E.$ 1245^b 19–26, $M. M.$ 1213^b 3–17   1171^a 21–^{b} 28
$= E. E.$ 1244^b 1–1245^b 19, 1245^b 26–1246^a 25, $M. M.$ 1213^b 3–17

BOOK I

1   EVERY art and every inquiry, and similarly every action **1094ᵃ** and pursuit, is thought to aim at some good; and for this reason the good has rightly been declared[1] to be that at which all things aim. But a certain difference is found among ends; some are activities, others are products apart from the activities that produce them. Where there are ends apart 5 from the actions, it is the nature of the products to be better than the activities. Now, as there are many actions, arts, and sciences, their ends also are many; the end of the medical art is health, that of shipbuilding a vessel, that of strategy victory, that of economics wealth. But where such arts fall under a single capacity—as bridle-making and the other 10 arts concerned with the equipment of horses fall under the art of riding, and this and every military action under strategy, in the same way other arts fall under yet others— in all of these the ends of the master arts are to be preferred to all the subordinate ends; for it is for the sake of the 15 former that the latter are pursued. It makes no difference whether the activities themselves are the ends of the actions, or something else apart from the activities, as in the case of the sciences just mentioned.

2   If, then, there is some end of the things we do, which we desire for its own sake (everything else being desired for the sake of this), and if we do not choose everything for the sake of something else (for at that rate the process would 20 go on to infinity, so that our desire would be empty and vain), clearly this must be the good and the chief good. Will not the knowledge of it, then, have a great influence on life? Shall we not, like archers who have a mark to aim at, be more likely to hit upon what is right? If so, we 25

[1] Perhaps by Eudoxus; cf. 1172ᵇ9.

must try, in outline at least, to determine what it is, and of which of the sciences or capacities it is the object. It would seem to belong to the most authoritative art and that which is most truly the master art. And politics appears to be of this nature; for it is this that ordains which of the sciences **1094**^b should be studied in a state, and which each class of citizens should learn and up to what point they should learn them; and we see even the most highly esteemed of capacities to fall under this, e. g. strategy, economics, rhetoric; now, since 5 politics uses the rest of the sciences, and since, again, it legislates as to what we are to do and what we are to abstain from, the end of this science must include those of the others, so that this end must be the good for man. For even if the end is the same for a single man and for a state, that of the state seems at all events something greater and more complete whether to attain or to preserve; though it is worth while to attain the end merely for one man, it is finer and more godlike to attain it for a nation or for city-10 states. These, then, are the ends at which our inquiry aims, since it is political science, in one sense of that term.

Our discussion will be adequate if it has as much clear- **3** ness as the subject-matter admits of, for precision is not to be sought for alike in all discussions, any more than in all the products of the crafts. Now fine and just actions, which 15 political science investigates, admit of much variety and fluctuation of opinion, so that they may be thought to exist only by convention, and not by nature. And goods also give rise to a similar fluctuation because they bring harm to many people; for before now men have been undone by reason of their wealth, and others by reason of their courage. We must be content, then, in speaking of such subjects and 20 with such premises to indicate the truth roughly and in outline, and in speaking about things which are only for the most part true and with premises of the same kind to reach conclusions that are no better. In the same spirit, therefore, should each type of statement be *received*; for it is the mark of an educated man to look for precision in each 25 class of things just so far as the nature of the subject admits;

it is evidently equally foolish to accept probable reasoning from a mathematician and to demand from a rhetorician scientific proofs.

Now each man judges well the things he knows, and of these he is a good judge. And so the man who has been educated in a subject is a good judge of that subject, and 1095[a] the man who has received an all-round education is a good judge in general. Hence a young man is not a proper hearer of lectures on political science;[1] for he is inexperienced in the actions that occur in life, but its discussions start from these and are about these; and, further, since he tends to follow his passions, his study will be vain and unprofitable, because the end aimed at is not knowledge but action. 5 And it makes no difference whether he is young in years or youthful in character; the defect does not depend on time, but on his living, and pursuing each successive object, as passion directs. For to such persons, as to the incontinent, knowledge brings no profit; but to those who desire and 10 act in accordance with a rational principle[2] knowledge about such matters will be of great benefit.

These remarks about the student, the sort of treatment to be expected, and the purpose of the inquiry, may be taken as our preface.

[1] Cf.   'Young men, whom Aristotle thought
            Unfit to hear moral philosophy.'
                   (*Troilus and Cressida*, II. ii. 166 f.)

[2] Of all the words of common occurrence in the *Ethics*, the hardest to translate is λόγος. Till recently the accepted translation was 'reason'. But it is, I think, quite clear that normally λόγος in Aristotle does not stand for the faculty of reason, but for something grasped by reason, or perhaps sometimes for an operation of reason. Its connexion with reason is so close as to make 'irrational' the most natural translation of ἄλογος. But for λόγος I have used, according to the shade of meaning uppermost in each context, such renderings as 'rational principle', 'rational ground', 'rule' (ὀρθὸς λόγος I always render 'right rule'), 'argument', 'reasoning', 'course of reasoning'. The connexion between reason and its object is for Aristotle so close that not infrequently λόγος occurs where strict logic would require him to be naming the faculty of reason, and it is possible that in some of the latest passages of his works in which λόγος occurs it has come to mean 'reason'—which it certainly had come to mean, not much later in the history of philosophy.

The meaning of λόγος in Aristotle is discussed by Professor J. L. Stocks in *Journal of Philology*, xxxiii (1914), 182–94, *Classical Quarterly*, viii (1914), 9–12, and by Professor J. Cook Wilson in *Classical Review*, xxvii (1913), 113–17.

Let us resume our inquiry and state, in view of the fact **4**
that all knowledge and every pursuit aims at some good,
15 what it is that we say political science aims at and what is
the highest of all goods achievable by action. Verbally
there is very general agreement; for both the general run
of men and people of superior refinement say that it is
happiness, and identify living well and doing well with
20 being happy; but with regard to what happiness is they
differ, and the many do not give the same account as the
wise. For the former think it is some plain and obvious
thing, like pleasure, wealth, or honour; they differ, however,
from one another—and often even the same man identifies
it with different things, with health when he is ill, with
25 wealth when he is poor; but, conscious of their ignorance,
they admire those who proclaim some great ideal that is
above their comprehension. Now some[1] thought that apart
from these many goods there is another which is self-
subsistent and causes the goodness of all these as well.
To examine all the opinions that have been held were
perhaps somewhat fruitless; enough to examine those that
are most prevalent or that seem to be arguable.

30 Let us not fail to notice, however, that there is a difference
between arguments from and those to the first principles.
For Plato, too, was right in raising this question and asking,
as he used to do, 'are we on the way from or to the first
principles?'[2] There is a difference, as there is in a racecourse between the course from the judges to the turning-
1095ᵇ point and the way back. For, while we must begin with what
is known, things are objects of knowledge in two senses
—some to us, some without qualification. Presumably,
then, *we* must begin with things known to *us*. Hence any
one who is to listen intelligently to lectures about what is
5 noble and just and, generally, about the subjects of political
science must have been brought up in good habits. For
the fact is the starting-point, and if this is sufficiently plain
to him, he will not at the start need the reason as well;
and the man who has been well brought up has or can

---

[1] The Platonic School; cf. ch. 6.
[2] Cf. *Rep.* 511 B.

easily get starting-points. And as for him who neither
has nor can get them, let him hear the words of Hesiod : [1]

> Far best is he who knows all things himself ;   10
> Good, he that hearkens when men counsel right ;
> But he who neither knows, nor lays to heart
> Another's wisdom, is a useless wight.

5   Let us, however, resume our discussion from the point at
which we digressed.[2] To judge from the lives that men
lead, most men, and men of the most vulgar type, seem (not
without some ground) to identify the good, or happiness, 15
with pleasure ; which is the reason why they love the life
of enjoyment. For there are, we may say, three prominent
types of life—that just mentioned, the political, and thirdly
the contemplative life. Now the mass of mankind are
evidently quite slavish in their tastes, preferring a life suit- 20
able to beasts, but they get some ground for their view from
the fact that many of those in high places share the tastes
of Sardanapallus. A consideration of the prominent types
of life shows that people of superior refinement and of
active disposition identify happiness with honour ; [3] for
this is, roughly speaking, the end of the political life.
But it seems too superficial to be what we are looking
for, since it is thought to depend on those who bestow
honour rather than on him who receives it, but the good 25
we divine to be something proper to a man and not
easily taken from him. Further, men seem to pursue
honour in order that they may be assured of their goodness ; at least it is by men of practical wisdom that they
seek to be honoured, and among those who know them, and
on the ground of their virtue ; clearly, then, according to
them, at any rate, virtue is better. And perhaps one might 30
even suppose this to be, rather than honour, the end of the
political life. But even this appears somewhat incomplete ;
for possession of virtue seems actually compatible with
being asleep, or with lifelong inactivity, and, further, with

---

[1] *Op.* 293, 295–7 Rzach.   [2] ^a 30.
[3] Mr. C. M. Mulvany has pointed out (*C. Q.* xv (1921), 87) that there
is a continuous sentence from l. 14 to l. 30, and that τὸ ἀγαθὸν καὶ τὴν
εὐδαιμονίαν οὐκ ἀλόγως ἐοίκασιν ἐκ τῶν βίων ὑπολαμβάνειν (14–16) goes
with οἱ δὲ χαρίεντες ... τιμήν as with οἱ μὲν πολλοὶ ... ἡδονήν.

1096ª the greatest sufferings and misfortunes; but a man who was living so no one would call happy, unless he were maintaining a thesis at all costs. But enough of this; for the subject has been sufficiently treated even in the current discussions. Third comes the contemplative life, which we shall consider later.[1]

5   The life of money-making is one undertaken under compulsion, and wealth is evidently not the good we are seeking; for it is merely useful and for the sake of something else. And so one might rather take the aforenamed objects to be ends; for they are loved for themselves. But it is evident that not even these are ends; yet many arguments have
10 been thrown away in support of them. Let us leave this subject, then.

We had perhaps better consider the universal good and **6** discuss thoroughly what is meant by it, although such an inquiry is made an uphill one by the fact that the Forms have been introduced by friends of our own. Yet it would perhaps be thought to be better, indeed to be our duty, for the sake of maintaining the truth even to destroy what
15 touches us closely, especially as we are philosophers or lovers of wisdom; for, while both are dear, piety requires us to honour truth above our friends.

The men who introduced this doctrine did not posit Ideas of classes within which they recognized priority and posteriority (which is the reason why they did not maintain the existence of an Idea embracing all numbers); but the term 'good' is used both in the category of substance and
20 in that of quality and in that of relation, and that which is *per se*, i. e. substance, is prior in nature to the relative (for the latter is like an offshoot and accident of being); so that there could not be a common Idea set over all these goods. Further, since 'good' has as many senses as 'being' (for it is predicated both in the category of substance, as of God
25 and of reason, and in quality, i. e. of the virtues, and in quantity, i. e. of that which is moderate, and in relation, i. e. of the useful, and in time, i. e. of the right opportunity,

---

[1] 1177ª 12–1178ª 8, 1178ª 22–1179ª 32.

and in place, i. e. of the right locality and the like), clearly
it cannot be something universally present in all cases and
single; for then it could not have been predicated in all
the categories but in one only. Further, since of the things
answering to one Idea there is one science, there would have ₃₀
been one science of all the goods; but as it is there are
many sciences even of the things that fall under one
category, e. g. of opportunity, for opportunity in war is
studied by strategics and in disease by medicine, and the
moderate in food is studied by medicine and in exercise
by the science of gymnastics. And one might ask the
question, what in the world they *mean* by 'a thing itself',
if (as is the case) in 'man himself' and in a particular man ₃₅
the account of man is one and the same. For in so far as **1096ᵇ**
they are man, they will in no respect differ; and if this is
so, neither will 'good itself' and particular goods, in so far
as they are good. But again it will not be good any the
more for being eternal, since that which lasts long is no
whiter than that which perishes in a day. The Pythagoreans ₅
seem to give a more plausible account of the good, when
they place the one in the column of goods; and it is they
that Speusippus seems to have followed.

But let us discuss these matters elsewhere[1]; an objection
to what we have said, however, may be discerned in the
fact that the Platonists have not been speaking about *all*
goods, and that the goods that are pursued and loved for ₁₀
themselves are called good by reference to a single Form,
while those which tend to produce or to preserve these
somehow or to prevent their contraries are called so by
reference to these, and in a secondary sense. Clearly, then,
goods must be spoken of in two ways, and some must be
good in themselves, the others by reason of these. Let us
separate, then, things good in themselves from things useful,
and consider whether the former are called good by reference ₁₅
to a single Idea. What sort of goods would one call good
in themselves? Is it those that are pursued even when
isolated from others, such as intelligence, sight, and certain

[1] Cf. *Met.* 986ᵃ 22-6, 1028ᵇ 21-4, 1072ᵇ 30-1073ᵃ 3, 1091ᵃ 29-ᵇ 3, ᵇ 13-
1092ᵃ 17.

pleasures and honours? Certainly, if we pursue these als
for the sake of something else, yet one would place thei
among things good in themselves. Or is nothing oth
20 than the Idea of good good in itself? In that case the For
will be empty. But if the things we have named are al
things good in themselves, the account of the good wi
have to appear as something identical in them all, as tha
of whiteness is identical in snow and in white lead. But o
honour, wisdom, and pleasure, just in respect of their good
25 ness, the accounts are distinct and diverse. The good, there
fore, is not some common element answering to one Idea.

But what then do we mean by the good? It is surely
not like the things that only chance to have the same name.
Are goods one, then, by being derived from one good or by all
contributing to one good, or are they rather one by analogy?
Certainly as sight is in the body, so is reason in the soul,
30 and so on in other cases. But perhaps these subjects
had better be dismissed for the present; for perfect precision about them would be more appropriate to another
branch of philosophy.[1] And similarly with regard to the
Idea; even if there is some one good which is universally
predicable of goods or is capable of separate and independent
existence, clearly it could not be achieved or attained by
man; but we are now seeking something attainable.
35 Perhaps, however, some one might think it worth while to
recognize this with a view to the goods that *are* attainable
1097ᵃ and achievable; for having this as a sort of pattern we shall
know better the goods that are good for us, and if we
know them shall attain them. This argument has some
plausibility, but seems to clash with the procedure of the
5 sciences; for all of these, though they aim at some good
and seek to supply the deficiency of it, leave on one side
the knowledge of *the* good. Yet that all the exponents of
the arts should be ignorant of, and should not even seek, so
great an aid is not probable. It is hard, too, to see how
a weaver or a carpenter will be benefited in regard to his
10 own craft by knowing this 'good itself', or how the man
who has viewed the Idea itself will be a better doctor or

[1] Cf. *Met.* Γ. 2.

general thereby. For a doctor seems not even to study health in this way, but the health of man, or perhaps rather the health of a particular man; it is individuals that he is healing. But enough of these topics.

7   Let us again return to the good we are seeking, and ask what it can be. It seems different in different actions and arts; it is different in medicine, in strategy, and in the other arts likewise. What then is the good of each? Surely that for whose sake everything else is done. In medicine this is health, in strategy victory, in architecture a house, in any other sphere something else, and in every action and pursuit the end; for it is for the sake of this that all men do whatever else they do. Therefore, if there is an end for all that we do, this will be the good achievable by action, and if there are more than one, these will be the goods achievable by action.

So the argument has by a different course reached the same point; but we must try to state this even more clearly. Since there are evidently more than one end, and we choose some of these (e. g. wealth, flutes,[1] and in general instruments) for the sake of something else, clearly not all ends are final ends; but the chief good is evidently something final. Therefore, if there is only one final end, this will be what we are seeking, and if there are more than one, the most final of these will be what we are seeking. Now we call that which is in itself worthy of pursuit more final than that which is worthy of pursuit for the sake of something else, and that which is never desirable for the sake of something else more final than the things that are desirable both in themselves and for the sake of that other thing, and therefore we call final without qualification that which is always desirable in itself and never for the sake of something else.

Now such a thing happiness, above all else, is held to be; for this we choose always for itself and never for the sake **1097[b]** of something else, but honour, pleasure, reason, and every virtue we choose indeed for themselves (for if nothing

---

[1] Cf. Pl. *Euthyd.* 289 c.

resulted from them we should still choose each of them), but we choose them also for the sake of happiness, judging 5 that by means of them we shall be happy. Happiness, on the other hand, no one chooses for the sake of these, nor, in general, for anything other than itself.

From the point of view of self-sufficiency the same result seems to follow; for the final good is thought to be self-sufficient. Now by self-sufficient we do not mean that which is sufficient for a man by himself, for one who lives 10 a solitary life, but also for parents, children, wife, and in general for his friends and fellow citizens, since man is born for citizenship. But some limit must be set to this; for if we extend our requirement to ancestors and descendants and friends' friends we are in for an infinite series. Let us examine this question, however, on another occasion;[1] the self-sufficient we now define as that which when isolated 15 makes life desirable and lacking in nothing; and such we think happiness to be; and further we think it most desirable of all things, without being counted as one good thing among others—if it were so counted it would clearly be made more desirable by the addition of even the least of goods; for that which is added becomes an excess of goods, 20 and of goods the greater is always more desirable. Happiness, then, is something final and self-sufficient, and is the end of action.

Presumably, however, to say that happiness is the chief good seems a platitude, and a clearer account of what it is is still desired. This might perhaps be given, if we could 25 first ascertain the function of man. For just as for a flute-player, a sculptor, or any artist, and, in general, for all things that have a function or activity, the good and the 'well' is thought to reside in the function, so would it seem to be for man, if he has a function. Have the carpenter, then, and the tanner certain functions or activities, and has 30 man none? Is he born without a function? Or as eye, hand, foot, and in general each of the parts evidently has a function, may one lay it down that man similarly has a function apart from all these? What then can this be?

[1] i. 10, 11, ix. 10.

Life seems to be common even to plants, but we are seeking
what is peculiar to man.   Let us exclude, therefore, the life
of nutrition and growth.[1]   Next there would be a life of 1098^a
perception, but *it* also seems to be common even to the
horse, the ox, and every animal.   There remains, then, an
active life of the element that has a rational principle ;
of this, one part has such a principle in the sense of being
obedient to one, the other in the sense of possessing one
and exercising thought.   And, as 'life of the rational 5
element' also has two meanings, we must state that life
in the sense of activity is what we mean ; for this seems to
be the more proper sense of the term.   Now if the function
of man is an activity of soul which follows or implies a
rational principle, and if we say 'a so-and-so' and 'a good
so-and-so' have a function which is the same in kind, e. g. a
lyre-player and a good lyre-player, and so without qualification in all cases, eminence in respect of goodness being 10
added to the name of the function (for the function of a
lyre-player is to play the lyre, and that of a good lyre-
player is to do so well) : if this is the case, [and we state
the function of man to be a certain kind of life, and this to
be an activity or actions of the soul implying a rational
principle, and the function of a good man to be the good
and noble performance of these, and if any action is well 15
performed when it is performed in accordance with the
appropriate excellence : if this is the case,] human good
turns out to be activity of soul in accordance with virtue,
and if there are more than one virtue, in accordance with
the best and most complete.

But we must add 'in a complete life'.   For one swallow
does not make a summer, nor does one day ; and so too one
day, or a short time, does not make a man blessed and happy.

Let this serve as an outline of the good ; for we must 20
presumably first sketch it roughly, and then later fill in the
details.   But it would seem that any one is capable of
carrying on and articulating what has once been well out-
lined, and that time is a good discoverer or partner in such
a work ; to which facts the advances of the arts are due ;

---

[1] Omitting τε and τὴν in l. 1, with most MSS.

25 for any one can add what is lacking. And we must also remember what has been said before,[1] and not look for precision in all things alike, but in each class of things such precision as accords with the subject-matter, and so much as is appropriate to the inquiry. For a carpenter and a geometer investigate the right angle in different 30 ways; the former does so in so far as the right angle is useful for his work, while the latter inquires what it is or what sort of thing it is; for he is a spectator of the truth. We must act in the same way, then, in all other matters as well, that our main task may not be subordinated to minor questions. Nor must we demand the cause in all matters **1098ᵇ** alike; it is enough in some cases that the *fact* be well established, as in the case of the first principles; the fact is the primary thing or first principle. Now of first principles we see some by induction, some by perception, some by a certain habituation, and others too in other ways. But each set of principles we must try to investigate in the 5 natural way, and we must take pains to state them definitely, since they have a great influence on what follows. For the beginning is thought to be more than half of the whole, and many of the questions we ask are cleared up by it.

We must consider it, however, in the light not only of our **8** 10 conclusion and our premises, but also of what is commonly said about it; for with a true view all the data harmonize, but with a false one the facts soon clash. Now goods have been divided into three classes,[2] and some are described as external, others as relating to soul or to body; we call those that relate to soul most properly and truly goods, 15 and psychical actions and activities we class as relating to soul. Therefore our account must be sound, at least according to this view, which is an old one and agreed on by philosophers. It is correct also in that we identify the end with certain actions and activities; for thus it falls among goods of the soul and not among external goods. 20 Another belief which harmonizes with our account is that the happy man lives well and does well; for we have practi-

---

[1] 1094ᵇ 11–27.   [2] Pl. *Euthyd.* 279 AB, *Phil.* 48 E, *Laws*, 743 E.

cally defined happiness as a sort of good life and good action. The characteristics that are looked for in happiness seem also, all of them, to belong to what we have defined happiness as being. For some identify happiness with virtue, some with practical wisdom, others with a kind of philosophic wisdom, others with these, or one of these, accompanied by 25 pleasure or not without pleasure; while others include also external prosperity. Now some of these views have been held by many men and men of old, others by a few eminent persons; and it is not probable that either of these should be entirely mistaken, but rather that they should be right in at least some one respect or even in most respects.

With those who identify happiness with virtue or some 30 one virtue our account is in harmony; for to virtue belongs virtuous activity. But it makes, perhaps, no small difference whether we place the chief good in possession or in use, in state of mind or in activity. For the state of mind may exist without producing any good result, as in a man who **1099ᵃ** is asleep or in some other way quite inactive, but the activity cannot; for one who has the activity will of necessity be acting, and acting well. And as in the Olympic Games it is not the most beautiful and the strongest that are crowned but those who compete (for it is some of these that are victorious), so those who act win, and rightly win, the noble 5 and good things in life.

Their life is also in itself pleasant. For pleasure is a state of *soul*, and to each man that which he is said to be a lover of is pleasant; e. g. not only is a horse pleasant to the lover of horses, and a spectacle to the lover of sights, but 10 also in the same way just acts are pleasant to the lover of justice and in general virtuous acts to the lover of virtue. Now for most men their pleasures are in conflict with one another because these are not by nature pleasant, but the lovers of what is noble find pleasant the things that are by nature pleasant; and virtuous actions are such, so that these are pleasant for such men as well as in their own nature. Their life, therefore, has no further need 15 of pleasure as a sort of adventitious charm, but has its pleasure in itself. For, besides what we have said, the man

who does not rejoice in noble actions is not even good;
since no one would call a man just who did not enjoy acting
justly, nor any man liberal who did not enjoy liberal actions;
20 and similarly in all other cases. If this is so, virtuous
actions must be in themselves pleasant. But they are also
good and *noble*, and have each of these attributes in the
highest degree, since the good man judges well about these
attributes; his judgement is such as we have described.[1]
Happiness then is the best, noblest, and most pleasant thing
25 in the world, and these attributes are not severed as in the
inscription at Delos—

> Most noble is that which is justest, and best is health;
> But pleasantest is it to win what we love.

For all these properties belong to the best activities; and
30 these, or one—the best—of these, we identify with happiness.

Yet evidently, as we said,[2] it needs the external goods as
well; for it is impossible, or not easy, to do noble acts with-
1099ᵇ out the proper equipment. In many actions we use friends
and riches and political power as instruments; and there are
some things the lack of which takes the lustre from happiness, as good birth, goodly children, beauty; for the man who
is very ugly in appearance or ill-born or solitary and child-
5 less is not very likely to be happy, and perhaps a man would
be still less likely if he had thoroughly bad children or
friends or had lost good children or friends by death. As
we said,[2] then, happiness seems to need this sort of prosperity
in addition; for which reason some identify happiness with
good fortune, though others identify it with virtue.

For this reason also the question is asked, whether 9
happiness is to be acquired by learning or by habituation or
10 some other sort of training, or comes in virtue of some
divine providence or again by chance. Now if there is *any*
gift of the gods to men, it is reasonable that happiness
should be god-given, and most surely god-given of all human
things inasmuch as it is the best. But this question would
perhaps be more appropriate to another inquiry; happiness

---

[1] I. e., he judges that virtuous actions are good and noble in the
highest degree. [2] 1098ᵇ 26–9.

seems, however, even if it is not god-sent but comes as a 15
result of virtue and some process of learning or training, to
be among the most godlike things; for that which is the
prize and end of virtue seems to be the best thing in the
world, and something godlike and blessed.

It will also on this view be very generally shared; for all
who are not maimed as regards their potentiality for virtue
may win it by a certain kind of study and care. But if it is 20
better to be happy thus than by chance, it is reasonable that
the facts should be so, since everything that depends on the
action of nature is by nature as good as it can be, and
similarly everything that depends on art or any rational
cause, and especially if it depends on the best of all causes.
To entrust to chance what is greatest and most noble would
be a very defective arrangement.

The answer to the question we are asking is plain also 25
from the definition of happiness; for it has been said [1] to be
a virtuous activity of soul, of a certain kind. Of the
remaining goods, some must necessarily pre-exist as conditions of happiness, and others are naturally co-operative and
useful as instruments. And this will be found to agree with
what we said at the outset; [2] for we stated the end of
political science to be the best end, and political science 30
spends most of its pains on making the citizens to be of a
certain character, viz. good and capable of noble acts.

It is natural, then, that we call neither ox nor horse nor
any other of the animals happy; for none of them is capable
of sharing in such activity. For this reason also a boy is 1100^a
not happy; for he is not yet capable of such acts, owing to
his age; and boys who are called happy are being congratu-
lated by reason of the hopes we have for them. For there
is required, as we said, [3] not only complete virtue but also a
complete life, since many changes occur in life, and all 5
manner of chances, and the most prosperous may fall into
great misfortunes in old age, as is told of Priam in the
Trojan Cycle; and one who has experienced such chances
and has ended wretchedly no one calls happy.

[1] 1098^a 16.   [2] 1094^a 27.

[3] 1098^a 16-18.

10   Must no one at all, then, be called happy while he lives; 10 must we, as Solon says,[1] see the end? Even if we are to lay down this doctrine, is it also the case that a man *is* happy when he is *dead*? Or is not this quite absurd, especially for us who say that happiness is an activity? But if we do not

15 call the dead man happy, and if Solon does not mean this, but that one can then safely *call* a man blessed as being at last beyond evils and misfortunes, this also affords matter for discussion; for both evil and good are thought to exist for a dead man, as much as for one who is alive but not

20 aware of them; e. g. honours and dishonours and the good or bad fortunes of children and in general of descendants. And this also presents a problem; for though a man has lived happily up to old age and has had a death worthy of his life, many reverses may befall his descendants—some

25 of them may be good and attain the life they deserve, while with others the opposite may be the case; and clearly too the degrees of relationship between them and their ancestors may vary indefinitely. It would be odd, then, if the dead man were to share in these changes and become at one time happy, at another wretched; while it would also be odd if

30 the fortunes of the descendants did not for *some* time have *some* effect on the happiness of their ancestors.

But we must return to our first difficulty;[2] for perhaps by a consideration of it our present problem might be solved. Now if we must see the end and only then call a man happy, not as being happy but as having been so

35 before, surely this is a paradox, that when he is happy the attribute that belongs to him is not to be truly predicated 1100ᵇ of him because we do not wish to call living men happy, on account of the changes that may befall them, and because we have assumed happiness to be something permanent and by no means easily changed, while a single man may suffer many turns of fortune's wheel. For clearly if we

5 were to keep pace with his fortunes, we should often call the same man happy and again wretched, making the happy man out to be a 'chameleon and insecurely based'.[3] Or is this keeping pace with his fortunes quite wrong? Success

---

[1] Hdt. i. 32.   [2] Cf. l. 10.   [3] Source unknown.

or failure in life does not depend on these, but human life,
as we said,[1] needs these as mere additions, while virtuous
activities or their opposites are what constitute happiness
or the reverse.   10

The question we have now discussed confirms our definition. For no function of man has so much permanence as
virtuous activities (these are thought to be more durable even
than knowledge of the sciences), and of these themselves the   15
most valuable are more durable because those who are happy
spend their life most readily and most continuously in these;
for this seems to be the reason why we do not forget them.
The attribute in question,[2] then, will belong to the happy
man, and he will be happy throughout his life; for always,
or by preference to everything else, he will be engaged in
virtuous action and contemplation, and he will bear the   20
chances of life most nobly and altogether decorously, if he
is 'truly good' and 'foursquare beyond reproach'.[3]

Now many events happen by chance, and events differing
in importance; small pieces of good fortune or of its opposite
clearly do not weigh down the scales of life one way or the
other, but a multitude of great events if they turn out well   25
will make life happier (for not only are they themselves
such as to add beauty to life, but the way a man deals with
them may be noble and good), while if they turn out ill
they crush and maim happiness; for they both bring pain
with them and hinder many activities. Yet even in these   30
nobility shines through, when a man bears with resignation
many great misfortunes, not through insensibility to pain
but through nobility and greatness of soul.

If activities are, as we said,[4] what gives life its character,
no happy man can become miserable; for he will never do
the acts that are hateful and mean. For the man who is   35
truly good and wise, we think, bears all the chances of life   1101^a
becomingly and always makes the best of circumstances, as
a good general makes the best military use of the army at
his command and a good shoemaker makes the best shoes
out of the hides that are given him; and so with all other   5

---

[1] 1099^a 31–^{b} 7.   [2] Durability.
[3] Simonides, fr. 4 Diehl.   [4] l. 9.

craftsmen. And if this is the case, the happy man can never become miserable—though he will not reach *blessedness*, if he meet with fortunes like those of Priam.

Nor, again, is he many-coloured and changeable; for 10 neither will he be moved from his happy state easily or by any ordinary misadventures, but only by many great ones, nor, if he has had many great misadventures, will he recover his happiness in a short time, but if at all, only in a long and complete one in which he has attained many splendid successes.

Why then should we not say that he is happy who is 15 active in accordance with complete virtue and is sufficiently equipped with external goods, not for some chance period but throughout a complete life? Or must we add 'and who is destined to live thus and die as befits his life'? Certainly the future is obscure to us, while happiness, we claim, is an end and something in every way final. If so, we shall call happy those among living men in whom these conditions 20 are, and are to be, fulfilled—but happy *men*. So much for these questions.

¹That the fortunes of descendants and of all a man's 11 friends should not affect his happiness at all seems a very unfriendly doctrine, and one opposed to the opinions men hold; but since the events that happen are numerous and 25 admit of all sorts of difference, and some come more near to us and others less so, it seems a long—nay, an infinite—task to discuss each in detail; a general outline will perhaps suffice. If, then, as some of a man's own misadventures have a certain weight and influence on life while others are, as it 30 were, lighter, so too there are differences among the misadventures of our friends taken as a whole, and it makes a difference whether the various sufferings befall the living or the dead (much more even than whether lawless and terrible deeds are presupposed in a tragedy or done on the stage), this difference also must be taken into account; or rather, 35 perhaps, the fact that doubt is felt whether the dead share 1101ᵇ in any good or evil. For it seems, from these considerations,

---

¹ Aristotle now returns to the question stated in 1100ᵃ 18-30.

that even if anything whether good or evil penetrates to them, it must be something weak and negligible, either in itself or for them, or if not, at least it must be such in degree and kind as not to make happy those who are not happy nor to take away their blessedness from those who are. The good or bad fortunes of friends, then, seem to have some 5 effects on the dead, but effects of such a kind and degree as neither to make the happy unhappy nor to produce any other change of the kind.

12 These questions having been definitely answered, let 10 us consider whether happiness is among the things that are praised or rather among the things that are prized; for clearly it is not to be placed among *potentialities*.[1] Everything that is praised seems to be praised because it is of a certain kind and is related somehow to something else; for we praise the just or brave man and in general both the good man and virtue itself because of the actions and 15 functions involved, and we praise the strong man, the good runner, and so on, because he is of a certain kind and is related in a certain way to something good and important. This is clear also from the praises of the gods; for it seems absurd that the gods should be referred to our standard, but this *is* done because praise involves a reference, as we 20 said, to something else. But if praise is for things such as we have described, clearly what applies to the best things is not praise, but something greater and better, as is indeed obvious; for what we do to the gods and the most godlike of men is to call them blessed and happy. And so too 25 with good *things*; no one praises happiness as he does justice, but rather calls it blessed, as being something more divine and better.

Eudoxus also seems to have been right in his method of advocating the supremacy of pleasure; he thought that the fact that, though a good, it is not praised indicated it to be better than the things that are praised, and that this is what God and the good are; for by reference to these all other 30 things are judged. *Praise* is appropriate to virtue, for as a result of virtue men tend to do noble deeds; but *encomia* are

---

[1] Cf. *Top.* 126^{b} 4; *M. M.* 1183^{b} 20.

bestowed on acts, whether of the body or of the soul. But
perhaps nicety in these matters is more proper to those who
35 have made a study of encomia; to us it is clear from what
IIO2^a has been said that happiness is among the things that are
prized and perfect. It seems to be so also from the fact
that it is a first principle; for it is for the sake of this that we
all do all that we do, and the first principle and cause of
goods is, we claim, something prized and divine.

5 Since happiness is an activity of soul in accordance with **13**
perfect virtue, we must consider the nature of virtue; for
perhaps we shall thus see better the nature of happiness.
The true student of politics, too, is thought to have
studied virtue above all things; for he wishes to make
10 his fellow citizens good and obedient to the laws. As
an example of this we have the lawgivers of the Cretans
and the Spartans, and any others of the kind that there
may have been. And if this inquiry belongs to political
science, clearly the pursuit of it will be in accordance with
our original plan. But clearly the virtue we must study
is human virtue; for the good we were seeking was human
15 good and the happiness human happiness. By human
virtue we mean not that of the body but that of the soul;
and happiness also we call an activity of soul. But if this
is so, clearly the student of politics must know somehow the
facts about soul, as the man who is to heal the eyes or the
body as a whole must know about the eyes or the body;
20 and all the more since politics is more prized and better
than medicine; but even among doctors the best educated
spend much labour on acquiring knowledge of the body.
The student of politics, then, must study the soul, and must
study it with these objects in view, and do so just to the
extent which is sufficient for the questions we are discussing;
25 for further precision is perhaps something more laborious
than our purposes require.

Some things are said about it, adequately enough, even
in the discussions outside our school, and we must use
these; e. g. that one element in the soul is irrational and one
has a rational principle. Whether these are separated as the

parts of the body or of anything divisible are, or are distinct 30
by definition but by nature inseparable, like convex and con-
cave in the circumference of a circle, does not affect the
present question.

Of the irrational element one division seems to be widely
distributed, and vegetative in its nature, I mean that which
causes nutrition and growth ; for it is this kind of power of the
soul that one must assign to all nurslings and to embryos, 1102ᵇ
and this same power to full-grown creatures; this is more
reasonable than to assign some different power to them.
Now the excellence of this seems to be common to all
species and not specifically human ; for this part or faculty 5
seems to function most in sleep, while goodness and badness
are least manifest in sleep (whence comes the saying that
the happy are no better off than the wretched for half their
lives ; and this happens naturally enough, since sleep is an
inactivity of the soul in that respect in which it is called good
or bad), unless perhaps to a small extent some of the move- 10
ments actually penetrate to the soul, and in this respect the
dreams of good men are better than those of ordinary people.
Enough of this subject, however ; let us leave the nutritive
faculty alone, since it has by its nature no share in human
excellence.

There seems to be also another irrational element in the
soul—one which in a sense, however, shares in a rational
principle. For we praise the rational principle of the
continent man and of the incontinent, and the part of their 15
soul that has such a principle, since it urges them aright and
towards the best objects; but there is found in them
also another element naturally opposed to the rational
principle, which fights against and resists that principle.
For exactly as paralysed limbs when we intend to move 20
them to the right turn on the contrary to the left, so is
it with the soul ; the impulses of incontinent people move
in contrary directions. But while in the body we see
that which moves astray, in the soul we do not. No doubt,
however, we must none the less suppose that in the soul
too there is something contrary to the rational principle, 25
resisting and opposing it. In what sense it is distinct from

the other elements does not concern us. Now even this seems to have a share in a rational principle, as we said ;[1] at any rate in the continent man it obeys the rational principle—and presumably in the temperate and brave man it is still more obedient ; for in him it speaks, on all matters, with the same voice as the rational principle.

Therefore the irrational element also appears to be twofold. For the vegetative element in no way shares in a rational principle, but the appetitive and in general the desiring element in a sense shares in it, in so far as it listens to and obeys it; this is the sense in which we speak of 'taking account' of one's father or one's friends, not that in which we speak of 'accounting' for a mathematical property.[2] That the irrational element is in some sense persuaded by a rational principle is indicated also by the giving of advice and by all reproof and exhortation. And if this element also must be said to have a rational principle, that which has a rational principle (as well as that which has not) will be twofold, one subdivision having it in the strict sense and in itself, and the other having a tendency to obey as one does one's father.

Virtue too is distinguished into kinds in accordance with this difference ; for we say that some of the virtues are intellectual and others moral, philosophic wisdom and understanding and practical wisdom being intellectual, liberality and temperance moral. For in speaking about a man's character we do not say that he is wise or has understanding but that he is good-tempered or temperate ; yet we praise the wise man also with respect to his state of mind ; and of states of mind we call those which merit praise virtues.

[1] l. 13.

[2] It is impossible in English to reproduce the play on the meanings of λόγον ἔχειν, translated above 'have a rational principle' and here 'take account of' and 'account for'. Aristotle's point is that the ἄλογον (the faculty of desire) can be said to have λόγος only in the sense that it can obey a λόγος presented to it by reason, not in the sense that it can originate a λόγος—just as many people can 'take account of' a father's advice who could not 'account for' a mathematical property.

BOOK II

1 VIRTUE, then, being of two kinds, intellectual and moral, intellectual virtue in the main owes both its birth 15 and its growth to teaching (for which reason it requires experience and time), while moral virtue comes about as a result of habit, whence also its name (ἠθική) is one that is formed by a slight variation from the word ἔθος (habit). From this it is also plain that none of the moral virtues arises in us by nature; for nothing that exists by nature can form a habit contrary to its nature. For instance the stone 20 which by nature moves downwards cannot be habituated to move upwards, not even if one tries to train it by throwing it up ten thousand times; nor can fire be habituated to move downwards, nor can anything else that by nature behaves in one way be trained to behave in another. Neither by nature, then, nor contrary to nature do the virtues arise in us; rather we are adapted by nature to receive them, and are made perfect by habit. 25

Again, of all the things that come to us by nature we first acquire the potentiality and later exhibit the activity (this is plain in the case of the senses; for it was not by often seeing or often hearing that we got these senses, but on the 30 contrary we had them before we used them, and did not come to have them by using them); but the virtues we get by first exercising them, as also happens in the case of the arts as well. For the things we have to learn before we can do them, we learn by doing them, e. g. men become builders by building and lyre-players by playing the lyre; so too we become just by doing just acts, temperate by 1103ᵇ doing temperate acts, brave by doing brave acts.

This is confirmed by what happens in states; for legislators make the citizens good by forming habits in them, and this is the wish of every legislator, and those who do not effect 5 it miss their mark, and it is in this that a good constitution differs from a bad one.

Again, it is from the same causes and by the same means that every virtue is both produced and destroyed, and similarly every art; for it is from playing the lyre that both good and bad lyre-players are produced. And the corresponding statement is true of builders and of all the
10 rest ; men will be good or bad builders as a result of building well or badly. For if this were not so, there would have been no need of a teacher, but all men would have been born good or bad at their craft. This, then, is the case with the virtues also ; by doing the acts that we do in our transactions
15 with other men we become just or unjust, and by doing the acts that we do in the presence of danger, and being habituated to feel fear or confidence, we become brave or cowardly. The same is true of appetites and feelings of anger; some men become temperate and good-tempered, others self-
20 indulgent and irascible, by behaving in one way or the other in the appropriate circumstances. Thus, in one word, states of character arise out of like activities. This is why the activities we exhibit must be of a certain kind ; it is because the states of character correspond to the differences between these. It makes no small difference, then, whether we form
25 habits of one kind or of another from our very youth ; it makes a very great difference, or rather *all* the difference.

Since, then, the present inquiry does not aim at theoretical **2** knowledge like the others (for we are inquiring not in order to know what virtue is, but in order to become good, since otherwise our inquiry would have been of no use), we must examine the nature of actions, namely how we ought to do
30 them ; for these determine also the nature of the states of character that are produced, as we have said.[1] Now, that we must act according to the right rule is a common principle and must be assumed—it will be discussed later,[2] i. e. both what the right rule is, and how it is related to the
1104ᵃ other virtues. But this must be agreed upon beforehand, that the whole account of matters of conduct must be given in outline and not precisely, as we said at the very beginning[3] that the accounts we demand must be in accordance with

---

[1] ᵃ 31–ᵇ 25.   [2] vi. 13.   [3] 1094ᵇ 11–27.

the subject-matter; matters concerned with conduct and questions of what is good for us have no fixity, any more than matters of health. The general account being of this 5 nature, the account of particular cases is yet more lacking in exactness; for they do not fall under any art or precept but the agents themselves must in each case consider what is appropriate to the occasion, as happens also in the art of medicine or of navigation.

But though our present account is of this nature we must 10 give what help we can. First, then, let us consider this, that it is the nature of such things to be destroyed by defect and excess, as we see in the case of strength and of health (for to gain light on things imperceptible we must use the evidence of sensible things); both excessive and defective 15 exercise destroys the strength, and similarly drink or food which is above or below a certain amount destroys the health, while that which is proportionate both produces and increases and preserves it. So too is it, then, in the case of temperance and courage and the other virtues. For the man who 20 flies from and fears everything and does not stand his ground against anything becomes a coward, and the man who fears nothing at all but goes to meet every danger becomes rash; and similarly the man who indulges in every pleasure and abstains from none becomes self-indulgent, while the man who shuns every pleasure, as boors do, becomes in a way insensible; temperance and courage, then, are destroyed by 25 excess and defect, and preserved by the mean.

But not only are the sources and causes of their origination and growth the same as those of their destruction, but also the sphere of their actualization will be the same; for this is also true of the things which are more evident to sense, e.g. of strength; it is produced by taking much 30 food and undergoing much exertion, and it is the strong man that will be most able to do these things. So too is it with the virtues; by abstaining from pleasures we become temperate, and it is when we have become so that we are most able to abstain from them; and similarly too in the 35 case of courage; for by being habituated to despise things 1104ᵇ that are terrible and to stand our ground against them

we become brave, and it is when we have become so
that we shall be most able to stand our ground against them.

We must take as a sign of states of character the pleasure **3**
5 or pain that ensues on acts; for the man who abstains from
bodily pleasures and delights in this very fact is temperate,
while the man who is annoyed at it is self-indulgent, and he
who stands his ground against things that are terrible and
delights in this or at least is not pained is brave, while
the man who is pained is a coward. For moral excellence
is concerned with pleasures and pains; it is on account of the
10 pleasure that we do bad things, and on account of the pain
that we abstain from noble ones. Hence we ought to have
been brought up in a particular way from our very youth,
as Plato says,[1] so as both to delight in and to be pained by
the things that we ought; for this is the right education.

Again, if the virtues are concerned with actions and passions, and every passion and every action is accompanied by
15 pleasure and pain, for this reason also virtue will be concerned
with pleasures and pains. This is indicated also by the fact
that punishment is inflicted by these means; for it is a kind of
cure, and it is the nature of cures to be effected by contraries.

Again, as we said but lately,[2] every state of soul has
20 a nature relative to and concerned with the kind of things
by which it tends to be made worse or better; but it is
by reason of pleasures and pains that men become bad, by
pursuing and avoiding these—either the pleasures and pains
they ought not or when they ought not or as they ought not,
or by going wrong in one of the other similar ways that may
be distinguished. Hence men[3] even define the virtues as
25 certain states of impassivity and rest; not well, however,
because they speak absolutely, and do not say 'as one ought'
and 'as one ought not' and 'when one ought or ought not',
and the other things that may be added. We assume, then,
that this kind of excellence tends to do what is best with
regard to pleasures and pains, and vice does the contrary.

The following facts also may show us that virtue and vice
30 are concerned with these same things. There being three

---

[1] *Laws*, 653 A ff., *Rep.* 401 E-402 A.   [2] a 27-b 3.
[3] Probably Speusippus is referred to.

objects of choice and three of avoidance, the noble, the
advantageous, the pleasant, and their contraries, the base,
the injurious, the painful, about all of these the good man
tends to go right and the bad man to go wrong, and
especially about pleasure ; for this is common to the animals,
and also it accompanies all objects of choice ; for even the 35
noble and the advantageous appear pleasant.

Again, it has grown up with us all from our infancy ; this **1105**^a
is why it is difficult to rub off this passion, engrained as it is
in our life. And we measure even our actions, some of us
more and others less, by the rule of pleasure and pain. For 5
this reason, then, our whole inquiry must be about these ;
for to feel delight and pain rightly or wrongly has no small
effect on our actions.

Again, it is harder to fight with pleasure than with anger, to
use Heraclitus' phrase [1], but both art and virtue are always
concerned with what is harder ; for even the good is better
when it is harder. Therefore for this reason also the whole 10
concern both of virtue and of political science is with
pleasures and pains ; for the man who uses these well will
be good, he who uses them badly bad.

That virtue, then, is concerned with pleasures and pains,
and that by the acts from which it arises it is both increased
and, if they are done differently, destroyed, and that the 15
acts from which it arose are those in which it actualizes
itself—let this be taken as said.

4   The question might be asked, what we mean by saying [2]
that we must become just by doing just acts, and temperate
by doing temperate acts ; for if men do just and temperate
acts, they are already just and temperate, exactly as, if they 20
do what is in accordance with the laws of grammar and of
music, they are grammarians and musicians.

Or is this not true even of the arts ? It is possible to do
something that is in accordance with the laws of grammar,
either by chance or at the suggestion of another. A man
will be a grammarian, then, only when he has both done

---

[1] Fr. 85 Diels, θυμῶι μάχεσθαι χαλεπόν· ὅ τι γὰρ ἂν θέληι, ψυχῆς
ὠνεῖται.

[2] 1103^a 31–^b 25, 1104^a 27–^b 3.

25 something grammatical and done it grammatically; and this means doing it in accordance with the grammatical knowledge in himself.

Again, the case of the arts and that of the virtues are not similar; for the products of the arts have their goodness in themselves, so that it is enough that they should have a certain character, but if the acts that are in accordance with the virtues have themselves a certain character it does 30 not follow that they are done justly or temperately. The agent also must be in a certain condition when he does them; in the first place he must have knowledge, secondly he must choose the acts, and choose them for their own sakes, and thirdly his action must proceed from a firm and unchangeable character. These are not reckoned in as 1105ᵇ conditions of the possession of the arts, except the bare knowledge; but as a condition of the possession of the virtues knowledge has little or no weight, while the other conditions count not for a little but for everything, i. e. the very conditions which result from often doing just and temperate acts.

5 Actions, then, are called just and temperate when they are such as the just or the temperate man would do; but it is not the man who does these that is just and temperate, but the man who also does them *as* just and temperate men do them. It is well said, then, that it is by doing just acts that the 10 just man is produced, and by doing temperate acts the temperate man; without doing these no one would have even a prospect of becoming good.

But most people do not do these, but take refuge in theory and think they are being philosophers and will become 15 good in this way, behaving somewhat like patients who listen attentively to their doctors, but do none of the things they are ordered to do. As the latter will not be made well in body by such a course of treatment, the former will not be made well in soul by such a course of philosophy.

Next we must consider what virtue is. Since things that 5 20 are found in the soul are of three kinds—passions, faculties, states of character, virtue must be one of these. By passions

I mean appetite, anger, fear, confidence, envy, joy, friendly
feeling, hatred, longing, emulation, pity, and in general the
feelings that are accompanied by pleasure or pain; by
faculties the things in virtue of which we are said to be
capable of feeling these, e.g. of becoming angry or being
pained or feeling pity; by states of character the things in 25
virtue of which we stand well or badly with reference to the
passions, e.g. with reference to anger we stand badly if we
feel it violently or too weakly, and well if we feel it moderately; and similarly with reference to the other passions.

Now neither the virtues nor the vices are *passions*, because
we are not called good or bad on the ground of our
passions, but are so called on the ground of our virtues and 30
our vices, and because we are neither praised nor blamed
for our passions (for the man who feels fear or anger is not
praised, nor is the man who simply feels anger blamed, but
the man who feels it in a certain way), but for our virtues 1106^a
and our vices we *are* praised or blamed.

Again, we feel anger and fear without choice, but the
virtues are modes of choice or involve choice.   Further, in
respect of the passions we are said to be moved, but in 5
respect of the virtues and the vices we are said not to be
moved but to be disposed in a particular way.

For these reasons also they are not *faculties*; for we
are neither called good nor bad, nor praised nor blamed, for
the simple capacity of feeling the passions; again, we have
the faculties by nature, but we are not made good or bad
by nature; we have spoken of this before.[1]

If, then, the virtues are neither passions nor faculties, all 10
that remains is that they should be *states of character*.

Thus we have stated what virtue is in respect of its genus.

6   We must, however, not only describe virtue as a state of
character, but also say what sort of state it is.   We may 15
remark, then, that every virtue or excellence both brings
into good condition the thing of which it is the excellence
and makes the work of that thing be done well; e.g. the
excellence of the eye makes both the eye and its work good;

[1] 1103^a 18–^b 2.

for it is by the excellence of the eye that we see well. Simi-
20 larly the excellence of the horse makes a horse both good in
itself and good at running and at carrying its rider and at
awaiting the attack of the enemy. Therefore, if this is true
in every case, the virtue of man also will be the state of
character which makes a man good and which makes him
do his own work well.

How this is to happen we have stated already,[1] but it
25 will be made plain also by the following consideration
of the specific nature of virtue. In everything that is
continuous and divisible it is possible to take more, less, or
an equal amount, and that either in terms of the thing
itself or relatively to us; and the equal is an intermediate
between excess and defect. By the intermediate in the
object I mean that which is equidistant from each of the
30 extremes, which is one and the same for all men; by
the intermediate relatively to us that which is neither too
much nor too little—and this is not one, nor the same for all.
For instance, if ten is many and two is few, six is the intermediate, taken in terms of the object; for it exceeds and is
35 exceeded by an equal amount; this is intermediate according to arithmetical proportion. But the intermediate relatively to us is not to be taken so; if ten pounds are too
1106ᵇ much for a particular person to eat and two too little, it does
not follow that the trainer will order six pounds; for this also
is perhaps too much for the person who is to take it, or too
little—too little for Milo,[2] too much for the beginner in athletic
5 exercises. The same is true of running and wrestling. Thus
a master of any art avoids excess and defect, but seeks the
intermediate and chooses this—the intermediate not in the
object but relatively to us.

If it is thus, then, that every art does its work well—by
looking to the intermediate and judging its works by this
10 standard (so that we often say of good works of art that it
is not possible either to take away or to add anything,
implying that excess and defect destroy the goodness
of works of art, while the mean preserves it; and good
artists, as we say, look to this in their work), and if, further,

---

[1] 1104ᵃ 11-27.   [2] A famous wrestler.

virtue is more exact and better than any art, as nature also is, then virtue must have the quality of aiming at the 15 intermediate. I mean moral virtue; for it is this that is concerned with passions and actions, and in these there is excess, defect, and the intermediate. For instance, both fear and confidence and appetite and anger and pity and in general pleasure and pain may be felt both too much and too little, and in both cases not well; but to feel them at the 20 right times, with reference to the right objects, towards the right people, with the right motive, and in the right way, is what is both intermediate and best, and this is characteristic of virtue. Similarly with regard to actions also there is excess, defect, and the intermediate. Now virtue is con- cerned with passions and actions, in which excess is a form 25 of failure, and so is defect, while the intermediate is praised and is a form of success; and being praised and being successful are both characteristics of virtue. Therefore virtue is a kind of mean, since, as we have seen, it aims at what is intermediate.

Again, it is possible to fail in many ways (for evil belongs to the class of the unlimited, as the Pythagoreans conjectured, and good to that of the limited), while to succeed is possible 30 only in one way (for which reason also one is easy and the other difficult—to miss the mark easy, to hit it difficult); for these reasons also, then, excess and defect are characteristic of vice, and the mean of virtue;

For men are good in but one way, but bad in many.[1]   35

Virtue, then, is a state of character concerned with choice, lying in a mean, i. e. the mean relative to us, this being 1107[a] determined by a rational principle, and by that principle by which the man of practical wisdom would determine it. Now it is a mean between two vices, that which depends on excess and that which depends on defect; and again it is a mean because the vices respectively fall short of or exceed what is right in both passions and actions, while virtue both 5 finds and chooses that which is intermediate. Hence ˙n respect of its substance and the definition which states its

---

[1] Fr. eleg. adesp. 16, Diehl.

essence virtue is a mean, with regard to what is best and right an extreme.

But not every action nor every passion admits of a mean;
10 for some have names that already imply badness, e. g. spite, shamelessness, envy, and in the case of actions adultery, theft, murder; for all of these and suchlike things imply by their names that they are themselves bad, and not the excesses or deficiencies of them. It is not possible, then, ever to be right with regard to them; one must always be
15 wrong. Nor does goodness or badness with regard to such things depend on committing adultery with the right woman, at the right time, and in the right way, but simply to do any of them is to go wrong. It would be equally absurd, then, to expect that in unjust, cowardly, and voluptuous action
20 there should be a mean, an excess, and a deficiency; for at that rate there would be a mean of excess and of deficiency, an excess of excess, and a deficiency of deficiency. But as there is no excess and deficiency of temperance and courage because what is intermediate is in a sense an extreme, so too of the actions we have mentioned there is no mean nor any excess and deficiency, but however they are done they are
25 wrong; for in general there is neither a mean of excess and deficiency, nor excess and deficiency of a mean.

We must, however, not only make this general statement, **7** but also apply it to the individual facts. For among statements about conduct those which are general apply more
30 widely, but those which are particular are more genuine, since conduct has to do with individual cases, and our statements must harmonize with the facts in these cases. We may take these cases from our table. With regard to feelings of
1107^b fear and confidence courage is the mean; of the people who exceed, he who exceeds in fearlessness has no name (many of the states have no name), while the man who exceeds in confidence is rash, and he who exceeds in fear and falls short in confidence is a coward. With regard to pleasures and pains—not all of them, and not so much with regard to the
5 pains—the mean is temperance, the excess self-indulgence. Persons deficient with regard to the pleasures are not often

found ; hence such persons also have received no name. But let us call them 'insensible'.

With regard to giving and taking of money the mean is liberality, the excess and the defect prodigality and meanness. In these actions people exceed and fall short in contrary ways ; the prodigal exceeds in spending and falls short in taking, while the mean man exceeds in taking and falls short in spending. (At present we are giving a mere outline or summary, and are satisfied with this ; later these states will be more exactly determined.[1]) With regard to money there are also other dispositions—a mean, magnificence (for the magnificent man differs from the liberal man ; the former deals with large sums, the latter with small ones), an excess, tastelessness and vulgarity, and a deficiency, niggardliness ; these differ from the states opposed to liberality, and the mode of their difference will be stated later.[2]

With regard to honour and dishonour the mean is proper pride, the excess is known as a sort of 'empty vanity', and the deficiency is undue humility ; and as we said [3] liberality was related to magnificence, differing from it by dealing with small sums, so there is a state similarly related to proper pride, being concerned with small honours while that is concerned with great. For it is possible to desire honour as one ought, and more than one ought, and less, and the man who exceeds in his desires is called ambitious, the man who falls short unambitious, while the intermediate person has no name. The dispositions also are nameless, except that that of the ambitious man is called ambition. Hence the people who are at the extremes lay claim to the middle place ; and we ourselves sometimes call the intermediate person ambitious and sometimes unambitious, and sometimes praise the ambitious man and sometimes the unambitious. The reason of our doing this will be stated **1108^a** in what follows ; [4] but now let us speak of the remaining states according to the method which has been indicated.

With regard to anger also there is an excess, a deficiency, and a mean. Although they can scarcely be said to have

[1] iv. 1.   [2] 1122ᵃ 20–9, ᵇ 10–18.
[3] ll. 17–19.   [4] ᵇ 11–26, 1125ᵇ 14–18.

names, yet since we call the intermediate person good-tempered let us call the mean good temper; of the persons at the extremes let the one who exceeds be called irascible, and his vice irascibility, and the man who falls short an inirascible sort of person, and the deficiency inirascibility.

There are also three other means, which have a certain 10 likeness to one another, but differ from one another: for they are all concerned with intercourse in words and actions, but differ in that one is concerned with truth in this sphere, the other two with pleasantness; and of this one kind is exhibited in giving amusement, the other in all the circumstances of life. We must therefore speak of these too, that we may the better see that in all things the mean is praise-15 worthy, and the extremes neither praiseworthy nor right, but worthy of blame. Now most of these states also have no names, but we must try, as in the other cases, to invent names ourselves so that we may be clear and easy to follow. 20 With regard to truth, then, the intermediate is a truthful sort of person and the mean may be called truthfulness, while the pretence which exaggerates is boastfulness and the person characterized by it a boaster, and that which understates is mock modesty and the person characterized by it mock-modest. With regard to pleasantness in the giving of amusement the intermediate person is ready-witted and the disposition ready wit, the excess is buffoonery and the 25 person characterized by it a buffoon, while the man who falls short is a sort of boor and his state is boorishness. With regard to the remaining kind of pleasantness, that which is exhibited in life in general, the man who is pleasant in the right way is friendly and the mean is friendliness, while the man who exceeds is an obsequious person if he has no end in view, a flatterer if he is aiming at his own advantage, and the man who falls short and is unpleasant in all circumstances is a quarrelsome and surly sort of person.

30 There are also means in the passions and concerned with the passions; since shame is not a virtue, and yet praise is extended to the modest man. For even in these matters one man is said to be intermediate, and another to exceed,

as for instance the bashful man who is ashamed of everything; while he who falls short or is not ashamed of anything at all is shameless, and the intermediate person is
modest. Righteous indignation is a mean between envy 35
and spite, and these states are concerned with the pain and **1108ᵇ**
pleasure that are felt at the fortunes of our neighbours; the
man who is characterized by righteous indignation is pained
at undeserved good fortune, the envious man, going beyond
him, is pained at all good fortune, and the spiteful man falls 5
so far short of being pained that he even rejoices.[1] But
these states there will be an opportunity of describing elsewhere;[2] with regard to justice, since it has not one simple
meaning, we shall, after describing the other states, distinguish its two kinds and say how each of them is a mean;[3]
and similarly we shall treat also of the rational virtues.[4]   10

8   There are three kinds of disposition, then, two of them
vices, involving excess and deficiency respectively, and one
a virtue, viz. the mean, and all are in a sense opposed to all;
for the extreme states are contrary both to the intermediate state and to each other, and the intermediate to
the extremes; as the equal is greater relatively to the less, 15
less relatively to the greater, so the middle states are
excessive relatively to the deficiencies, deficient relatively
to the excesses, both in passions and in actions. For the
brave man appears rash relatively to the coward, and
cowardly relatively to the rash man; and similarly the 20
temperate man appears self-indulgent relatively to the insensible man, insensible relatively to the self-indulgent, and the
liberal man prodigal relatively to the mean man, mean relatively to the prodigal. Hence also the people at the extremes
push the intermediate man each over to the other, and the

---

[1] Aristotle must mean that while the envious man is pained at the
good fortune of others, whether deserved or not, the spiteful man is
pleased at the *bad* fortune of others, whether deserved or not. But if
he had stated this in full, he would have seen that there is no real
opposition.

[2] The reference may be to the whole treatment of the moral virtues
in iii. 6–iv. 9, or to the discussion of shame in iv. 9 and an intended
corresponding discussion of righteous indignation, or to the discussion
of these two states in *Rhet.* ii. 6, 9, 10.

[3] 1129ᵃ 26–ᵇ1, 1130ᵃ 14–ᵇ5, 1131ᵇ 9–15, 1132ᵃ 24–30, 1133ᵇ 30–1134ᵃ 1.

[4] Bk. vi.

brave man is called rash by the coward, cowardly by the
25 rash man, and correspondingly in the other cases.

These states being thus opposed to one another, the
greatest contrariety is that of the extremes to each other,
rather than to the intermediate; for these are further from
each other than from the intermediate, as the great is
further from the small and the small from the great than
30 both are from the equal. Again, to the intermediate some
extremes show a certain likeness, as that of rashness to
courage and that of prodigality to liberality; but the
extremes show the greatest unlikeness to each other; now
contraries are defined as the things that are furthest from
each other, so that things that are further apart are more
35 contrary.

1109ᵃ To the mean in some cases the deficiency, in some the
excess is more opposed; e. g. it is not rashness, which is an
excess, but cowardice, which is a deficiency, that is more
opposed to courage, and not insensibility, which is a deficiency, but self-indulgence, which is an excess, that is more
5 opposed to temperance. This happens from two reasons,
one being drawn from the thing itself; for because one
extreme is nearer and liker to the intermediate, we oppose
not this but rather its contrary to the intermediate. E. g.,
since rashness is thought liker and nearer to courage, and
cowardice more unlike, we oppose rather the latter to
10 courage; for things that are further from the intermediate
are thought more contrary to it. This, then, is one cause,
drawn from the thing itself; another is drawn from ourselves; for the things to which we ourselves more naturally
tend seem more contrary to the intermediate. For instance,
15 we ourselves tend more naturally to pleasures, and hence
are more easily carried away towards self-indulgence than
towards propriety. We describe as contrary to the mean,
then, rather the directions in which we more often go to
great lengths; and therefore self-indulgence, which is an
excess, is the more contrary to temperance.

20 That moral virtue is a mean, then, and in what sense it is 9
so, and that it is a mean between two vices, the one involving

excess, the other deficiency, and that it is such because its
character is to aim at what is intermediate in passions and
in actions, has been sufficiently stated.   Hence also it is no
easy task to be good.   For in everything it is no easy task
to find the middle, e. g. to find the middle of a circle is not 25
for every one but for him who knows; so, too, any one can
get angry—that is easy—or give or spend money; but to
do this to the right person, to the right extent, at the right
time, with the right motive, and in the right way, *that* is
not for every one, nor is it easy ; wherefore goodness is both
rare and laudable and noble.

Hence he who aims at the intermediate must first depart 30
from what is the more contrary to it, as Calypso advises—

Hold the ship out beyond that surf and spray.[1]

For of the extremes one is more erroneous, one less so ;
therefore, since to hit the mean is hard in the extreme,
we must as a second best, as people say, take the least of
the evils ; and this will be done best in the way we 35
describe.

But we must consider the things towards which we our- 1109ᵇ
selves also are easily carried away ; for some of us tend to
one thing, some to another ; and this will be recognizable
from the pleasure and the pain we feel.   We must drag
ourselves away to the contrary extreme ; for we shall get 5
into the intermediate state by drawing well away from
error, as people do in straightening sticks that are bent.

Now in everything the pleasant or pleasure is most to be
guarded against ; for we do not judge it impartially.   We
ought, then, to feel towards pleasure as the elders of the
people felt towards Helen, and in all circumstances repeat 10
their saying ;[2] for if we dismiss pleasure thus we are less
likely to go astray.   It is by doing this, then, (to sum the
matter up) that we shall best be able to hit the mean.

But this is no doubt difficult, and especially in individual
cases ; for it is not easy to determine both how and with 15

---

[1] *Od.* xii. 219 f. (Mackail's trans.).   But it was Circe who gave the
advice (xii. 108), and the actual quotation is from Odysseus' orders to
his steersman.

[2] *Il.* iii. 156–60.

whom and on what provocation and how long one should be
angry; for we too sometimes praise those who fall short
and call them good-tempered, but sometimes we praise
those who get angry and call them manly. The man,
however, who deviates little from goodness is not blamed,
whether he do so in the direction of the more or of the less,
but only the man who deviates more widely; for *he* does
20 not fail to be noticed. But up to what point and to what
extent a man must deviate before he becomes blameworthy
it is not easy to determine by reasoning, any more than
anything else that is perceived by the senses; such things
depend on particular facts, and the decision rests with
perception. So much, then, is plain, that the intermediate
state is in all things to be praised, but that we must incline
25 sometimes towards the excess, sometimes towards the deficiency; for so shall we most easily hit the mean and what
is right.

BOOK III

1   SINCE virtue is concerned with passions and actions, and 30
on voluntary passions and actions praise and blame are
bestowed, on those that are involuntary pardon, and sometimes also pity, to distinguish the voluntary and the involuntary is presumably necessary for those who are
studying the nature of virtue, and useful also for legislators
with a view to the assigning both of honours and of punishments.

Those things, then, are thought involuntary, which take 35
place under compulsion or owing to ignorance; and that is 1110^a
compulsory of which the moving principle is outside, being
a principle in which nothing is contributed by the person
who is acting or is feeling the passion, e. g. if he were to be
carried somewhere by a wind, or by men who had him in
their power.

But with regard to the things that are done from fear of
greater evils or for some noble object (e. g. if a tyrant were 5
to order one to do something base, having one's parents and
children in his power, and if one did the action they were to
be saved, but otherwise would be put to death), it may be
debated whether such actions are involuntary or voluntary.
Something of the sort happens also with regard to the
throwing of goods overboard in a storm; for in the abstract
no one throws goods away voluntarily, but on condition of 10
its securing the safety of himself and his crew any sensible
man does so.   Such actions, then, are mixed, but are more
like voluntary actions; for they are worthy of choice at the
time when they are done, and the end of an action is relative to the occasion.   Both the terms, then, 'voluntary' and
'involuntary', must be used with reference to the moment
of action.   Now the man acts voluntarily; for the principle 15
that moves the instrumental parts of the body in such actions
is in him, and the things of which the moving principle is in

a man himself are in his power to do or not to do.   Such actions, therefore, are voluntary, but in the abstract perhaps involuntary; for no one would choose any such act in itself.

20   For such actions men are sometimes even praised, when they endure something base or painful in return for great and noble objects gained; in the opposite case they are blamed, since to endure the greatest indignities for no noble end or for a trifling end is the mark of an inferior person. On some actions praise indeed is not bestowed, but pardon

25 is, when one does what he ought not under pressure which overstrains human nature and which no one could withstand.   But some acts, perhaps, we cannot be forced to do, but ought rather to face death after the most fearful sufferings; for the things that ' forced ' Euripides' Alcmaeon to slay his mother [1] seem absurd.   It is difficult sometimes to determine what should be chosen at what cost, and what

30 should be endured in return for what gain, and yet more difficult to abide by our decisions; for as a rule what is expected is painful, and what we are forced to do is base, whence praise and blame are bestowed on those who have been compelled or have not.

1110^b   What sort of acts, then, should be called compulsory? We answer that without qualification actions are so when the cause is in the external circumstances and the agent contributes nothing.   But the things that in themselves are involuntary, but now and in return for these gains are worthy of choice, and whose moving principle is in the

5 agent, are in themselves involuntary, but now and in return for these gains voluntary.   They are more like voluntary acts; for actions are in the class of particulars, and the particular acts here are voluntary.   What sort of things are to be chosen, and in return for what, it is not easy to state; for there are many differences in the particular cases.

But if some one were to say that pleasant and noble objects have a compelling power, forcing us from without,

10 all acts would be for him compulsory; for it is for these

---

[1] Μάλιστα μέν μ᾽ ἐπῆρ᾽ ἐπισκήψας πατήρ,
ὅθ᾽ ἅρματ᾽ εἰσέβαινεν εἰς Θήβας ἰών,

Alcmeon, fr. 69, Nauck.

objects that all men do everything they do. And those
who act under compulsion and unwillingly act with pain,
but those who do acts for their pleasantness and nobility do
them with pleasure; it is absurd to make external circumstances responsible, and not oneself, as being easily caught
by such attractions, and to make oneself responsible for
noble acts but the pleasant objects responsible for base acts.
The compulsory, then, seems to be that whose moving prin- 15
ciple is outside, the person compelled contributing nothing.

Everything that is done by reason of ignorance is *not*
voluntary; it is only what produces pain and repentance
that is *in*voluntary. For the man who has done something
owing to ignorance, and feels not the least vexation at his
action, has not acted voluntarily, since he did not know 20
what he was doing, nor yet involuntarily, since he is not
pained. Of people, then, who act by reason of ignorance
he who repents is thought an involuntary agent, and the
man who does not repent may, since he is different, be
called a not voluntary agent; for, since he differs from the
other, it is better that he should have a name of his own.

Acting by reason of ignorance seems also to be different
from acting *in* ignorance; for the man who is drunk or in 25
a rage is thought to act as a result not of ignorance but
of one of the causes mentioned, yet not knowingly but in
ignorance.

Now every wicked man is ignorant of what he ought to
do and what he ought to abstain from, and it is by reason
of error of this kind that men become unjust and in general
bad; but the term 'involuntary' tends to be used not if 30
a man is ignorant of what is to his advantage—for it is not
mistaken purpose that causes involuntary action (it leads
rather to wickedness), nor ignorance of the universal (for
that men are *blamed*), but ignorance of particulars, i. e. of
the circumstances of the action and the objects with which
it is concerned. For it is on these that both pity and 1111^a
pardon depend, since the person who is ignorant of any of
these acts involuntarily.

Perhaps it is just as well, therefore, to determine their
nature and number. A man may be ignorant, then, of who

he is, what he is doing, what or whom he is acting on, and
sometimes also what (e. g. what instrument) he is doing it
5 with, and to what end (e. g. he may think his act will
conduce to some one's safety), and how he is doing it
(e. g. whether gently or violently). Now of all of these no
one could be ignorant unless he were mad, and evidently
also he could not be ignorant of the agent; for how could
he not know himself? But of what he is doing a man
might be ignorant, as for instance people say 'it slipped
out of their mouths as they were speaking',[1] or 'they did
not know it was a secret', as Aeschylus said of the mysteries,[2]
10 or a man might say he 'let it go off when he merely wanted
to show its working', as the man did with the catapult.
Again, one might think one's son was an enemy, as Merope
did,[3] or that a pointed spear had a button on it, or that
a stone was pumice-stone ; or one might give a man a
draught to save him, and really kill him ; or one might
want to touch a man, as people do in sparring, and really
15 wound him. The ignorance may relate, then, to any of
these things, i. e. of the circumstances of the action, and
the man who was ignorant of any of these is thought to
have acted involuntarily, and especially if he was ignorant
on the most important points ; and these are thought to be
the circumstances of the action and its end. Further,[4] the
doing of an act that is called involuntary in virtue of igno-
20 rance of this sort must be painful and involve repentance.

Since that which is done under compulsion or by reason
of ignorance is involuntary, the voluntary would seem to be
that of which the moving principle is in the agent himself,

---

[1] Reading in l. 9 λέγοντάς with (apparently) Aspasius and αὐτούς
with the Aldine edition.

[2] Aeschylus was acquitted by the Areopagus on a charge of revealing
the Eleusinian mysteries. In Pl. *Rep.* 563 C we have οὐκοῦν κατ'
Αἰσχύλον, ἔφη, ἐροῦμεν ὅτι νῦν ἦλθ' ἐπὶ στόμα. Professor H. Jackson (in
J. of P. xxvii. 159 f.) connects the two references and suggests that
Aeschylus, charged with betraying the mysteries, replied, 'I said the
first thing which occurred to me', and perhaps added, 'not knowing
that there was anything in it which had to do with the mysteries'.
He conjectures, further, that the true reading of the present passage is
οἷον λέγοντές φασιν ἐκπεσεῖν αὐτοὺς ἃ οὐκ εἰδέναι ὅτι ἀπόρρητα ἦν. This
emendation is, however, not very probable.

[3] In the *Cresphontes* of Euripides ; v. Nauck², 497 f.

[4] Reading τοῦ δέ in l. 19, with Thurot.

he being aware of the particular circumstances of the action. Presumably acts done by reason of anger or appetite are not rightly called involuntary.[1] For in the first place, on 25 that showing none of the other animals will act voluntarily, nor will children; and secondly, is it meant that we do not do voluntarily *any* of the acts that are due to appetite or anger, or that we do the noble acts voluntarily and the base acts involuntarily? Is not this absurd, when one and the same thing is the cause? But it would surely be odd to describe as involuntary the things one ought to desire; and 30 we ought both to be angry at certain things and to have an appetite for certain things, e. g. for health and for learning. Also what is involuntary is thought to be painful, but what is in accordance with appetite is thought to be pleasant. Again, what is the difference in respect of involuntariness between errors committed upon calculation and those committed in anger? Both are to be avoided, but the irrational **IIII**ᵇ passions are thought not less human than reason is, and therefore also the actions which proceed from anger or appetite are the man's actions. It would be odd, then, to treat them as involuntary.

2   Both the voluntary and the involuntary having been delimited, we must next discuss choice;[2] for it is thought 5 to be most closely bound up with virtue and to discriminate characters better than actions do.

Choice, then, seems to be voluntary, but not the same thing as the voluntary; the latter extends more widely. For both children and the lower animals share in voluntary action, but not in choice, and acts done on the spur of the moment we describe as voluntary, but not as chosen.

Those who say it is appetite or anger or wish or a kind 10 of opinion do not seem to be right. For choice is not common to irrational creatures as well, but appetite and anger are. Again, the incontinent man acts with appetite,

---

[1] A reference to Pl. *Laws* 863 B, ff., where anger and appetite are coupled with ignorance as sources of wrong action.

[2] Προαίρεσις is a very difficult word to translate. Sometimes 'intention', 'will', or 'purpose' would bring out the meaning better; but I have for the most part used 'choice'. The etymological meaning is 'preferential choice'.

but not with choice; while the continent man on the
15 contrary acts with choice, but not with appetite. Again,
appetite is contrary to choice, but not appetite to appetite.
Again, appetite relates to the pleasant and the painful,
choice neither to the painful nor to the pleasant.

Still less is it anger; for acts due to anger are thought to
be less than any others objects of choice.

20 But neither is it wish, though it seems near to it; for
choice cannot relate to impossibles, and if any one said he
chose them he would be thought silly; but there may be a
wish even for impossibles, e. g. for immortality. And wish
may relate to things that could in no way be brought about
by one's own efforts, e. g. that a particular actor or athlete
25 should win in a competition; but no one chooses such
things, but only the things that he thinks could be brought
about by his own efforts. Again, wish relates rather to the
end, choice to the means; for instance, we wish to be
healthy, but we choose the acts which will make us healthy,
and we wish to be happy and say we do, but we cannot
well say we choose to be so; for, in general, choice seems to
relate to the things that are in our own power.

30 For this reason, too, it cannot be opinion; for opinion
is thought to relate to all kinds of things, no less to eternal
things and impossible things than to things in our own
power; and it is distinguished by its falsity or truth, not by
its badness or goodness, while choice is distinguished rather
by these.

Now with opinion in general perhaps no one even says it
III2^a is identical. But it is not identical even with any kind
of opinion; for by choosing what is good or bad we are men
of a certain character, which we are not by holding certain
opinions. And we choose to get or avoid something good
or bad, but we have opinions about what a thing is or whom
it is good for or how it is good for him; we can hardly be
5 said to opine to get or avoid anything. And choice is praised
for being related to the right object rather than for being
rightly related to it, opinion for being truly related to its
object. And we choose what we best know to be good, but
we opine what we do not quite know; and it is not the same

people that are thought to make the best choices and to
have the best opinions, but some are thought to have fairly
good opinions, but by reason of vice to choose what they 10
should not. If opinion precedes choice or accompanies it,
that makes no difference ; for it is not this that we are considering, but whether it is *identical* with some kind of opinion.

What, then, or what kind of thing is it, since it is none of
the things we have mentioned? It seems to be voluntary,
but not all that is voluntary to be an object of choice. Is 15
it, then, what has been decided on by previous deliberation?
At any rate choice involves a rational principle and
thought. Even the name seems to suggest that it is what
is chosen before other things.

3   Do we deliberate about everything, and is everything
a possible subject of deliberation, or is deliberation impossible
about some things? We ought presumably to call not what 20
a fool or a madman would deliberate about, but what
a sensible man would deliberate about, a subject of deliberation. Now about eternal things no one deliberates,
e. g. about the material universe or the incommensurability
of the diagonal and the side of a square. But no more do
we deliberate about the things that involve movement but
always happen in the same way, whether of necessity
or by nature or from any other cause, e. g. the solstices and 25
the risings of the stars ; nor about things that happen now
in one way, now in another, e. g. droughts and rains ; nor
about chance events, like the finding of treasure. But we
do not deliberate even about all human affairs ; for instance,
no Spartan deliberates about the best constitution for the
Scythians. For none of these things can be brought about
by our own efforts.

We deliberate about things that are in our power and can 30
be done ; and these are in fact what is left. For nature,
necessity, and chance are thought to be causes, and also
reason and everything that depends on man. Now every
class of men deliberates about the things that can be done by
their own efforts. And in the case of exact and self-contained
sciences there is no deliberation, e. g. about the letters of the III2^b

alphabet (for we have no doubt how they should be written);
but the things that are brought about by our own efforts, but
not always in the same way, are the things about which we
deliberate, e. g. questions of medical treatment or of money-
5 making. And we do so more in the case of the art of navigation than in that of gymnastics, inasmuch as it has been
less exactly worked out, and again about other things in the
same ratio, and more also in the case of the arts than in that
of the sciences; for we have more doubt about the former.
Deliberation is concerned with things that happen in a certain way for the most part, but in which the event is obscure,
10 and with things in which it is indeterminate. We call in
others to aid us in deliberation on important questions,
distrusting ourselves as not being equal to deciding.

We deliberate not about ends but about means. For
a doctor does not deliberate whether he shall heal, nor
an orator whether he shall persuade, nor a statesman
whether he shall produce law and order, nor does
15 any one else deliberate about his end. They assume the end
and consider how and by what means it is to be attained;
and if it seems to be produced by several means they
consider by which it is most easily and best produced, while
if it is achieved by one only they consider how it will
be achieved by this and by what means *this* will be achieved,
till they come to the first cause, which in the order of
20 discovery is last. For the person who deliberates seems
to investigate and analyse in the way described as though
he were analysing a geometrical construction [1] (not all
investigation appears to be deliberation—for instance mathematical investigations—but all deliberation is investigation),
and what is last in the order of analysis seems to be
first in the order of becoming. And if we come on an
25 impossibility, we give up the search, e. g. if we need money
and this cannot be got; but if a thing appears possible we

---

[1] Aristotle has in mind the method of discovering the solution of
a geometrical problem. The problem being to construct a figure of a
certain kind, we suppose it constructed and then analyse it to see if
there is some figure by constructing which we can construct the
required figure, and so on till we come to a figure which our existing
knowledge enables us to construct.

try to do it.   By ' possible ' things I mean things that might
be brought about by our own efforts ; and these in a sense
include things that can be brought about by the efforts of our
friends, since the moving principle is in ourselves.   The
subject of investigation is sometimes the instruments, sometimes the use of them ; and similarly in the other cases— 30
sometimes the means, sometimes the mode of using it or the
means of bringing it about.   It seems, then, as has been
said, that man is a moving principle of actions ; now deliberation is about the things to be done by the agent himself,
and actions are for the sake of things other than themselves.
For the end cannot be a subject of deliberation, but only the
means ;   nor indeed can the particular facts be a subject
of it, as whether this is bread or has been baked as it should ; III3^a
for these are matters of perception.   If we are to be always
deliberating, we shall have to go on to infinity.

The same thing is deliberated upon and is chosen, except
that the object of choice is already determinate, since it is
that which has been decided upon as a result of deliberation that is the object of choice.   For every one ceases to 5
inquire how he is to act when he has brought the moving
principle back to himself and to the ruling part of himself ;
for this is what chooses.   This is plain also from the ancient
constitutions, which Homer represented ; for the kings an-
nounced their choices to the people.   The object of choice
being one of the things in our own power which is desired 10
after deliberation, choice will be deliberate desire of things
in our own power ; for when we have decided as a result of
deliberation, we desire in accordance with our deliberation.

We may take it, then, that we have described choice in
outline, and stated the nature of its objects and the fact that
it is concerned with means.

4   That *wish* is for the end has already been stated ;[1] some 15
think it is for the good, others for the apparent good.   Now
those who say that the good is the object of wish must admit
in consequence that that which the man who does not choose
aright wishes for is not an object of wish (for if it is to be

[1] IIII^b26.

so, it must also be good; but it was, if it so happened,
20 bad); while those who say the apparent good is the object
of wish must admit that there is no natural object of wish,
but only what seems good to each man. Now different
things appear good to different people, and, if it so happens,
even contrary things.

If these consequences are unpleasing, are we to say that
absolutely and in truth the good is the object of wish, but
25 for each person the apparent good; that that which is in
truth an object of wish is an object of wish to the good man,
while any chance thing may be so to the bad man, as in the
case of bodies also the things that are in truth wholesome are
wholesome for bodies which are in good condition, while for
those that are diseased other things are wholesome—or bitter
or sweet or hot or heavy, and so on; since the good man judges
30 each class of things rightly, and in each the truth appears to
him? For each state of character has its own ideas of the noble
and the pleasant, and perhaps the good man differs from
others most by seeing the truth in each class of things, being
as it were the norm and measure of them. In most things
the error seems to be due to pleasure; for it appears a good
1113ᵇ when it is not. We therefore choose the pleasant as a
good, and avoid pain as an evil.

The end, then, being what we wish for, the means what
we deliberate about and choose, actions concerning means
5 must be according to choice and voluntary. Now the
exercise of the virtues is concerned with means. Therefore
virtue also is in our own power, and so too vice. For where
it is in our power to act it is also in our power not to act,
and *vice versa*; so that, if to act, where this is noble, is in
our power, not to act, which will be base, will also be in our
10 power, and if not to act, where this is noble, is in our power,
to act, which will be base, will also be in our power. Now
if it is in our power to do noble or base acts, and likewise in
our power not to do them, and this was what being good or
bad meant,[1] then it is in our power to be virtuous or vicious.
The saying[2] that 'no one is voluntarily wicked nor involun-

---

[1] 1112ᵃ 1 f.   [2] Fr. adesp. (? Solon), Bergk³, p. 1356 f.

tarily happy' seems to be partly false and partly true; for 15
no one is involuntarily happy, but wickedness *is* voluntary.
Or else we shall have to dispute what has just been said, at
any rate, and deny that man is a moving principle or begetter
of his actions as of children. But if these facts are evident
and we cannot refer actions to moving principles other than
those in ourselves, the acts whose moving principles are in 20
us must themselves also be in our power and voluntary.

Witness seems to be borne to this both by individuals in
their private capacity and by legislators themselves; for
these punish and take vengeance on those who do wicked
acts (unless they have acted under compulsion or as a result
of ignorance for which they are not themselves responsible),
while they honour those who do noble acts, as though they 25
meant to encourage the latter and deter the former. But no
one is encouraged to do the things that are neither in our
power nor voluntary; it is assumed that there is no gain in
being persuaded not to be hot or in pain or hungry or the like,
since we shall experience these feelings none the less. Indeed,[1] we punish a man for his very ignorance, if he is thought 30
responsible for the ignorance, as when penalties are doubled
in the case of drunkenness;[2] for the moving principle is in the
man himself, since he had the power of not getting drunk and
his getting drunk was the cause of his ignorance. And we
punish those who are ignorant of anything in the laws that
they ought to know and that is not difficult, and so too in the 1114^{a}
case of anything else that they are thought to be ignorant
of through carelessness; we assume that it is in their power
not to be ignorant, since they have the power of taking care.

But perhaps a man is the kind of man not to take care.
Still they are themselves by their slack lives responsible for
becoming men of that kind, and men make themselves
responsible for being unjust or self-indulgent, in the one case 5
by cheating and in the other by spending their time in
drinking bouts and the like; for it is activities exercised on
particular objects that make the corresponding character.

---

[1] This connects with the words of l. 24 f. 'unless they have acted . . .
as a result of ignorance for which they are not themselves responsible.'
[2] As by the law of Pittacus; cf. *Pol.* 1274^{b} 19, *Rhet.* 1402^{b} 9.

This is plain from the case of people training for any contest or action; they practise the activity the whole time. Now not to know that it is from the exercise of activities on 10 particular objects that states of character are produced is the mark of a thoroughly senseless person. Again, it is irrational to suppose that a man who acts unjustly does not wish to be unjust or a man who acts self-indulgently to be self-indulgent. But if *without* being ignorant a man does the things which will make him unjust, he will be unjust voluntarily. Yet it does not follow that if he wishes he will cease to be unjust and will be just. For neither does the 15 man who is ill become well on those terms. We may suppose a case in which he is ill voluntarily, through living incontinently and disobeying his doctors. In that case it was *then* open to him not to be ill, but not now, when he has thrown away his chance, just as when you have let a stone go it is too late to recover it; but yet it was in your power to throw it, since the moving principle was in you. So, 20 too, to the unjust and to the self-indulgent man it was open at the beginning not to become men of this kind, and so they are unjust and self-indulgent voluntarily; but now that they have become so it is not possible for them not to be so.

But not only are the vices of the soul voluntary, but those of the body also for some men, whom we accordingly blame; while no one blames those who are ugly by nature, we blame 25 those who are so owing to want of exercise and care. So it is, too, with respect to weakness and infirmity; no one would reproach a man blind from birth or by disease or from a blow, but rather pity him, while every one would blame a man who was blind from drunkenness or some other form of self-indulgence. Of vices of the body, then, those in our own power are blamed, those not in our power are not. 30 And if this be so, in the other cases also the vices that are blamed must be in our own power.

Now some one may say that all men desire the apparent good, but have no control over the appearance, but the end appears to each man in a form answering to his character. **1114ᵇ** We reply that if each man is somehow responsible for his state of mind, he will also be himself somehow responsible

for the appearance ; but if not, no one is responsible for his
own evildoing, but every one does evil acts through ignorance
of the end, thinking that by these he will get what is best, and 5
the aiming at the end is not self-chosen but one must be
born with an eye, as it were, by which to judge rightly and
choose what is truly good, and he is well endowed by nature
who is well endowed with this. For it is what is greatest and
most noble, and what we cannot get or learn from another,
but must have just such as it was when given us at birth,
and to be well and nobly endowed with this will be perfect 10
and true excellence of natural endowment. If this is true,
then, how will virtue be more voluntary than vice ? To
both men alike, the good and the bad, the end appears and
is fixed by nature or however it may be, and it is by refer- 15
ring everything else to this that men do whatever they do.

Whether, then, it is not by nature that the end appears to
each man such as it does appear, but something also depends
on him, or the end is natural but because the good man
adopts the means voluntarily virtue is voluntary, vice also
will be none the less voluntary ; for in the case of the bad 20
man there is equally present that which depends on himself in
his actions even if not in his end. If, then, as is asserted, the
virtues are voluntary (for we are ourselves somehow partly responsible for our states of character, and it is by being persons
of a certain kind that we assume the end to be so and so),
the vices also will be voluntary ; for the same is true of them. 25

With regard to the virtues in *general* we have stated their
genus in outline, viz. that they are means and that they are
states of character, and that they tend, and by their own
nature, to the doing of the acts by which they are produced,
and that they are in our power and voluntary, and act as the
right rule prescribes. But actions and states of character 30
are not voluntary in the same way ; for we are masters of
our actions from the beginning right to the end, if we know
the particular facts, but though we control the beginning of
our states of character the gradual progress is not obvious, III5^a
any more than it is in illnesses; because it was in our power,
however, to act in this way or not in this way, therefore the
states are voluntary.

Let us take up the several virtues, however, and say which they are and what sort of things they are concerned with and 5 how they are concerned with them ; at the same time it will become plain how many they are.　And first let us speak of courage.

That it is a mean with regard to feelings of fear and **6** confidence has already been made evident;[1] and plainly the things we fear are terrible things, and these are, to speak without qualification, evils; for which reason 10 people even define fear as expectation of evil.　Now we fear all evils, e. g. disgrace, poverty, disease, friend-lessness, death, but the brave man is not thought to be concerned with all ; for to fear some things is even right and noble, and it is base not to fear them—e. g. disgrace ; he who fears this is good and modest, and he who does not is shameless.　He is, however, by some people called brave, 15 by a transference of the word to a new meaning ; for he has in him something which is like the brave man, since the brave man also is a fearless person.　Poverty and disease we perhaps ought not to fear, nor in general the things that do not proceed from vice and are not due to a man himself. But not even the man who is fearless of these is brave.　Yet 20 we apply the word to him also in virtue of a similarity ; for some who in the dangers of war are cowards are liberal and are confident in face of the loss of money.　Nor is a man a coward if he fears insult to his wife and children or envy or anything of the kind ; nor brave if he is confident when he is about to be flogged.　With what sort of terrible things, 25 then, is the brave man concerned?　Surely with the greatest; for no one is more likely than he to stand his ground against what is awe-inspiring.　Now death is the most terrible of all things ; for it is the end, and nothing is thought to be any longer either good or bad for the dead.　But the brave man would not seem to be concerned even with death in *all* circumstances, e. g. at sea or in disease.　In 30 what circumstances, then?　Surely in the noblest.　Now such deaths are those in battle ; for these take place in the greatest and noblest danger.　And these are corre-

[1] 1107^a 33–^b 4.

spondingly honoured in city-states and at the courts of
monarchs. Properly, then, he will be called brave who is
fearless in face of a noble death, and of all emergencies that
involve death; and the emergencies of war are in the highest
degree of this kind. Yet at sea also, and in disease, the 35
brave man is fearless, but not in the same way as the seamen ; III5ᵇ
for he has given up hope of safety, and is disliking the
thought of death in this shape, while they are hopeful
because of their experience. At the same time, we show
courage in situations where there is the opportunity of 5
showing prowess or where death is noble; but in these
forms of death neither of these conditions is fulfilled.

7   What is terrible is not the same for all men; but we say
there are things terrible even beyond human strength.
These, then, are terrible to every one—at least to every
sensible man; but the terrible things that are *not* beyond
human strength differ in magnitude and degree, and so too
do the things that inspire confidence. Now the brave man 10
is as dauntless as man may be. Therefore, while he will
fear even the things that are not beyond human strength,
he will face them as he ought and as the rule directs,
for honour's sake; for this is the end of virtue. But it is
possible to fear these more, or less, and again to fear things
that are not terrible as if they were. Of the faults that are 15
committed one consists in fearing what one should not,
another in fearing as we should not, another in fearing
when we should not, and so on; and so too with respect to
the things that inspire confidence. The man, then, who faces
and who fears the right things and from the right motive,
in the right way and at the right time, and who feels
confidence under the corresponding conditions, is brave;
for the brave man feels and acts according to the merits of
the case and in whatever way the rule directs. Now the end 20
of every activity is conformity to the corresponding state
of character. This is true, therefore, of the brave man as
well as of others. But courage is noble.[1] Therefore the
end also is noble; for each thing is defined by its end.

---

[1] Reading, as Ramsauer suggests, καὶ τῷ ἀνδρείῳ δή· ἡ ⟨δὲ⟩ ἀνδρεία
καλόν.

Therefore it is for a noble end that the brave man endures and acts as courage directs.

Of those who go to excess he who exceeds in fearlessness 25 has no name (we have said previously that many states of character have no names[1]), but he would be a sort of madman or insensible person if he feared nothing, neither earthquakes nor the waves, as they say the Celts do not ; while the man who exceeds in confidence about what really is terrible is rash. The rash man, however, is also 30 thought to be boastful and only a pretender to courage ; at all events, as the brave man *is* with regard to what is terrible, so the rash man wishes to *appear* ; and so he imitates him in situations where he can. Hence also most of them are a mixture of rashness and cowardice ; for, while in these situations they display confidence, they do not hold their ground against what is really terrible. The man who exceeds in fear is a coward ; for he fears both 35 what he ought not and as he ought not, and all the similar **1116ᵃ** characterizations attach to him. He is lacking also in confidence ; but he is more conspicuous for his excess of fear in painful situations. The coward, then, is a despairing sort of person ; for he fears everything. The brave man, on the other hand, has the opposite disposition ; for confidence is the mark of a hopeful disposition. The coward, the rash man, and the brave man, then, are concerned with the same 5 objects but are differently disposed towards them ; for the first two exceed and fall short, while the third holds the middle, which is the right, position ; and rash men are precipitate, and wish for dangers beforehand but draw back when they are in them, while brave men are keen in the moment of action, but quiet beforehand.

10   As we have said, then, courage is a mean with respect to things that inspire confidence or fear, in the circumstances that have been stated ;[2] and it chooses or endures things because it is noble to do so, or because it is base not to do so.[3] But to die to escape from poverty or love or anything painful is not the mark of a brave man, but rather of a coward ;

---

[1] 1107ᵇ 2, cf. 1107ᵇ 29, 1108ᵃ 5.   [2] Ch. 6.
          [3] 1115ᵇ 11–24.

for it is softness to fly from what is troublesome, and such a
man endures death not because it is noble but to fly from
evil.

8   Courage, then, is something of this sort, but the name is 15
also applied to five other kinds. (1) First comes the courage
of the citizen-soldier; for this is most like true courage.
Citizen-soldiers seem to face dangers because of the penalties
imposed by the laws and the reproaches they would otherwise incur, and because of the honours they win by such
action; and therefore those peoples seem to be bravest 20
among whom cowards are held in dishonour and brave men
in honour. This is the kind of courage that Homer depicts,
e. g. in Diomede and in Hector:

First will Polydamas be to heap reproach on me then;[1]
and

> For Hector one day 'mid the Trojans shall utter   25
>   his vaulting harangue:
> "Afraid was Tydeides, and fled from my face."[2]

This kind of courage is most like to that which we described
earlier,[3] because it is due to virtue; for it is due to shame
and to desire of a noble object (i. e. honour) and avoidance of
disgrace, which is ignoble. One might rank in the same class
even those who are compelled by their rulers; but they are 30
inferior, inasmuch as they do what they do not from shame but
from fear, and to avoid not what is disgraceful but what is
painful; for their masters compel them, as Hector[4] does:

But if I shall spy any dastard that cowers far from the
    fight,
Vainly will such an one hope to escape from the dogs. 35

And those who give them their posts, and beat them
if they retreat,[5] do the same, and so do those who draw **1116ᵇ**
them up with trenches or something of the sort behind
them; all of these apply compulsion. But one ought to be
brave not under compulsion but because it is noble to be so.

---

[1] *Il.* xxii. 100.   [2] *Il.* viii. 148, 149.   [3] Chs. 6, 7.
[4] Aristotle's quotation is more like *Il.* ii. 391–3, where Agamemnon
speaks, than xv. 348–51, where Hector speaks.   [5] Cf. Hdt. vii. 223.

(2) Experience with regard to particular facts is also thought to be courage; this is indeed the reason why 5 Socrates thought courage was knowledge.[1] Other people exhibit this quality in other dangers, and professional soldiers exhibit it in the dangers of war; for there seem to be many empty alarms in war, of which these have had the most comprehensive experience; therefore they seem brave, because the others do not know the nature of the facts. Again, their experience makes them most capable 10 in attack and in defence, since they can use their arms and have the kind that are likely to be best both for attack and for defence; therefore they fight like armed men against unarmed or like trained athletes against amateurs; for in such contests too it is not the bravest men that fight best, but those who are strongest and have their bodies in the 15 best condition. Professional soldiers turn cowards, however, when the danger puts too great a strain on them and they are inferior in numbers and equipment; for they are the first to fly, while citizen-forces die at their posts, as in fact happened at the temple of Hermes.[2] For to the latter 20 flight is disgraceful and death is preferable to safety on those terms; while the former from the very beginning faced the danger on the assumption that they were stronger, and when they know the facts they fly, fearing death more than disgrace; but the brave man is not that sort of person.

(3) Passion also is sometimes reckoned as courage; those who act from passion, like wild beasts rushing at those 25 who have wounded them, are thought to be brave, because brave men also are passionate; for passion above all things is eager to rush on danger, and hence Homer's 'put strength into his passion'[3] and 'aroused their spirit and passion'[4] and 'hard he breathed panting'[5] and 'his blood boiled'.[6] For all such expressions seem to indicate the stirring and 30 onset of passion. Now brave men act for honour's sake,

---

[1] Xen. *Mem.* iii. 9. 1 f., iv. 6. 10 f., Pl. *Prot.* 350, 360.

[2] The reference is to a battle at Coronea in the Sacred War, c. 353 B.C., in which the Phocians defeated the citizens of Coronea and some Boeotian regulars.

[3] This is a conflation of *Il.* xi. 11 or xiv. 151 and xvi. 529.

[4] Cf. *Il.* v. 470, xv. 232, 594.   [5] Cf. *Od.* xxiv. 318 f.

[6] The phrase does not occur in Homer; it is found in Theocr. xx. 15.

but passion aids them; while wild beasts act under the influence of pain; for they attack because they have been wounded or because they are afraid, since if they are in a forest they do not come near one. Thus they are not brave because, driven by pain and passion, they rush on danger without foreseeing any of the perils, since at that rate even 35 asses would be brave when they are hungry; for blows will not drive them from their food;[1] and lust also makes 1117[a] adulterers do many daring things. [Those creatures are not brave, then, which are driven on to danger by pain or passion.] The 'courage' that is due to passion seems to be the most natural, and to be courage if choice and motive be added.

Men, then, as well as beasts, suffer pain when they are 5 angry, and are pleased when they exact their revenge; those who fight for these reasons, however, are pugnacious but not brave; for they do not act for honour's sake nor as the rule directs, but from strength of feeling; they have, however, something akin to courage.

(4) Nor are sanguine people brave; for they are confident 10 in danger only because they have conquered often and against many foes. Yet they closely resemble brave men, because both are confident; but brave men are confident for the reasons stated earlier,[2] while these are so because they think they are the strongest and can suffer nothing. (Drunken men also behave in this way; they become sanguine). When their adventures do not succeed, however, 15 they run away; but it was[2] the mark of a brave man to face things that are, and seem, terrible for a man, because it is noble to do so and disgraceful not to do so. Hence also it is thought the mark of a braver man to be fearless and undisturbed in sudden alarms than to be so in those that are foreseen; for it must have proceeded more from a state of character, because less from preparation; acts that are 20 foreseen may be chosen by calculation and rule, but sudden actions must be in accordance with one's state of character.

(5) People who are ignorant of the danger also appear brave, and they are not far removed from those of a

---

[1] Cf. *Il.* xi. 558-62.   [2] 1115[b] 11-24.

sanguine temper, but are inferior inasmuch as they have
no self-reliance while these have. Hence also the sanguine
25 hold their ground for a time; but those who have been
deceived about the facts fly if they know or suspect that
these are different from what they supposed, as happened
to the Argives when they fell in with the Spartans and
took them for Sicyonians.[1]

We have, then, described the character both of brave men 9
and of those who are thought to be brave.

Though courage is concerned with feelings of confidence
and of fear, it is not concerned with both alike, but more
30 with the things that inspire fear; for he who is undisturbed
in face of these and bears himself as he should towards these
is more truly brave than the man who does so towards the
things that inspire confidence. It is for facing what is
painful, then, as has been said,[2] that men are called brave.
Hence also courage involves pain, and is justly praised; for
it is harder to face what is painful than to abstain from what
35 is pleasant. Yet the end which courage sets before it would
1117^b seem to be pleasant, but to be concealed by the attending
circumstances, as happens also in athletic contests; for the
end at which boxers aim is pleasant—the crown and the
honours—but the blows they take are distressing to flesh
5 and blood, and painful, and so is their whole exertion; and
because the blows and the exertions are many the end,
which is but small, appears to have nothing pleasant in it.
And so, if the case of courage is similar, death and wounds
will be painful to the brave man and against his will, but he
will face them because it is noble to do so or because it is
base not to do so. And the more he is possessed of virtue in
10 its entirety and the happier he is, the more he will be pained
at the thought of death; for life is best worth living for such
a man, and he is knowingly losing the greatest goods, and
this is painful. But he is none the less brave, and perhaps
all the more so, because he chooses noble deeds of war at
15 that cost. It is not the case, then, with all the virtues that
the exercise of them is pleasant, except in so far as it

---

[1] At the Long Walls of Corinth, 392 B.C. Cf. Xen. *Hell.* iv. 4. 10.
[2] 1115^b7–13.

reaches its end. But it is quite possible that the best soldiers may be not men of this sort but those who are less brave but have no other good; for these are ready to face danger, and they sell their life for trifling gains.

So much, then, for courage; it is not difficult to grasp its 20 nature in outline, at any rate, from what has been said.

After courage let us speak of temperance; for these seem 10 to be the virtues of the irrational parts. We have said[1] that temperance is a mean with regard to pleasures (for it 25 is less, and not in the same way, concerned with pains); self-indulgence also is manifested in the same sphere. Now, therefore, let us determine with what sort of pleasures they are concerned. We may assume the distinction between bodily pleasures and those of the soul, such as love of honour and love of learning; for the lover of each of these delights in that of which he is a lover, the body being in no 30 way affected, but rather the mind; but men who are concerned with such pleasures are called neither temperate nor self-indulgent. Nor, again, are those who are concerned with the other pleasures that are not bodily; for those who are fond of hearing and telling stories and who spend their days on anything that turns up are called gossips, but not 35 self-indulgent, nor are those who are pained at the loss of money or of friends.

Temperance must be concerned with bodily pleasures, 1118^a but not all even of these; for those who delight in objects of vision, such as colours and shapes and painting, are called neither temperate nor self-indulgent; yet it would seem 5 possible to delight even in these either as one should or to excess or to a deficient degree.

And so too is it with objects of hearing; no one calls those who delight extravagantly in music or acting self-indulgent, nor those who do so as they ought temperate.

Nor do we apply these names to those who delight in odour, unless it be incidentally; we do not call those self- 10 indulgent who delight in the odour of apples or roses or incense, but rather those who delight in the odour of

---

[1] 1107^b 4–6.

unguents or of dainty dishes; for self-indulgent people delight in these because these remind them of the objects of their appetite. And one may see even other people, 15 when they are hungry, delighting in the smell of food; but to delight in this kind of thing is the mark of the self-indulgent man; for these are objects of appetite to him.

Nor is there in animals other than man any pleasure connected with these senses, except incidentally. For dogs do not delight in the scent of hares, but in the eating of them, 20 but the scent told them the hares were there; nor does the lion delight in the lowing of the ox, but in eating it; but he perceived by the lowing that it was near, and therefore appears to delight in the lowing; and similarly he does not delight because he sees 'a stag or a wild goat ',[1] but because he is going to make a meal of it. Temperance and self-indulgence, however, are concerned with the kind of 25 pleasures that the other animals share in, which therefore appear slavish and brutish; these are touch and taste. But even of taste they appear to make little or no use; for the business of taste is the discriminating of flavours, which is done by wine-tasters and people who season dishes; but they hardly take pleasure in making these discriminations, 30 or at least self-indulgent people do not, but in the actual enjoyment, which in all cases comes through touch, both in the case of food and in that of drink and in that of sexual intercourse. This is why a certain gourmand[2] prayed that his throat might become longer than a crane's, implying that 1118ᵇ it was the contact that he took pleasure in. Thus the sense with which self-indulgence is connected is the most widely shared of the senses; and self-indulgence would seem to be justly a matter of reproach, because it attaches to us not as men but as animals. To delight in such things, then, and to love them above all others, is brutish. For even of the pleasures of touch the most liberal have been eliminated, 5 e. g. those produced in the gymnasium by rubbing and by the consequent heat; for the contact characteristic of the self-indulgent man does not affect the whole body but only certain parts.

---

[1] *Il.* iii. 24.   [2] Philoxenus; cf. *E.E.* 1231ᵃ 17, *Probl.*, 950ᵃ 3.

11 Of the appetites some seem to be common, others to be peculiar to individuals and acquired; e. g. the appetite for food is natural, since every one who is without it craves for 10 food or drink, and sometimes for both, and for love also (as Homer says)[1] if he is young and lusty; but not every one craves for this[2] or that kind of nourishment or love, nor for the same things. Hence such craving appears to be our very own. Yet it has of course something natural about it; for different things are pleasant to different kinds of people, and some things are more pleasant to every one than chance objects. Now in the natural appetites few go 15 wrong, and only in one direction, that of excess; for to eat or drink whatever offers itself till one is surfeited is to exceed the natural amount, since natural appetite is the replenishment of one's deficiency. Hence these people are called belly-gods, this implying that they fill their belly beyond what is right. It is people of entirely slavish 20 character that become like this. But with regard to the pleasures peculiar to individuals many people go wrong and in many ways. For while the people who are 'fond of so and so' are so called because they delight either in the wrong things, or more than most people do, or in the wrong way, the self-indulgent exceed in all three ways; they both 25 delight in some things that they ought not to delight in (since they are hateful), and if one ought to delight in some of the things they delight in, they do so more than one ought and than most men do.

Plainly, then, excess with regard to pleasures is self-indulgence and is culpable; with regard to pains one is not, as in the case of courage, called temperate for facing them or self-indulgent for not doing so, but the self-indulgent man 30 is so called because he is pained more than he ought at not getting pleasant things (even his pain being caused by pleasure), and the temperate man is so called because he is not pained at the absence of what is pleasant and at his abstinence from it.

---

[1] *Il.* xxiv. 130.
[2] Reading τῆς δὲ τοιᾶσδε as Bywater suggests, and omitting the comma before οὐκέτι.

The self-indulgent man, then, craves for all pleasant things or those that are most pleasant, and is led by his appetite to choose these at the cost of everything else; hence he is pained both when he fails to get them and when he is merely craving for them (for appetite involves pain); but it seems
5 absurd to be pained for the sake of pleasure. People who fall short with regard to pleasures and delight in them less than they should are hardly found; for such insensibility is not human. Even the other animals distinguish different kinds of food and enjoy some and not others; and if there is any one who finds nothing pleasant and nothing more attractive than anything else, he must be something quite
10 different from a man; this sort of person has not received a name because he hardly occurs. The temperate man occupies a middle position with regard to these objects. For he neither enjoys the things that the self-indulgent man enjoys most—but rather dislikes them—nor in general the things that he should not, nor anything of this sort to excess, nor does he feel pain or craving when they are absent, or does so only to a moderate degree, and not more than he should,
15 nor when he should not, and so on; but the things that, being pleasant, make for health or for good condition, he will desire moderately and as he should, and also other pleasant things if they are not hindrances to these ends, or contrary to what is noble, or beyond his means. For he who neglects these conditions loves such pleasures more than they
20 are worth, but the temperate man is not that sort of person, but the sort of person that the right rule prescribes.

Self-indulgence is more like a voluntary state than 12 cowardice. For the former is actuated by pleasure, the latter by pain, of which the one is to be chosen and the other to be avoided; and pain upsets and destroys the nature of the person who feels it, while pleasure does nothing of the sort.
25 Therefore self-indulgence is more voluntary. Hence also it is more a matter of reproach; for it is easier to become accustomed to its objects, since there are many things of this sort in life, and the process of habituation to them is free from danger, while with terrible objects the reverse is

the case. But cowardice would seem to be voluntary in a different degree from its particular manifestations; for it is itself painless, but in these we are upset by pain, so that we even throw down our arms and disgrace ourselves in other ways; hence our acts are even thought to be done 30 under compulsion. For the self-indulgent man, on the other hand, the particular acts are voluntary (for he does them with craving and desire), but the whole state is less so; for no one craves to be self-indulgent.

The name self-indulgence is applied also to childish faults;[1] for they bear a certain resemblance to what we have been considering. Which is called after which, makes no differ- 1119ᵇ ence to our present purpose; plainly, however, the later is called after the earlier. The transference of the name seems not a bad one; for that which desires what is base and which develops quickly ought to be kept in a chastened condition, and these characteristics belong above all to appetite and to the child, since children in fact live at the 5 beck and call of appetite, and it is in them that the desire for what is pleasant is strongest. If, then, it is not going to be obedient and subject to the ruling principle, it will go to great lengths; for in an irrational being the desire for pleasure is insatiable even if it tries every source of gratification, and the exercise of appetite increases its innate force, and if 10 appetites are strong and violent they even expel the power of calculation. Hence they should be moderate and few, and should in no way oppose the rational principle—and this is what we call an obedient and chastened state—and as the child should live according to the direction of his tutor, so the appetitive element should live according to rational principle. Hence the appetitive element in a 15 temperate man should harmonize with the rational principle; for the noble is the mark at which both aim, and the temperate man craves for the things he ought, as he ought, and when he ought; and this is what rational principle directs.

Here we conclude our account of temperance.

[1] ἀκόλαστος, which we have translated 'self-indulgent', meant originally 'unchastened' and was applied to the ways of spoilt children.

BOOK IV

LET us speak next of liberality. It seems to be the mean with regard to wealth; for the liberal man is praised not in respect of military matters, nor of those in respect of which the temperate man is praised, nor of judicial decisions, 25 but with regard to the giving and taking of wealth, and especially in respect of giving. Now by 'wealth' we mean all the things whose value is measured by money. Further, prodigality and meanness are excesses and defects with regard to wealth; and meanness we always impute to those 30 who care more than they ought for wealth, but we sometimes apply the word 'prodigality' in a complex sense; for we call those men prodigals who are incontinent and spend money on self-indulgence. Hence also they are thought the poorest characters; for they combine more vices than one. Therefore the application of the word to them is not its proper use; for a 'prodigal' means a man who has a 1120^{a} single evil quality, that of wasting his substance; since a prodigal is one who is being ruined by his own fault,[1] and the wasting of substance is thought to be a sort of ruining of oneself, life being held to depend on possession of substance.

This, then, is the sense in which we take the word 'prodigality'. Now the things that have a use may be 5 used either well or badly; and riches is a useful thing; and everything is used best by the man who has the virtue concerned with it; riches, therefore, will be used best by the man who has the virtue concerned with wealth; and this is the liberal man. Now spending and giving seem to be the using of wealth; taking and keeping rather the possession of it. Hence it is more the mark of the liberal man to 10 give to the right people than to take from the right sources and not to take from the wrong. For it is more characteristic

---

[1] ἄ-σωτος = one who is not saved, who is ruined.

of virtue to do good than to have good done to one, and more characteristic to do what is noble than not to do what is base; and it is not hard to see that giving implies doing good and doing what is noble, and taking implies having good done to one or not acting basely. And gratitude is 15 felt towards him who gives, not towards him who does not take, and praise also is bestowed more on him. It is easier, also, not to take than to give; for men are apter to give away their own too little than to take what is another's. Givers, too, are called liberal; but those who do not take are not praised for liberality but rather for justice; while 20 those who take are hardly praised at all. And the liberal are almost the most loved of all virtuous characters, since they are useful; and this depends on their giving.

Now virtuous actions are noble and done for the sake of the noble. Therefore the liberal man, like other virtuous men, will give for the sake of the noble, and rightly; for he will 25 give to the right people, the right amounts, and at the right time, with all the other qualifications that accompany right giving; and that too with pleasure or without pain; for that which is virtuous is pleasant or free from pain—least of all will it be painful. But he who gives to the wrong people or not for the sake of the noble but for some other cause, will be called not liberal but by some other name. Nor is he liberal who gives with pain; for he would prefer the 30 wealth to the noble act, and this is not characteristic of a liberal man. But no more will the liberal man take from wrong sources; for such taking is not characteristic of the man who sets no store by wealth. Nor will he be a ready asker; for it is not characteristic of a man who confers benefits to accept them lightly. But he will take from the right sources, e. g. from his own possessions, not as some- **1120^b** thing noble but as a necessity, that he may have something to give. Nor will he neglect his own property, since he wishes by means of this to help others. And he will refrain from giving to anybody and everybody, that he may have something to give to the right people, at the right time, and where it is noble to do so. It is highly characteristic of a liberal man also to go to excess in giving, so that he 5 leaves too little for himself; for it is the nature of a liberal man not to look to himself. The term 'liberality' is used relatively to a man's substance; for liberality resides not in the multitude of the gifts but in the state of character of the giver, and this is relative to the giver's substance.[1] There is therefore nothing to prevent the man who gives 10 less from being the more liberal man, if he has less to give. Those are thought to be more liberal who have not made their wealth but inherited it; for in the first place they have no experience of want, and secondly all men are fonder of their own productions, as are parents and poets. It is not 15 easy for the liberal man to be rich, since he is not apt either at taking or at keeping, but at giving away, and does not value wealth for its own sake but as a means to giving. Hence comes the charge that is brought against fortune, that those who deserve riches most get it least. But it is not unreasonable that it should turn out so; for he cannot have wealth, any more than anything else, if he does not 20 take pains to have it. Yet he will not give to the wrong people nor at the wrong time, and so on; for he would no longer be acting in accordance with liberality, and if he spent on these objects he would have nothing to spend on the right objects. For, as has been said, he is liberal who spends according to his substance and on the right objects; 25 and he who exceeds is prodigal. Hence we do not call despots prodigal; for it is thought not easy for them to give and spend beyond the amount of their possessions. Liberality, then, being a mean with regard to giving and taking of wealth, the liberal man will both give and spend the right amounts and on the right objects, alike in small 30 things and in great, and that with pleasure; he will also take the right amounts and from the right sources. For, the virtue being a mean with regard to both, he will do both as he ought; since this sort of taking accompanies proper giving, and that which is not of this sort is contrary to it, and accordingly the giving and taking that accompany each other are present together in the same man, while the **1121^a** contrary kinds evidently are not. But if he happens to

---

[1] Omitting διδωσιν, as Bywater suggests.

spend in a manner contrary to what is right and noble, he will be pained, but moderately and as he ought; for it is the mark of virtue both to be pleased and to be pained at the right objects and in the right way.   Further, the liberal man is easy to deal with in money matters; for he can be 5 got the better of, since he sets no store by money, and is more annoyed if he has not spent something that he ought than pained if he has spent something that he ought not, and does not agree with the saying of Simonides.[1]

The prodigal errs in these respects also; for he is neither pleased nor pained at the right things or in the right way; this will be more evident as we go on.   We have said[2] that 10 prodigality and meanness are excesses and deficiencies, and in two things, in giving and in taking; for we include spending under giving.   Now prodigality exceeds in giving and not taking, and falls short in taking, while meanness falls short in giving, and exceeds in taking, except in small 15 things.

The characteristics of prodigality are not often combined; for it is not easy to give to all if you take from none; private persons soon exhaust their substance with giving, and it is to these that the name of prodigals is applied—though a man of this sort would seem to be in no small degree better than a mean man.   For he is easily cured both by age and 20 by poverty, and thus he may move towards the middle state. For he has the characteristics of the liberal man, since he both gives and refrains from taking, though he does neither of these in the right manner or well.   Therefore if he were brought to do so by habituation or in some other way, he would be liberal; for he will then give to the right people, and will not take from the wrong sources.   This is why he 25 is thought to have not a bad character; it is not the mark of a wicked or ignoble man to go to excess in giving and not taking, but only of a foolish one.   The man who is prodigal in this way is thought much better than the mean man

---

[1] Reading Σιμωνίδου, as Bywater suggests.   The reference may be to any one of three sayings of Simonides, which are recorded in *Rhet.* 1391^a 8; Athenaeus xiv. 656 C–E; Plutarch, *An seni resp. gerenda sit*, I, p. 783 E.
[2] 1119^b 27.

both for the aforesaid reasons and because he benefits many while the other benefits no one, not even himself.

30 But most prodigal people, as has been said,[1] also take from the wrong sources, and are in this respect mean. They become apt to take because they wish to spend and cannot do this easily; for their possessions soon run short. Thus they are forced to provide means from some other source. **1121ᵇ** At the same time, because they care nothing for honour, they take recklessly and from any source; for they have an appetite for giving, and they do not mind how or from what source. Hence also their giving is not liberal; for it is not noble, nor does it aim at nobility, nor is it done in the 5 right way; sometimes they make rich those who should be poor, and will give nothing to people of respectable character, and much to flatterers or those who provide them with some other pleasure. Hence also most of them are self-indulgent; for they spend lightly and waste money on their indulgences, and incline towards pleasures because they do not live with a view to what is noble.

10 The prodigal man, then, turns into what we have described if he is left untutored, but if he is treated with care he will arrive at the intermediate and right state. But meanness is both incurable (for old age and every disability is thought 15 to make men mean) and more innate in men than prodigality; for most men are fonder of getting money than of giving. It also extends widely, and is multiform, since there seem to be many kinds of meanness.

For it consists in two things, deficiency in giving and excess in taking, and is not found complete in all men but is some- 20 times divided; some men go to excess in taking, others fall short in giving. Those who are called by such names as 'miserly', 'close', 'stingy', all fall short in giving, but do not covet the possessions of others nor wish to get them. In some this is due to a sort of honesty and avoidance of what 25 is disgraceful (for some seem, or at least profess, to hoard their money for this reason, that they may not some day be forced to do something disgraceful; to this class belong the cheeseparer and every one of the sort; he is so called from

[1] ll. 16–19.

his excess of unwillingness to give anything); while others
again keep their hands off the property of others from fear,
on the ground that it is not easy, if one takes the property
of others oneself, to avoid having one's own taken by them;
they are therefore content neither to take nor to give.   30

Others again exceed in respect of taking by taking anything and from any source, e. g. those who ply sordid trades,
pimps and all such people, and those who lend small sums
and at high rates. For all of these take more than they 1122[a]
ought and from wrong sources. What is common to them
is evidently sordid love of gain; they all put up with a bad
name for the sake of gain, and little gain at that. For those
who make great gains but from wrong sources, and not the
right gains, e. g. despots when they sack cities and spoil 5
temples, we do not call mean but rather wicked, impious,
and unjust. But the gamester and the footpad [and the
highwayman] [1] belong to the class of the mean, since they
have a sordid love of gain. For it is for gain that both of
them ply their craft and endure the disgrace of it, and the
one faces the greatest dangers for the sake of the booty,
while the other makes gain from his friends, to whom he 10
ought to be giving. Both, then, since they are willing to
make gain from wrong sources, are sordid lovers of gain;
therefore all such forms of taking are mean.

And it is natural that meanness is described as the
contrary of liberality; for not only is it a greater evil than
prodigality, but men err more often in this direction than 15
in the way of prodigality as we have described it.

So much, then, for liberality and the opposed vices.

2   It would seem proper to discuss magnificence next. For
this [2] also seems to be a virtue concerned with wealth; but 20
it does not like liberality extend to all the actions that are
concerned with wealth, but only to those that involve
expenditure; and in these it surpasses liberality in scale.
For, as the name itself suggests, it is a fitting expenditure
involving largeness of scale. But the scale is relative; for

---

[1] Omitting καὶ ὁ λῃστής, as Bywater suggests and as Aspasius seems
to do.
[2] Reading αὕτη in l. 19, with Coraes.

the expense of equipping a trireme is not the same as that
25 of heading a sacred embassy. It is what is fitting, then,
in relation to the agent, and to the circumstances and the
object. The man who in small or middling things spends
according to the merits of the case is not called magnificent
(e. g. the man who can say 'many a gift I gave the wanderer'),[1]
but only the man who does so in great things. For the
magnificent man is liberal, but the liberal man is not neces-
30 sarily magnificent. The deficiency of this state of character
is called niggardliness, the excess vulgarity, lack of taste,
and the like, which do not go to excess in the amount spent
on right objects, but by showy expenditure in the wrong
circumstances and the wrong manner; we shall speak of
these vices later.[2]

The magnificent man is like an artist; for he can see
35 what is fitting and spend large sums tastefully. For, as we
1122ᵇ said at the beginning,[3] a state of character is determined by
its activities and by its objects. Now the expenses of the
magnificent man are large and fitting. Such, therefore, are
also his results; for thus there will be a great expenditure
and one that is fitting to its result. Therefore the result
5 should be worthy of the expense, and the expense should
be worthy of the result, or should even exceed it. And the
magnificent man will spend such sums for honour's sake;
for this is common to the virtues. And further he will do
so gladly and lavishly; for nice calculation is a niggardly
thing. And he will consider how the result can be made
most beautiful and most becoming rather than for how
much it can be produced and how it can be produced
10 most cheaply. It is necessary, then, that the magnificent
man be also liberal. For the liberal man also will spend
what he ought and as he ought; and it is in these matters
that the greatness implied in the name of the magnificent
man—his bigness, as it were—is manifested, since liberality
is concerned with these matters; and at an equal expense
he will produce a more magnificent work of art. For a
possession and a work of art have not the same excellence.

---

[1] *Od.* xvii. 420.   [2] 1123ᵃ 19–33.
[3] Not in so many words, but cf. 1103ᵇ 21–23, 1104ᵃ 27–29.

The most valuable possession is that which is worth most, 15
e. g. gold, but the most valuable work of art is that which
is great and beautiful (for the contemplation of such a
work inspires admiration, and so does magnificence) ; and a
work has an excellence—viz. magnificence—which involves
magnitude. Magnificence is an attribute of expenditures of
the kind which we call honourable, e. g. those connected
with the gods—votive offerings, buildings, and sacrifices—
and similarly with any form of religious worship, and all 20
those that are proper objects of public-spirited ambition,
as when people think they ought to equip a chorus or
a trireme, or entertain the city, in a brilliant way. But in
all cases, as has been said,[1] we have regard to the agent as
well and ask who he is and what means he has; for the 25
expenditure should be worthy of his means, and suit not
only the result but also the producer. Hence a poor man
cannot be magnificent, since he has not the means with
which to spend large sums fittingly ; and he who tries is
a fool, since he spends beyond what can be expected of
him and what is proper, but it is *right* expenditure that is
virtuous. But great expenditure is becoming to those who 30
have suitable means to start with, acquired by their own
efforts or from ancestors or connexions, and to people of
high birth or reputation, and so on ; for all these things
bring with them greatness and prestige. Primarily, then,
the magnificent man is of this sort, and magnificence
is shown in expenditures of this sort, as has been said ;[2]
for these are the greatest and most honourable. Of *private* 35
occasions of expenditure the most suitable are those that
take place once for all, e. g. a wedding or anything of the
kind, or anything that interests the whole city or the people **1123**^a
of position in it, and also the receiving of foreign guests and
the sending of them on their way, and gifts and counter-
gifts ; for the magnificent man spends not on himself but
on public objects, and gifts bear some resemblance to votive 5
offerings. A magnificent man will also furnish his house
suitably to his wealth (for even a house is a sort of public
ornament), and will spend by preference on those works

---

[1] ^a 24–26.   [2] ll. 19–23.

that are lasting (for these are the most beautiful), and on every class of things he will spend what is becoming; for the same things are not suitable for gods and for men, nor in 10 a temple and in a tomb. And since each expenditure may be great of its kind, and what is most magnificent absolutely is great expenditure on a great object, but what is magnificent *here* is what is great in *these* circumstances, and greatness in the work differs from greatness in the expense (for the most beautiful ball or bottle is magnificent as a gift to 15 a child, but the price of it is small and mean),—therefore it is characteristic of the magnificent man, whatever kind of result he is producing, to produce it magnificently (for such a result is not easily surpassed) and to make it worthy of the expenditure.

Such, then, is the magnificent man; the man who goes to excess and is vulgar exceeds, as has been said,[1] by 20 spending beyond what is right. For on small objects of expenditure he spends much and displays a tasteless showiness; e. g. he gives a club dinner on the scale of a wedding banquet, and when he provides the chorus for a comedy he brings them on to the stage in purple, as they do at Megara. 25 And all such things he will do not for honour's sake but to show off his wealth, and because he thinks he is admired for these things, and where he ought to spend much he spends little and where little, much. The niggardly man on the other hand will fall short in everything, and after spending the greatest sums will spoil the beauty of the result for a trifle, and whatever he is doing he will hesitate and consider 30 how he may spend least, and lament even that, and think he is doing everything on a bigger scale than he ought.

These states of character, then, are vices; yet they do not bring *disgrace* because they are neither harmful to one's neighbour nor very unseemly.

Pride seems even from its name[2] to be concerned with **3** great things; what sort of great things, is the first question

---

[1] 1122ᵃ 31–33.

[2] 'Pride' of course has not the etymological associations of μεγαλο-ψυχία, but seems in other respects the best translation.

we must try to answer. It makes no difference whether we 35 consider the state of character or the man characterized by it. Now the man is thought to be proud who thinks him- **1123ᵃ** self worthy of great things, being worthy of them; for he who does so beyond his deserts is a fool, but no virtuous man is foolish or silly. The proud man, then, is the man we have described. For he who is worthy of little and 5 thinks himself worthy of little is temperate, but not proud; for pride implies greatness, as beauty implies a good-sized body, and little people may be neat and well-proportioned but cannot be beautiful. On the other hand, he who thinks himself worthy of great things, being unworthy of them, is vain; though not every one who thinks himself worthy of more than he really is worthy of is vain. The man who thinks himself worthy of less than he is really worthy of is unduly humble, whether his deserts be great or moderate, or his 10 deserts be small but his claims yet smaller. And the man whose deserts are great would seem *most* unduly humble; for what would he have done if they had been less? The proud man, then, is an extreme in respect of the greatness of his claims, but a mean in respect of the rightness of them; for he claims what is in accordance with his merits, while the others go to excess or fall short.

If, then, he deserves and claims great things, and above all 15 the greatest things, he will be concerned with one thing in particular. Desert is relative to external goods; and the greatest of these, we should say, is that which we render to the gods, and which people of position most aim at, and which is the prize appointed for the noblest deeds; and 20 this is honour; that is surely the greatest of external goods. Honours and dishonours, therefore, are the objects with respect to which the proud man is as he should be. And even apart from argument it is with honour that proud men appear to be concerned; for it is honour that they chiefly claim, but in accordance with their deserts. The unduly humble man falls short both in comparison with his own merits and in comparison with the proud man's claims. The vain man goes to excess in comparison with his own 25 merits, but does not exceed the proud man's claims.

Now the proud man, since he deserves most, must be good in the highest degree; for the better man always deserves more, and the best man most. Therefore the truly proud
30 man must be good. And greatness in every virtue would seem to be characteristic of a proud man. And it would be most unbecoming for a proud man to fly from danger, swinging his arms by his sides, or to wrong another; for to what end should he do disgraceful acts, he to whom nothing is great? If we consider him point by point we shall see the utter absurdity of a proud man who is not good. Nor, again, would he be worthy of honour if he were
35 bad; for honour is the prize of virtue, and it is to the good
1124^a that it is rendered. Pride, then, seems to be a sort of crown of the virtues; for it makes them greater, and it is not found without them. Therefore it is hard to be truly proud; for it is impossible without nobility and goodness of character. It is chiefly with honours and dishonours, then, that the
5 proud man is concerned; and at honours that are great and conferred by good men he will be moderately pleased, thinking that he is coming by his own or even less than his own; for there can be no honour that is worthy of perfect virtue, yet he will at any rate accept it since they have
10 nothing greater to bestow on him; but honour from casual people and on trifling grounds he will utterly despise, since it is not this that he deserves, and dishonour too, since in his case it cannot be just. In the first place, then, as has been said,[1] the proud man is concerned with honours; yet he will also bear himself with moderation towards wealth and power and all good or evil fortune, whatever may befall
15 him, and will be neither over-joyed by good fortune nor over-pained by evil. For not even towards honour does he bear himself as if it were a very great thing. Power and wealth are desirable for the sake of honour (at least those who have them wish to get honour by means of them); and for him to whom even honour is a little thing the others must be so too. Hence proud men are thought to be disdainful.

[1] 1123^b 15–22.

The goods of fortune also are thought to contribute 20 towards pride. For men who are well-born are thought worthy of honour, and so are those who enjoy power or wealth; for they are in a superior position, and everything that has a superiority in something good is held in greater honour. Hence even such things make men prouder; for they are honoured by some for having them; but in truth 25 the good man alone is to be honoured; he, however, who has both advantages is thought the more worthy of honour. But those who without virtue have such goods are neither justified in making great claims nor entitled to the name of ' proud '; for these things imply perfect virtue. Disdainful and insolent, however, even those who have such goods become. For without virtue it is not easy to bear grace- 30 fully the goods of fortune; and, being unable to bear them, and thinking themselves · superior to others, they 1124^{b} despise others and themselves do what they please. They imitate the proud man without being like him, and this they do where they can; so they do not act virtuously, but they do despise others. For the proud man despises 5 justly (since he thinks truly), but the many do so at random.

He does not run into trifling dangers, nor is he fond of danger, because he honours few things; but he will face great dangers, and when he is in danger he is unsparing of his life, knowing that there are conditions on which life is not worth having. And he is the sort of man to confer benefits, but he is ashamed of receiving them; for the one is the mark 10 of a superior, the other of an inferior. And he is apt to confer greater benefits in return; for thus the original benefactor besides being paid will incur a debt to him, and will be the gainer by the transaction. They seem also to remember any service they have done, but not those they have received (for he who receives a service is inferior to him who has done it, but the proud man wishes to be superior), and to hear of the former with pleasure, of the latter with displeasure; this, 15 it seems, is why Thetis did not mention to Zeus the services she had done him,[1] and why the Spartans did not recount

[1] In fact she did, *Il.* i. 503.

their services to the Athenians, but those they had received.¹
It is a mark of the proud man also to ask for nothing or
scarcely anything, but to give help readily, and to be dignified
towards people who enjoy high position and good fortune,
20 but unassuming towards those of the middle class; for it is
a difficult and lofty thing to be superior to the former, but
easy to be so to the latter, and a lofty bearing over the
former is no mark of ill-breeding, but among humble people
it is as vulgar as a display of strength against the weak.
Again, it is characteristic of the proud man not to aim at
the things commonly held in honour, or the things in which
others excel; to be sluggish and to hold back except where
25 great honour or a great work is at stake, and to be a man of
few deeds, but of great and notable ones.   He must also be
open in his hate and in his love (for to conceal one's feelings,
i. e. to care less for truth than for what people will think,
is a coward's part), and must speak and act openly; for he
is free of speech because he is contemptuous, and he is
30 given to telling the truth, except when he speaks in irony
to the vulgar.   He must be unable to make his life revolve
1125ᵃ round another, unless it be a friend; for this is slavish, and
for this reason all flatterers are servile and people lacking
in self-respect are flatterers.   Nor is he given to admiration; for nothing to him is great.   Nor is he mindful of
wrongs; for it is not the part of a proud man to have
a long memory, especially for wrongs, but rather to over-
5 look them.   Nor is he a gossip; for he will speak neither
about himself nor about another, since he cares not to be
praised nor for others to be blamed; nor again is he given
to praise; and for the same reason he is not an evil-speaker,
even about his enemies, except from haughtiness.   With
regard to necessary or small matters he is least of all men
10 given to lamentation or the asking of favours; for it is the
part of one who takes such matters seriously to behave so
with respect to them.   He is one who will possess beautiful
and profitless things rather than profitable and useful ones;

¹ The Aldine scholiast quotes Callisthenes as stating that the
Spartans behaved in this way when they were asking for help from
the Athenians on the occasion of an invasion by the Thebans.   If the
reference is to B.C. 369, it does not agree with Xen. *Hell*. vi. 5. 33 f.

for this is more proper to a character that suffices to itself.

Further, a slow step is thought proper to the proud man, a deep voice, and a level utterance; for the man who takes few things seriously is not likely to be hurried, nor the man who thinks nothing great to be excited, while a shrill voice ¹⁵ and a rapid gait are the results of hurry and excitement.

Such, then, is the proud man; the man who falls short of him is unduly humble, and the man who goes beyond him is vain. Now even these are not thought to be bad (for they are not malicious), but only mistaken. For the unduly humble man, being worthy of good things, robs himself of what he deserves, and seems to have something bad about him from ²⁰ the fact that he does not think himself worthy of good things, and seems also not to know himself; else he would have desired the things he was worthy of, since these were good. Yet such people are not thought to be fools, but rather unduly retiring. Such a reputation, however, seems actually to make them worse; for each class of people ²⁵ aims at what corresponds to its worth, and these people stand back even from noble actions and undertakings, deeming themselves unworthy, and from external goods no less. Vain people, on the other hand, are fools and ignorant of themselves, and that manifestly; for, not being worthy of them, they attempt honourable undertakings, and then are found out; and they adorn themselves with clothing and outward show ³⁰ and such things, and wish their strokes of good fortune to be made public, and speak about them as if they would be honoured for them. But undue humility is more opposed to pride than vanity is; for it is both commoner and worse.

Pride, then, is concerned with honour on the grand scale, as has been said.¹   35

4   There seems to be in the sphere of honour also, as was 1125ᵇ said in our first remarks on the subject,² a virtue which would appear to be related to pride as liberality is to magnificence. For neither of these has anything to do with the grand scale, but both dispose us as is right with ₅

¹ 1107ᵇ 26, 1123ᵃ 34–ᵇ 22.   ² Ib. 24–27.

regard to middling and unimportant objects; as in getting
and giving of wealth there is a mean and an excess and
defect, so too honour may be desired more than is right, or
less, or from the right sources and in the right way. We
blame both the ambitious man as aiming at honour more
10 than is right and from wrong sources, and the unambitious
man as not willing to be honoured even for noble reasons.
But sometimes we praise the ambitious man as being manly
and a lover of what is noble, and the unambitious man as
being moderate and self-controlled, as we said in our first
treatment of the subject.[1] Evidently, since 'fond of such
and such an object' has more than one meaning, we do not
assign the term 'ambition' or 'love of honour' always to
15 the same thing, but when we praise the quality we think of
the man who loves honour more than most people, and
when we blame it we think of him who loves it more than
is right. The mean being without a name, the extremes
seem to dispute for its place as though that were vacant by
default. But where there is excess and defect, there is also
an intermediate; now men desire honour both more than
20 they should and less; therefore it is possible also to do so
as one should; at all events this is the state of character that
is praised, being an unnamed mean in respect of honour.
Relatively to ambition it seems to be unambitiousness, and
relatively to unambitiousness it seems to be ambition, while
relatively to both severally it seems in a sense to be both
together. This appears to be true of the other virtues also.
But in this case the extremes seem to be contradictories
25 because the mean has not received a name.

Good temper is a mean with respect to anger; the middle **5**
state being unnamed, and the extremes almost without a
name as well, we place good temper in the middle position,
though it inclines towards the deficiency, which is without
a name. The excess might be called a sort of 'irascibility'.
30 For the passion is anger, while its causes are many and diverse.
The man who is angry at the right things and with the
right people, and, further, as he ought, when he ought, and as

[1] 1107^b 33.

long as he ought, is praised.   This will be the good-tempered
man, then, since good temper is praised.   For the good-
tempered man tends to be unperturbed and not to be led
by passion, but to be angry in the manner, at the things, 35
and for the length of time, that the rule dictates; but he is **1126ᵃ**
thought to err rather in the direction of deficiency; for the
good-tempered man is not revengeful, but rather tends to
make allowances.

The deficiency, whether it is a sort of 'inirascibility' or
whatever it is, is blamed.   For those who are not angry at
the things they should be angry at are thought to be fools, 5
and so are those who are not angry in the right way, at
the right time, or with the right persons; for such a man is
thought not to feel things nor to be pained by them, and,
since he does not get angry, he is thought unlikely to defend
himself; and to endure being insulted and put up with insult
to one's friends is slavish.

The excess can be manifested in all the points that have
been named (for one can be angry with the wrong persons, at the wrong things, more than is right, too quickly, 10
or too long); yet *all* are not found in the same person.
Indeed they could not; for evil destroys even itself, and if
it is complete becomes unbearable.   Now *hot-tempered*
people get angry quickly and with the wrong persons and
at the wrong things and more than is right, but their anger
ceases quickly—which is the best point about them.   This 15
happens to them because they do not restrain their anger
but retaliate openly owing to their quickness of temper, and
then their anger ceases.   By reason of excess *choleric* people
are quick-tempered and ready to be angry with everything
and on every occasion; whence their name.   *Sulky* people
are hard to appease, and retain their anger long; for they 20
repress their passion.   But it ceases when they retaliate;
for revenge relieves them of their anger, producing in them
pleasure instead of pain.   If this does not happen they
retain their burden; for owing to its not being obvious no
one even reasons with them, and to digest one's anger in
oneself takes time.[1]   Such people are most troublesome to 25

---

[1] Reading in l. 25 δεῖται as Γ apparently does and Bywater suggests.

themselves and to their dearest friends. We call *bad-tempered* those who are angry at the wrong things, more than is right, and longer, and cannot be appeased until they inflict vengeance or punishment.

To good temper we oppose the excess rather than the defect ; for not only is it commoner (since revenge is the 30 more human), but bad-tempered people are worse to live with.

What we have said in our earlier treatment of the subject[1] is plain also from what we are now saying ; viz. that it is not easy to define how, with whom, at what, and how long one should be angry, and at what point right action ceases 35 and wrong begins. For the man who strays a little from the path, either towards the more or towards the less, is not blamed ; since sometimes we praise those who exhibit the 1126ᵇ deficiency, and call them good-tempered, and sometimes we call angry people manly, as being capable of ruling. How far, therefore, and how a man must stray before he becomes blameworthy, it is not easy to state in words ; for the decision depends on the particular facts and on perception. 5 But so much at least is plain, that the middle state is praiseworthy—that in virtue of which we are angry with the right people, at the right things, in the right way, and so on, while the excesses and defects are blameworthy— slightly so if they are present in a low degree, more if in a higher degree, and very much if in a high degree. Evidently, then, we must cling to the middle state.—Enough 10 of the states relative to anger.

In gatherings of men, in social life and the interchange **6** of words and deeds, some men are thought to be obsequious, viz. those who to give pleasure praise everything and never 15 oppose, but think it their duty 'to give no pain to the people they meet' ; while those who, on the contrary, oppose everything and care not a whit about giving pain are called churlish and contentious. That the states we have named are culpable is plain enough, and that the middle state is laudable—that in virtue of which a man will

[1] 1109ᵇ 14–26.

put up with, and will resent, the right things and in the
right way ; but no name has been assigned to it, though it
most resembles friendship.   For the man who corresponds 20
to this middle state is very much what, with affection
added, we call a good friend.   But the state in question
differs from friendship in that it implies no passion or
affection for one's associates ; since it is not by reason of
loving or hating that such a man takes everything in the
right way, but by being a man of a certain kind.   For he 25
will behave so alike towards those he knows and those he
does not know, towards intimates and those who are not so,
except that in each of these cases he will behave as is
befitting ; for it is not proper to have the same care for
intimates and for strangers, nor again is it the same conditions that make it right to give pain to them.   Now we
have said generally that he will associate with people in the
right way ; but it is by reference to what is honourable and
expedient that he will aim at not giving pain or at contributing pleasure.   For he seems to be concerned with the 30
pleasures and pains of social life ; and wherever it is not
honourable, or is harmful, for him to contribute pleasure,
he will refuse, and will choose rather to give pain ; also if
his acquiescence in another's action would bring disgrace,
and that in a high degree, or injury, *on that other*, while his
opposition brings a little pain, he will not acquiesce but will 35
decline.   He will associate differently with people in high
station and with ordinary people, with closer and more distant 1127^a
acquaintances, and so too with regard to all other differences,
rendering to each class what is befitting, and while for its
own sake he chooses to contribute pleasure, and avoids the
giving of pain, he will be guided by the consequences, if
these are greater, i.e. honour and expediency.   For the sake 5
of a great future pleasure, too, he will inflict small pains.

The man who attains the mean, then, is such as we have
described, but has not received a name ; of those who
contribute pleasure, the man who aims at being pleasant
with no ulterior object is obsequious, but the man who
does so in order that he may get some advantage in the
direction of money or the things that money buys is a

10 flatterer; while the man who quarrels with everything is, as has been said,[1] churlish and contentious. And the extremes seem to be contradictory to each other because the mean is without a name.

The mean opposed to boastfulness[2] is found in almost **7** the same sphere; and this[3] also is without a name. It will be no bad plan to describe these states as well; 15 for we shall both know the facts about character better if we go through them in detail, and we shall be convinced that the virtues are means if we see this to be so in all cases. In the field of social life those who make the giving of pleasure or pain their object in associating with others have been described;[4] let us now describe those who pursue truth or falsehood alike in words 20 and deeds and in the claims they put forward. The boastful man, then, is thought to be apt to claim the things that bring glory, when he has not got them, or to claim more of them than he has, and the mock-modest man on the other hand to disclaim what he has or belittle it, while the man who observes the mean is one who calls a thing by its own name, being truthful both in life and in word, owning to 25 what he has, and neither more nor less. Now each of these courses may be adopted either with or without an object. But each man speaks and acts and lives in accordance with his character, if he is *not* acting for some ulterior object. And falsehood is *in itself*[5] mean and 30 culpable, and truth noble and worthy of praise. Thus the truthful man is another case of a man who, being in the mean, is worthy of praise, and both forms of untruthful man are culpable, and particularly the boastful man.

Let us discuss them both, but first of all the truthful man. We are not speaking of the man who keeps faith in his agreements, i. e. in the things that pertain to justice or injustice (for this would belong to another virtue), but the **1127ᵇ** man who in the matters in which nothing of this sort is at

---

[1] 1125 ᵇ 14-16.
[2] Omitting in l. 13 καὶ εἰρωνείας, which as Burnet observes is not necessary according to Greek idiom.
[3] Reading αὔτη in l. 14, with Lᵇ Mᵇ.   [4] Ch. 6.
[5] I. e. apart from any ulterior object it may serve.

stake is true both in word and in life because his character
is such. But such a man would seem to be as a matter of
fact equitable. For the man who loves truth, and is truthful where nothing is at stake, will still more be truthful
where something is at stake; he will avoid falsehood as 5
something base, seeing that he avoided it even for its own
sake; and such a man is worthy of praise. He inclines
rather to understate the truth; for this seems in better
taste because exaggerations are wearisome.

He who claims more than he has with no ulterior
object is a contemptible sort of fellow (otherwise he would 10
not have delighted in falsehood), but seems futile rather
than bad; but if he does it for an object, he who does it for
the sake of reputation or honour is (for a boaster ¹) not very
much to be blamed, but he who does it for money, or the
things that lead to money, is an uglier character (it is not
the capacity that makes the boaster, but the purpose; for
it is in virtue of his state of character and by being a man
of a certain kind that he is a boaster); as one man is a liar 15
because he enjoys the lie itself, and another because he
desires reputation or gain. Now those who boast for the
sake of reputation claim such qualities as win praise or
congratulation, but those whose object is gain claim qualities which are of value to one's neighbours and one's lack
of which is not easily detected, e. g. the powers of a seer,
a sage, or a physician. For this reason it is such things as 20
these that most people claim and boast about; for in
them the above-mentioned qualities are found.

Mock-modest people, who understate things, seem more
attractive in character; for they are thought to speak not
for gain but to avoid parade; and here too it is qualities 25
which bring reputation that they disclaim, as Socrates used
to do. Those who disclaim trifling and obvious qualities
are called humbugs and are more contemptible; and sometimes this seems to be boastfulness, like the Spartan dress;
for both excess and great deficiency are boastful. But
those who use understatement with moderation and under- 30
state about matters that do not very much force themselves

¹ Reading ὡς ἀλαζών in l. 12.

on our notice seem attractive. And it is the boaster that seems to be opposed to the truthful man; for he is the worse character.

Since life includes rest as well as activity, and in this is **8** included leisure and amusement, there seems here also to **1128ᵃ** be a kind of intercourse which is tasteful; there is such a thing as saying—and again listening to—what one should and as one should. The kind of people one is speaking or listening to will also make a difference. Evidently here also there is both an excess and a deficiency as compared with the mean. Those who carry humour to 5 excess are thought to be vulgar buffoons, striving after humour at all costs, and aiming rather at raising a laugh than at saying what is becoming and at avoiding pain to the object of their fun; while those who can neither make a joke themselves nor put up with those who do are thought to be boorish and unpolished. But those who joke in a tasteful way are called ready-witted, which implies 10 a sort of readiness to turn this way and that; for such sallies are thought to be movements of the character, and as bodies are discriminated by their movements, so too are characters. The ridiculous side of things is not far to seek, however, and most people delight more than they should in amusement and in jesting, and so even buffoons are called 15 ready-witted because they are found attractive; but that they differ from the ready-witted man, and to no small extent, is clear from what has been said.

To the middle state belongs also tact; it is the mark of a tactful man to say and listen to such things as befit a good and well-bred man; for there are some things that it befits 20 such a man to say and to hear by way of jest, and the well-bred man's jesting differs from that of a vulgar man, and the joking of an educated man from that of an uneducated. One may see this even from the old and the new comedies; to the authors of the former indecency of language was amusing, to those of the latter innuendo is more so; and 25 these differ in no small degree in respect of propriety. Now should we define the man who jokes well by his saying

what is not unbecoming to a well-bred man, or by his not
giving pain, or even giving delight, to the hearer? Or is
the latter definition, at any rate, itself indefinite, since
different things are hateful or pleasant to different people?
The kind of jokes he will listen to will be the same; for
the kind he can put up with are also the kind he seems to
make. There are, then, jokes he will not make; for the
jest is a sort of abuse, and there are things that lawgivers 30
forbid us to abuse; and they should, perhaps, have for-
bidden us even to make a jest of such. The refined and
well-bred man, therefore, will be as we have described, being
as it were a law to himself.

Such, then, is the man who observes the mean, whether
he be called tactful or ready-witted. The buffoon, on the
other hand, is the slave of his sense of humour, and spares
neither himself nor others if he can raise a laugh, and says 35
things none of which a man of refinement would say, and to
some of which he would not even listen. The boor, again, 1128ᵇ
is useless for such social intercourse; for he contributes
nothing and finds fault with everything. But relaxation and
amusement are thought to be a necessary element in life.

The means in life that have been described, then, are
three in number, and are all concerned with an interchange 5
of words and deeds of some kind. They differ, however, in
that one is concerned with truth, and the other two with
pleasantness: Of those concerned with pleasure, one is dis-
played in jests, the other in the general social intercourse
of life.

9   Shame should not be described as a virtue; for it is more 10
like a feeling than a state of character. It is defined, at any
rate, as a kind of fear of dishonour, and produces an effect
similar to that[1] produced by fear of danger; for people who
feel disgraced blush, and those who fear death turn pale.
Both, therefore, seem to be in a sense bodily conditions,
which is thought to be characteristic of feeling rather than
of a state of character.

The feeling is not becoming to every age, but only 15

---

[1] Reading ἀποτελεῖ τι τῷ in l. 12.

to youth. For we think young people should be prone to
the feeling of shame because they live by feeling and
therefore commit many errors, but are restrained by shame;
and we praise young people who are prone to this feeling,
but an older person no one would praise for being prone to
20 the sense of disgrace, since we think he should not do
anything that need cause this sense. For the sense
of disgrace is not even characteristic of a good man,[1] since
it is consequent on bad actions (for such actions should not
be done; and if some actions are disgraceful in very truth
and others only according to common opinion, this makes no
difference; for neither class of actions should be done, so
25 that no disgrace should be felt); and it is a mark of a bad
man even to be such as to do any disgraceful action. To
be so constituted as to feel disgraced if one does such an
action, and for this reason to think oneself good, is absurd;
for it is for voluntary actions that shame is felt, and
the good man will never voluntarily do bad actions. But
30 shame may be said to be conditionally a good thing; *if* a
good man does such actions, he will feel disgraced; but the
virtues are not subject to such a qualification. And if
shamelessness—not to be ashamed of doing base actions—is
bad, that does not make it good to be ashamed of doing such
actions. Continence too is not virtue, but a mixed sort of
35 state; this will be shown later.[2] Now, however, let us
discuss justice.

---

[1] *Sc.* still less is it itself a virtue.   [2] vii. 1–10.

BOOK V

1 WITH regard to justice and injustice we must consider 1129^a
(1) what kind of actions they are concerned with, (2) what
sort of mean justice is, and (3) between what extremes the
just act is intermediate. Our investigation shall follow the 5
same course as the preceding discussions.

We see that all men mean by justice that kind of state
of character which makes people disposed to do what is just
and makes them act justly and wish for what is just; and
similarly by injustice that state which makes them act
unjustly and wish for what is unjust. Let us too, then, lay 10
this down as a general basis. For the same is not true
of the sciences and the faculties as of states of character. A
faculty or a science which is one and the same is held to
relate to contrary objects, but a state of character which is
one of two contraries does *not* produce the contrary results;
e. g. as a result of health we do not do what is the opposite of 15
healthy, but only what is healthy; for we say a man walks
healthily, when he walks as a healthy man would.

Now often one contrary state is recognized from its
contrary, and often states are recognized from the subjects
that exhibit them; for (A) if good condition is known, bad
condition also becomes known, and (B) good condition 20
is known from the things that are in good condition, and
they from it. If good condition is firmness of flesh, it
is necessary both that bad condition should be flabbiness
of flesh and that the wholesome should be that which
causes firmness in flesh. And it follows for the most part
that if one contrary is ambiguous the other also will be
ambiguous; e. g. if 'just' is so, that 'unjust' will be 25
so too.

Now 'justice' and 'injustice' seem to be ambiguous, but
because their different meanings approach near to one
another the ambiguity escapes notice and is not obvious as
it is, comparatively, when the meanings are far apart, e. g.

(for here the difference in outward form is great) as the
30 ambiguity in the use of κλείς for the collar-bone of an animal
and for that with which we lock a door. Let us take as
a starting-point, then, the various meanings of 'an unjust
man'. Both the lawless man and the grasping and unfair
man are thought to be unjust, so that evidently both the
law-abiding and the fair man will be just. The just, then, is
the lawful and the fair, the unjust the unlawful and the
unfair.

1129ᵇ   Since the unjust man is grasping, he must be concerned
with goods—not all goods, but those with which prosperity
and adversity have to do, which taken absolutely are
always good, but for a particular person are not always
5 good. Now men pray for and pursue these things; but they
should not, but should pray that the things that are good
absolutely may also be good for them, and should choose the
things that *are* good for them. The unjust man does not
always choose the greater, but also the less—in the case of
things bad absolutely; but because the lesser evil is itself
thought to be in a sense good, and graspingness is directed
10 at the good, therefore he is thought to be grasping. And
he is unfair; for this contains and is common to both.

Since the lawless man was seen[1] to be unjust and the
law-abiding man just, evidently all lawful acts are in a sense
just acts; for the acts laid down by the legislative art are
lawful, and each of these, we say, is just. Now the laws
15 in their enactments on all subjects aim at the common
advantage either of all or of the best or of those who hold
power, or something of the sort; so that in one sense we call
those acts just that tend to produce and preserve happiness
and its components for the political society. And the law
20 bids us do both the acts of a brave man (e. g. not to desert
our post nor take to flight nor throw away our arms), and
those of a temperate man (e. g. not to commit adultery nor
to gratify one's lust), and those of a good-tempered man
(e. g. not to strike another nor to speak evil), and similarly
with regard to the other virtues and forms of wickedness,
commanding some acts and forbidding others; and the

[1] a 32–b 1.

rightly-framed law does this rightly, and the hastily con-
ceived one less well.

This form of justice, then, is complete virtue, but not 25
absolutely, but in relation to our neighbour.   And therefore
justice is often thought to be the greatest of virtues, and
'neither evening nor morning star'[1] is so wonderful;
and proverbially 'in justice is every virtue comprehended'.[2]
And it is complete virtue in its fullest sense, because it is 30
the actual exercise of complete virtue.   It is complete
because he who possesses it can exercise his virtue not only
in himself but towards his neighbour also; for many men
can exercise virtue in their own affairs, but not in their
relations to their neighbour. This is why the saying of 1130^a
Bias is thought to be true, that 'rule will show the man';
for a ruler is necessarily in relation to other men and a
member of a society.   For this same reason justice, alone of
the virtues, is thought to be 'another's good',[3] because it is
related to our neighbour; for it does what is advantageous
to another, either a ruler or a copartner.   Now the worst man 5
is he who exercises his wickedness both towards himself
and towards his friends, and the best man is not he who
exercises his virtue towards himself but he who exercises
it towards another; for this is a difficult task. Justice
in this sense, then, is not part of virtue but virtue entire, nor
is the contrary injustice a part of vice but vice entire.   What 10
the difference is between virtue and justice in this sense
is plain from what we have said; they are the same
but their essence is not the same; what, as a relation to one's
neighbour, is justice is, as a certain kind of state without
qualification, virtue.

2   But at all events what we are investigating is the justice
which is a *part* of virtue; for there is a justice of this kind,
as we maintain.   Similarly it is with injustice in the 15
particular sense that we are concerned.

That there is such a thing is indicated by the fact that

---

[1] Eur., fr. from *Melanippe* (Nauck², fr. 486).   [2] Theog. 147.
[3] Pl. *Rep.* 343 C.

while the man who exhibits in action the other forms
of wickedness acts wrongly indeed, but not graspingly (e. g.
the man who throws away his shield through cowardice
or speaks harshly through bad temper or fails to help
a friend with money through meanness), when a man
20 acts graspingly he often exhibits none of these vices,—no,
nor all together, but certainly wickedness of some kind (for
we blame him) and injustice. There is, then, another kind
of injustice which is a part of injustice in the wide sense, and
a use of the word ' unjust' which answers to a part of what
is unjust in the wide sense of ' contrary to the law '. Again,
if one man commits adultery for the sake of gain and
25 makes money by it, while another does so at the bidding of
appetite though he loses money and is penalized for it,
the latter would be held to be self-indulgent rather than
grasping, but the former is unjust, but not self-indulgent ;
evidently, therefore, he is unjust by reason of his making
gain by his act. Again, all other unjust acts are ascribed
invariably to some particular kind of wickedness, e. g.
30 adultery to self-indulgence, the desertion of a comrade in
battle to cowardice, physical violence to anger ; but if a man
makes gain, his action is ascribed to no form of wickedness
but injustice. Evidently, therefore, there is apart from
injustice in the wide sense another, ' particular ', injustice
which shares the name and nature of the first, because its
1130^b definition falls within the same genus ; for the significance of
both consists in a relation to one's neighbour, but the
one is concerned with honour or money or safety—or
that which includes all these, if we had a single name for
it—and its motive is the pleasure that arises from gain ;
while the other is concerned with all the objects with which
5 the good man is concerned.

It is clear, then, that there is more than one kind of
justice, and that there is one which is distinct from virtue
entire ; we must try to grasp its genus and differentia.

The unjust has been divided into the unlawful and the
unfair, and the just into the lawful and the fair. To the
unlawful answers the afore-mentioned sense of injustice. But
10 since the unfair and the unlawful are not the same, but are

different as a part is from its whole (for all that is unfair is
unlawful, but not all that is unlawful is unfair), the unjust
and injustice in the sense of the unfair are not the same
as but different from the former kind, as part from whole;
for injustice in this sense is a part of injustice in the wide
sense, and similarly justice in the one sense of justice in the ¹⁵
other. Therefore we must speak also about particular
justice and particular injustice, and similarly about the just
and the unjust. The justice, then, which answers to the
whole of virtue, and the corresponding injustice, one being
the exercise of virtue as a whole, and the other that of vice
as a whole, towards one's neighbour, we may leave on one
side. And how the meanings of 'just' and 'unjust' which ²⁰
answer to these are to be distinguished is evident; for
practically the majority of the acts commanded by the law
are those which are prescribed from the point of view
of virtue taken as a whole; for the law bids us practise every
virtue and forbids us to practise any vice. And the things
that tend to produce virtue taken as a whole are those of ²⁵
the acts prescribed by the law which have been prescribed
with a view to education for the common good. But with
regard to the education of the individual as such, which
makes him without qualification a good *man*, we must
determine later ¹ whether this is the function of the political
art or of another; for perhaps it is not the same to be a
good man and a good citizen of any state taken at random.

　　Of particular justice and that which is just in the ³⁰
corresponding sense, (A) one kind is that which is manifested in distributions of honour or money or the other
things that fall to be divided among those who have a share
in the constitution (for in these it is possible for one man to
have a share either unequal or equal to that of another), and
(B) one is that which plays a rectifying part in transactions
between man and man. Of this there are two divisions; of 1131^a
transactions (1) some are voluntary and (2) others involuntary
—voluntary such transactions as sale, purchase, loan for
consumption, pledging, loan for use, depositing, letting (they

---

¹ 1179^b 20–1181^b 12.　*Pol.* 1276^b 16–1277^b 32, 1278^a 40–^b5, 1288^a 32–
^b2, 1333^a 11–16, 1337^a 11–14.

are called voluntary because the origin of these transactions
5 is voluntary), while of the involuntary (*a*) some are clandes-
tine, such as theft, adultery, poisoning, procuring, entice-
ment of slaves, assassination, false witness, and (*b*) others
are violent, such as assault, imprisonment, murder, robbery
with violence, mutilation, abuse, insult.

10   (A) We have shown that both the unjust man and the **3**
unjust act are unfair or unequal ; now it is clear that there
is also an intermediate between the two unequals involved
in either case. And this is the equal ; for in any kind of
action in which there is a more and a less there is also what
is equal. If, then, the unjust is unequal, the just is equal,
as all men suppose it to be, even apart from argument.
And since the equal is intermediate, the just will be an inter-
15 mediate. Now equality implies at least two things. The
just, then, must be both intermediate and equal and relative
(i. e for certain persons). And *qua* intermediate it must be
between certain things (which are respectively greater and
less) ; *qua* equal, it involves *two* things ; *qua* just, it is for certain people. The just, therefore, involves at least four terms ;
for the persons for whom it is in fact just are two, and the
things in which it is manifested, the objects distributed, are
20 two. And the same equality will exist between the persons
and between the things concerned ; for as the latter—the
things concerned—are related, so are the former; if they
are not equal, they will not have what is equal, but this is
the origin of quarrels and complaints—when either equals
have and are awarded unequal shares, or unequals equal
shares. Further, this is plain from the fact that awards
25 should be 'according to merit'; for all men agree that
what is just in distribution must be according to merit in
some sense, though they do not all specify the same sort of
merit, but democrats identify it with the status of freeman,
supporters of oligarchy with wealth (or with noble birth),
and supporters of aristocracy with excellence.
30   The just, then, is a species of the proportionate (proportion being not a property only of the kind of number which
consists of abstract units, but of number in general). For pro-

portion is equality of ratios, and involves four terms at least (that discrete proportion involves four terms is plain, but so does continuous proportion, for it uses one term as two and mentions it twice; e. g. 'as the line A is to the line B, so is **1131ᵇ** the line B to the line C'; the line B, then, has been mentioned twice, so that if the line B be assumed twice, the proportional terms will be four); and the just, too, involves at least four terms, and the ratio between one pair is the same as that between the other pair; for there is a similar distinction between the persons and between the things. As the term 5 A, then, is to B, so will C be to D, and therefore, *alternando*, as A is to C, B will be to D. Therefore also the whole is in the same ratio to the whole;[1] and this coupling the distribution effects, and, if the terms are so combined, effects justly. The conjunction, then, of the term A with C and of B with D is what is just in distribution,[2] and this species of the just 10 is intermediate, and the unjust is what violates the proportion; for the proportional is intermediate, and the just is proportional. (Mathematicians call this kind of proportion geometrical; for it is in geometrical proportion that it follows that the whole is to the whole as either part is to the corresponding part.) This proportion is not con- 15 tinuous; for we cannot get a single term standing for a person and a thing.

This, then, is what the just is—the proportional; the unjust is what violates the proportion. Hence one term becomes too great, the other too small, as indeed happens in practice; for the man who acts unjustly has too much, and the man who is unjustly treated too little, of what is good. In the case of evil the reverse is true; for the lesser 20 evil is reckoned a good in comparison with the greater evil, since the lesser evil is rather to be chosen than the greater,

---

[1] Person A + thing C to person B + thing D.

[2] The problem of distributive justice is to divide the distributable honour or reward into parts which are to one another as are the merits of the persons who are to participate. If
A (first person) : B (second person) :: C (first portion) : D (second portion),
then (*alternando*) A : C :: B : D,
and therefore (*componendo*) A + C : B + D :: A : B.
In other words the position established answers to the relative merits of the parties.

and what is worthy of choice is good, and what is worthier of choice a greater good.

This, then, is one species of the just.

25   (B) The remaining one is the rectificatory, which arises in **4** connexion with transactions both voluntary and involuntary. This form of the just has a different specific character from the former. For the justice which distributes common possessions is always in accordance with the kind of proportion mentioned above [1] (for in the case also in which the distribution is made from the common funds of a partner-
30 ship it will be according to the same ratio which the funds put into the business by the partners bear to one another); and the injustice opposed to this kind of justice is that which violates the proportion. But the justice in transactions between man and man is a sort of equality indeed,
1132^a and the injustice a sort of inequality; not according to that kind of proportion, however, but according to arithmetical proportion.[2] For it makes no difference whether a good man has defrauded a bad man or a bad man a good one, nor whether it is a good or a bad man that has committed adultery; the law looks only to the distinctive character
5 of the injury, and treats the parties as equal, if one is in the wrong and the other is being wronged, and if one inflicted injury and the other has received it. Therefore, this kind of injustice being an inequality, the judge tries to equalize it; for in the case also in which one has received and the other has inflicted a wound, or one has slain and the other been slain, the suffering and the action have been unequally distributed; but the judge tries to equalize things by means

---

[1] l. 12 f.

[2] The problem of 'rectificatory justice' has nothing to do with punishment proper but is only that of rectifying a wrong that has been done, by awarding damages; i.e. rectificatory justice is that of the civil, not that of the criminal courts. The parties are treated by the court as equal (since a law court is not a court of morals), and the wrongful act is reckoned as having brought equal gain to the wrong-doer and loss to his victim; it brings A to the position $A+C$, and B to the position $B-C$. The judge's task is to find the arithmetical mean between these, and this he does by transferring C from A to B. Thus (A being treated as $=$ B) we get the arithmetical 'proportion'
$$(A+C)-(A+C-C) = (A+C-C)-(B-C)$$
or $$(A+C)-(B-C+C) = (B-C+C)-(B-C).$$

of the penalty, taking away from the gain of the assailant. For the term 'gain' is applied generally to such cases, 10 even if it be not a term appropriate to certain cases, e. g. to the person who inflicts a wound—and 'loss' to the sufferer; at all events when the suffering has been estimated, the one is called loss and the other gain. Therefore the equal is intermediate between the greater and the less, 15 but the gain and the loss are respectively greater and less in contrary ways; more of the good and less of the evil are gain, and the contrary is loss; intermediate between them is, as we saw,¹ the equal, which we say is just; therefore corrective justice will be the intermediate between loss and gain. This is why, when people dispute, they take refuge in the judge; and to go to the judge is to go to justice; 20 for the nature of the judge is to be a sort of animate justice; and they seek the judge as an intermediate, and in some states they call judges mediators, on the assumption that if they get what is intermediate they will get what is just. The just, then, is an intermediate, since the judge is so. Now the judge restores equality; it is as though there were 25 a line divided into unequal parts, and he took away that by which the greater segment exceeds the half, and added it to the smaller segment. And when the whole has been equally divided, then they say they have 'their own'—i. e. when they have got what is equal. The equal is intermediate between the greater and the lesser line according to arithmetical proportion. It is for this reason also that 30 it is called just ($\delta i\kappa a\iota o\nu$), because it is a division into two equal parts ($\delta i\chi a$), just as if one were to call it $\delta i\chi a\iota o\nu$; and the judge ($\delta\iota\kappa a\sigma\tau\eta s$) is one who bisects ($\delta\iota\chi a\sigma\tau\eta s$). For when something is subtracted from one of two equals and added to the other, the other is in excess by these two; since if what was taken from the one had not been added to the other, the latter would have been in excess by one only. It therefore exceeds the intermediate by one, and 1132^b the intermediate exceeds by one that from which something was taken. By this, then, we shall recognize both what we must subtract from that which has more, and what we must

¹ l. 14.

add to that which has less; we must add to the latter that
5 by which the intermediate exceeds it, and subtract from the
greatest that by which it exceeds the intermediate. Let
the lines AA′, BB′, CC′ be equal to one another; from the
line AA′ let the segment AE have been subtracted, and to
the line CC′ let the segment CD [1] have been added, so that
the whole line DCC′ exceeds the line EA′ by the segment
CD and the segment CF; therefore it exceeds the line BB′
9 by the segment CD.

¹¹ These names, both loss and gain, have come from voluntary exchange; for to have more than one's own is called
gaining, and to have less than one's original share is called
¹⁵ losing, e. g. in buying and selling and in all other matters in
which the law has left people free to make their own terms;
but when they get neither more nor less but just what
belongs to themselves, they say that they have their own
and that they neither lose nor gain.

Therefore the just is intermediate between a sort of gain
and a sort of loss, viz. those which are involuntary; [2] it consists
²⁰ in having an equal amount before and after the transaction.

Some think that *reciprocity* is without qualification just, 5
as the Pythagoreans said; for they defined justice without
qualification as reciprocity.[3] Now 'reciprocity' fits neither
²⁵ distributive nor rectificatory justice—yet people *want* even
the justice of Rhadamanthus to mean this:

Should a man suffer what he did, right justice would be
      done [4]

—for in many cases reciprocity and rectificatory justice are
not in accord; e.g. (1) if an official has inflicted a wound,
he should not be wounded in return, and if some one has

¹ *Sc.* equal to AE.   ² I.e. for the loser.
³ Cf. Diels *Vors.* 45 B 4.   ⁴ Hes. fr. 174 Rzach.

wounded an official, he ought not to be wounded only but punished in addition. Further (2) there is a great difference 30 between a voluntary and an involuntary act. But in associations for exchange this sort of justice does hold men together—reciprocity in accordance with a proportion and not on the basis of precisely equal return. For it is by proportionate requital that the city holds together. Men seek to return either evil for evil—and if they cannot do so, think their position mere slavery—or good for good— 1133^a and if they cannot do so there is no exchange, but it is by exchange that they hold together. This is why they give a prominent place to the temple of the Graces—to promote the requital of services; for this is characteristic of grace—we should serve in return one who has shown grace to us, and should another time take the initiative in showing it.

Now proportionate return is secured by cross-conjunction.[1] 5 Let A be a builder, B a shoemaker, C a house, D a shoe. The builder, then, must get from the shoemaker the latter's work, and must himself give him in return his own. If, 10 then, first there is proportionate equality of goods, and then reciprocal action takes place, the result we mention will be effected. If not, the bargain is not equal, and does not hold; for there is nothing to prevent the work of the one being better than that of the other; they must therefore be equated. (And this is true of the other arts also; for they would have been destroyed if what the patient suf- 15 fered had not been just what the agent did, and of the same amount and kind.[2]) For it is not two doctors that associate for exchange, but a doctor and a farmer, or in

---

[1] The working of 'proportionate reciprocity' is not very clearly described by Aristotle, but seems to be as follows. A and B are workers in different trades, and will normally be of different degrees of 'worth'. Their products, therefore, will also have unequal worth, i.e. (though Aristotle does not expressly reduce the question to one of time) if A = nB, C (what A makes, say, in an hour) will be worth n times as much as D (what B makes in an hour). A fair exchange will then take place if A gets nD and B gets I C; i.e. if A gives what it takes him an hour to make, in exchange for what it takes B n hours to make.

[2] This sentence conveys a natural enough thought, and echoes closely the language of Pl. *Gorg.* 474 B-D. But it seems to have no relevance to the context, and probably here as in 1132^b 9-11 we have the unsuccessful attempt of an early editor to find a suitable place for an isolated note of Aristotle's.

general people who are different and unequal; but these
must be equated. This is why all things that are exchanged
must be somehow comparable. It is for this end that
money has been introduced, and it becomes in a sense an
20 intermediate; for it measures all things, and therefore the
excess and the defect—how many shoes are equal to a
house or to a given amount of food. The number of shoes
exchanged for a house [or for a given amount of food]¹
must therefore correspond to the ratio of builder to shoemaker. For if this be not so, there will be no exchange
25 and no intercourse. And this proportion will not be
effected unless the goods are somehow equal. All goods
must therefore be measured by some one thing, as we said
before.² Now this unit is in truth demand, which holds all
things together (for if men did not need one another's goods
at all, or did not need them equally, there would be either
no exchange or not the same exchange); but money has
30 become by convention a sort of representative of demand;
and this is why it has the name 'money' (νόμισμα)—because
it exists not by nature but by law (νόμος) and it is in our
power to change it and make it useless. There will, then,
be reciprocity when the terms have been equated so that
as farmer is to shoemaker, the amount of the shoemaker's
work is to that of the farmer's work for which it exchanges.
1133ᵇ But we must not bring them into a figure of proportion
when they have already exchanged (otherwise one extreme
will have both excesses), but when they still have their own
goods.³ Thus they are equals and associates just because

---

¹ ἢ τροφήν will not do here, and must surely be the work of a
copyist who has been misled by the occurrence of the farmer and his
product, food, as additional examples in the context (ᵃ 17, 22, 32, ᵇ 4).
So Ramsauer.   ² l. 19.

³ Aristotle's meaning, which has caused much difficulty, seems to be
explained by a reference to ix. 1. That chapter concludes with the
observation δεῖ δ' ἴσως οὐ τοσούτου τιμᾶν ὅσου ἔχοντι φαίνεται ἄξιον, ἀλλ'
ὅσου πρὶν ἔχειν ἐτίμα. The reasoning in that chapter shows that
Aristotle's meaning here must be that people must not exchange goods
in random amounts and *then* bring themselves into a 'figure of proportion'. For each will then set an unduly high value on the goods
he has parted with and an unduly low value on those he has received;
and any adjustment that is made will be decided by their respective
powers of bluff. One party will have 'both excesses' over the other,
since what he gets will exceed the mean and what the other man gets

this equality can be effected in their case. Let A be a farmer, C food, B a shoemaker, D his product equated to C. If it had not been possible for reciprocity to be thus effected, there would have been no association of the parties. That demand holds things together as a single unit is shown by the fact that when men do not need one another, i. e. when neither needs the other or one does not need the other, they do not exchange, as we do when some one wants what one has oneself, e. g. when people permit the exportation of corn in exchange for wine.[1] This equation therefore must be established. And for the future exchange—that if we do not need a thing now we shall have it if ever we do need it—money is as it were our surety; for it must be possible for us to get what we want by bringing the money. Now the same thing happens to money itself as to goods—it is not always worth the same; yet it tends to be steadier. This is why all goods must have a price set on them; for then there will always be exchange, and if so, association of man with man. Money, then, acting as a measure, makes goods commensurate and equates them; for neither would there have been association if there were not exchange, nor exchange if there were not equality, nor equality if there were not commensurability. Now in truth it is impossible that things differing so much should become commensurate, but with reference to demand they may become so sufficiently. There must, then, be a unit, and that fixed by agreement (for which reason it is called money[2]); for it is this that makes all things commensurate, since all things are measured by money. Let A be a house, B ten minae, C a bed. A is half of B, if the house is worth five minae or equal to them; the bed, C, is a tenth of B; it is plain, then, how many beds are equal to a house, viz. five. That exchange took place thus before there was money is plain; for it makes no difference whether it is five beds that exchange for a house, or the money value of five beds.

will fall short of it (cf. 1132ᵃ 32-ᵇ 2). The only fair method is for each to set a value on his own and on the other's goods *before* they exchange, and come to an agreement if they can.

[1] Omitting the comma after οἴνου in l. 9.   [2] Cf. ᵃ 30.

30 We have now defined the unjust and the just. These having been marked off from each other, it is plain that just action is intermediate between acting unjustly and being unjustly treated ; for the one is to have too much and the other to have too little. Justice is a kind of mean, but not in the same way as the other virtues, but because it relates to an intermediate amount, while injustice relates to the extremes.

1134^a And justice is that in virtue of which the just man is said to be a doer, by choice, of that which is just, and one who will distribute either between himself and another or between two others not so as to give more of what is desirable to himself and less to his neighbour (and conversely with what 5 is harmful), but so as to give what is equal in accordance with proportion ; and similarly in distributing between two other persons. Injustice on the other hand is similarly related to the unjust, which is excess and defect, contrary to proportion, of the useful or hurtful. For which reason injustice is excess and defect, viz. because it is productive of excess and defect—in one's own case excess of what is 10 in its own nature useful and defect of what is hurtful, while in the case of others it is as a whole like what it is in one's own case, but proportion may be violated in either direction. In the unjust act to have too little is to be unjustly treated ; to have too much is to act unjustly.

Let this be taken as our account of the nature of justice 15 and injustice, and similarly of the just and the unjust in general.

Since acting unjustly does not necessarily imply being **6** unjust, we must ask what sort of unjust acts imply that the doer is unjust with respect to each type of injustice, e.g. a thief, an adulterer, or a brigand. Surely the answer does not turn on the difference between these types. For a man might even lie with a woman knowing who she was, 20 but the origin of his act might be not deliberate choice but passion. He acts unjustly, then, but is not unjust; e.g. a man is not a thief, yet he stole, nor an adulterer, yet he committed adultery ; and similarly in all other cases.[1]

---

[1] This paragraph has no connexion with what follows; the subject of it is continued in ch. 8.

Now we have previously stated how the reciprocal is
related to the just ;[1] but we must not forget that what we 25
are looking for is not only what is just without qualification
but also political justice. This is found among men who
share their life with a view to self-sufficiency, men who are
free and either proportionately or arithmetically equal, so
that between those who do not fulfil this condition there is no
political justice but justice in a special sense and by analogy.
For justice exists only between men whose mutual relations 30
are governed by law ; and law exists for men between whom
there is injustice ; for legal justice is the discrimination of the
just and the unjust.   And between men between whom there
is injustice there is also unjust action (though there is not
injustice between all between whom there is unjust action),
and this is assigning too much to oneself of things good in
themselves and too little of things evil in themselves. This 35
is why we do not allow a *man* to rule, but *rational principle*,
because a man behaves thus in his own interests and becomes
a tyrant. The magistrate on the other hand is the guardian **1134**^b
of justice, and, if of justice, then of equality also. And since
he is assumed to have no more than his share, if he is just
(for he does not assign to himself more of what is good in
itself, unless such a share is proportional to his merits—so
that it is for others that he labours, and it is for this reason 5
that men, as we stated previously,[2] say that justice is
'another's good '), therefore a reward must be given him,
and this is honour and privilege ; but those for whom such
things are not enough become tyrants.

The justice of a master and that of a father are not the
same as the justice of citizens, though they are like it ; for
there can be no injustice in the unqualified sense towards
things that are one's own, but a man's chattel,[3] and his 10
child until it reaches a certain age and sets up for itself, are as
it were part of himself, and no one chooses to hurt himself
(for which reason there can be no injustice towards oneself).
Therefore the justice or injustice of citizens is not manifested
in these relations; for it was as we saw [4] according to law, and

---

[1] 1132^b 21–1133^b 28.   [2] 1130^a 3.
[3] I.e. his slave.   [4] ^a 30.

between people naturally subject to law, and these as we saw[1] are people who have an equal share in ruling and being
15 ruled. Hence justice can more truly be manifested towards a wife than towards children and chattels, for the former is household justice; but even this is different from political justice.

Of political justice part is natural, part legal,—natural, **7** that which everywhere has the same force and does not exist
20 by people's thinking this or that; legal, that which is originally indifferent, but when it has been laid down is not indifferent, e. g. that a prisoner's ransom shall be a mina, or that a goat and not two sheep shall be sacrificed, and again all the laws that are passed for particular cases, e. g. that sacrifice shall be made in honour of Brasidas,[2] and the provisions of decrees. Now some think that all justice
25 is of this sort, because that which is by nature is unchangeable and has everywhere the same force (as fire burns both here and in Persia), while they see change in the things recognized as just. This, however, is not true in this unqualified way, but is true in a sense; or rather, with the gods it is perhaps not true at all, while with us there is something that is just even by nature, yet all of it is changeable; but still some is by nature, some not by nature.
30 It is evident which sort of thing, among things capable of being otherwise, is by nature, and which is not but is legal and conventional, assuming that both are equally changeable. And in all other things the same distinction will apply; by nature the right hand is stronger, yet it is possible that all men should come to be ambidextrous. The things which are just by virtue of convention and
1135[a] expediency are like measures; for wine and corn measures are not everywhere equal, but larger in wholesale and smaller in retail markets. Similarly, the things which are just not by nature but by human enactment are not everywhere the same, since constitutions also are not the same, though there is but one which is everywhere by nature the best.

[1] [a] 26–8.　　　　　[2] Thuc. v. 11.

Of things just and lawful each is related as the universal 5
to its particulars; for the things that are done are many,
but of *them* each is one, since it is universal.

There is a difference between the act of injustice and
what is unjust, and between the act of justice and what
is just; for a thing is unjust by nature or by enactment;
and this very thing, when it has been done, is an act of 10
injustice, but before it is done is not yet that but is unjust.
So, too, with an act of justice (though the general term is
rather 'just action', and 'act of justice' is applied to the
correction of the act of injustice).

Each of these must later[1] be examined separately with
regard to the nature and number of its species and the
nature of the things with which it is concerned.

8   Acts just and unjust being as we have described them, 15
a man acts unjustly or justly whenever he does such acts
voluntarily; when involuntarily, he acts neither unjustly
nor justly except in an incidental way; for he does things
which happen to be just or unjust. Whether an act is or
is not one of injustice (or of justice) is determined by its
voluntariness or involuntariness; for when it is voluntary it 20
is blamed, and at the same time is then an act of injustice;
so that there will be things that are unjust but not yet acts
of injustice, if voluntariness be not present as well. By
the voluntary I mean, as has been said before,[2] any of the
things in a man's own power which he does with knowledge,
i. e. not in ignorance either of the person acted on or of the
instrument used or of the end that will be attained (e. g. 25
whom he is striking, with what, and to what end), each such
act being done not incidentally nor under compulsion
(e. g. if A takes B's hand and therewith strikes C, B does
not act voluntarily; for the act was not in his own power).
The person struck may be the striker's father, and the
striker may know that it is a man or one of the persons
present, but not know that it is his father; a similar 30
distinction may be made in the case of the end, and with

---

[1] Possibly a reference to an intended (or now lost) book of the
Politics on laws.

[2] 1109^b35–1111^a24.

regard to the whole action. Therefore that which is done in ignorance, or though not done in ignorance is not in the agent's power, or is done under compulsion, is involuntary (for many natural processes, even, we knowingly both per-

1135^b form and experience, none of which is either voluntary or involuntary; e. g. growing old or dying). But in the case of unjust and just acts alike the injustice or justice may be only incidental; for a man might return a deposit unwill-

5 ingly and from fear, and then he must not be said either to do what is just or to act justly, except in an incidental way. Similarly the man who under compulsion and unwillingly fails to return the deposit must be said to act unjustly, and to do what is unjust, only incidentally. Of voluntary acts

10 we do some by choice, others not by choice; by choice those which we do after deliberation, not by choice those which we do without previous deliberation. Thus there are three kinds of injury in transactions between man and man; those done in ignorance are *mistakes* when the person acted on, the act, the instrument, or the end that will be attained is other than the agent supposed; the agent thought either that he was not hitting any one or that he was not hitting with this missile or not hitting this person or to this end, but a result followed other than that which

15 he thought likely (e. g. he threw not with intent to wound but only to prick), or the person hit or the missile was other than he supposed. Now when (1) the injury takes place contrary to reasonable expectation, it is a *misadventure*. When (2) it is not contrary to reasonable expectation, but does not imply vice, it is a *mistake* (for a man makes a mistake when the fault originates in him, but is the victim of accident when the origin lies outside him). When (3) he acts with knowledge but not after deliberation,

20 it is an *act of injustice*—e. g. the acts due to anger or to other passions necessary or natural to man; for when men do such harmful and mistaken acts they act unjustly, and the acts are acts of injustice, but this does not imply that the doers are unjust or wicked; for the injury is not due to vice. But when (4) a man acts from choice, he is an

25 *unjust man* and a vicious man.

Hence acts proceeding from anger are rightly judged not to be done of malice aforethought; for it is not the man who acts in anger but he who enraged him that starts the mischief. Again, the matter in dispute is not whether the thing happened or not, but its justice; for it is apparent injustice that occasions rage. For they do not dispute about the occurrence of the act—as in commercial transactions where 30 one of the two parties *must* be vicious [1]—unless they do so owing to forgetfulness; but, agreeing about the fact, they dispute on which side justice lies (whereas a man who has deliberately injured another cannot help knowing that he has done so), so that the one thinks he is being treated unjustly and the other disagrees.[2]

But if a man harms another by choice, he acts unjustly; 1136[a] and *these* are the acts of injustice which imply that the doer is an unjust man, provided that the act violates proportion or equality. Similarly, a man *is just* when he acts justly by choice; but he *acts justly* if he merely acts voluntarily.

Of involuntary acts some are excusable, others not. For 5 the mistakes which men make not only in ignorance but also from ignorance are excusable, while those which men do not from ignorance but (though they do them *in* ignorance) owing to a passion which is neither natural nor such as man is liable to, are not excusable.

9 Assuming that we have sufficiently defined the suffering 10 and doing of injustice, it may be asked (1) whether the truth in expressed in Euripides' paradoxical words:

'I slew my mother, that's my tale in brief.'
'Were you both willing, or unwilling both?'[3]

---

[1] The plaintiff, if he brings a false accusation; the defendant, if he denies a true one.

[2] With Bywater's punctuation ὁ μέν means the person who acted in anger, ὁ δ' the person who angered him. I should prefer to treat ὁ δ' ἐπιβουλεύσας οὐκ ἀγνοεῖ as not parenthetical, in which case ὁ δ' οὔ will mean 'while a deliberate aggressor does not think he is being treated unjustly'. In any case, ὁ ἐπιβουλεύσας is apparently not one of the parties in the dispute περὶ τοῦ δικαίου, i.e. neither the θυμῷ ποιῶν nor the ὀργίσας, but is the μοχθηρός party to the dispute περὶ τοῦ γενέσθαι, i.e. either the guilty defendant or the fraudulent plaintiff.

[3] Fr. 68 (from the *Alcmeon*), Nauck².

15 Is it truly possible to be willingly treated unjustly, or is all suffering of injustice on the contrary involuntary, as all unjust action is voluntary? And is all suffering of injustice of the latter kind or else all of the former, or is it sometimes voluntary, sometimes involuntary? So, too, with the case of being justly treated; all just action is voluntary, so that it is reasonable that there should be a similar opposition in 20 either case—that both being unjustly and being justly treated should be either alike voluntary or alike involuntary. But it would be thought paradoxical even in the case of being justly treated, if it were always voluntary; for some are unwillingly treated justly. (2) One might raise this question also, whether every one who has suffered what is unjust is being unjustly treated, or on the other hand it is 25 with suffering as with acting. In action and in passivity alike it is possible to partake of justice incidentally, and similarly (it is plain) of injustice; for to do what is unjust is not the same as to act unjustly, nor to suffer what is unjust as to be treated unjustly, and similarly in the case of acting justly and being justly treated; for it is impossible 30 to be unjustly treated if the other does not act unjustly, or justly treated unless he acts justly. Now if to act unjustly is simply to harm some one voluntarily, and 'voluntarily' means 'knowing the person acted on, the instrument, and the manner of one's acting', and the incontinent man voluntarily harms himself, not only will he voluntarily be unjustly treated but it will be possible to treat oneself unjustly. (This also is one of the questions in doubt, whether a man 1136ᵇ can treat himself unjustly.) Again, a man may voluntarily, owing to incontinence, be harmed by another who acts voluntarily, so that it would be possible to be voluntarily treated unjustly. Or is our definition incorrect; must we to 'harming another, with knowledge both of the person acted on, of the instrument, and of the manner' add 'contrary to the 5 wish of the person acted on'? Then a man may be voluntarily harmed and voluntarily suffer what is unjust, but no one is voluntarily treated unjustly; for no one wishes to be unjustly treated, not even the incontinent man. He acts contrary to his wish; for no one *wishes* for what he does

not think to be good, but the incontinent man does *do*
things that he does not think he ought to do. Again, one
who gives what is his own, as Homer says Glaucus gave
Diomede

> Armour of gold for brazen, the price of a hundred beeves 10
>   for nine,[1]

is not unjustly treated ; for though to give is in his power,
to be unjustly treated is not, but there must be some one to
treat him unjustly. It is plain, then, that being unjustly
treated is not voluntary.

Of the questions we intended to discuss two still re- 15
main for discussion ; (3) whether it is the man who has
assigned to another more than his share that acts unjustly,
or he who has the excessive share, and (4) whether it is
possible to treat oneself unjustly. The questions are connected ; for if the former alternative is possible and the
distributor acts unjustly and not the man who has the
excessive share, then if a man assigns more to another than
to himself, knowingly and voluntarily, he treats himself
unjustly ; which is what modest people seem to do, since the 20
virtuous man tends to take less than his share. Or does this
statement too need qualification ? For (*a*) he perhaps gets
more than his share of some other good, e. g. of honour or
of intrinsic nobility. (*b*) The question is solved by applying
the distinction we applied to unjust action ;[2] for he suffers
nothing contrary to his own wish, so that he is not unjustly
treated as far as this goes, but at most only suffers harm.

It is plain too that the distributor acts unjustly, but not 25
always the man who has the excessive share ; for it is not
he to whom what is unjust appertains that acts unjustly,
but he to whom it appertains to do the unjust act voluntarily, i. e. the person in whom lies the origin of the action,
and this lies in the distributor, not in the receiver. Again,
since the word 'do' is ambiguous, and there is a sense in 30
which lifeless things, or a hand, or a servant who obeys an
order, may be said to slay, he who gets an excessive share
does not act unjustly, though he 'does' what is unjust.

Again, if the distributor gave his judgement in ignorance,

[1] *Il.* vi. 236.   [2] ll. 3-5.

he does not act unjustly in respect of legal justice, and his
judgement is not unjust in this sense, but in a sense it *is*
unjust (for legal justice and primordial justice are different) ;
1137ᵃ but if with knowledge he judged unjustly, he is himself
aiming at an excessive share either of gratitude or of
revenge. As much, then, as if he were to share in the
plunder, the man who has judged unjustly for these reasons
has got too much ; the fact that what he gets is different
from what he distributes makes no difference, for even if
he awards land with a view to sharing in the plunder he
gets not land but money.

5 Men think that acting unjustly is in their power, and
therefore that being just is easy. But it is not ; to lie with
one's neighbour's wife, to wound another, to deliver a bribe,
is easy and in our power, but to do these things as a result
of a certain state of character is neither easy nor in our
power. Similarly to know what is just and what is unjust
10 requires, men think, no great wisdom, because it is not hard
to understand the matters dealt with by the laws (though
these are not the things that are just, except incidentally) ;
but how actions must be done and distributions effected in
order to be just, to know *this* is a greater achievement than
knowing what is good for the health ; though even there, while
it is easy to know that honey, wine, hellebore, cautery, and
15 the use of the knife are so, to know how, to whom, and when
these should be applied with a view to producing health,
is no less an achievement than that of being a physician.
Again, for this very reason [1] men think that acting unjustly
is characteristic of the just man no less than of the unjust,
because he would be not less but even more capable of
doing each of these unjust acts ; [2] for he could lie with
20 a woman or wound a neighbour ; and the brave man could
throw away his shield and turn to flight in this direction or
in that. But to play the coward or to act unjustly consists
not in doing these things, except incidentally, but in doing
them as the result of a certain state of character, just as to
practise medicine and healing consists not in applying or

[1] i. e. that stated in l. 4 f., that acting unjustly is in our own power.
[2] Cf. ll. 6–8.

not applying the knife, in using or not using medicines, but 25 in doing so in a certain way.

Just acts occur between people who participate in things good in themselves and can have too much or too little of them; for some beings (e. g. presumably the gods) cannot have too much of them, and to others, those who are incurably bad, not even the smallest share in them is beneficial but all such goods are harmful, while to others they are beneficial up to a point; therefore justice is 30 essentially something human.

10   Our next subject is equity and the equitable (τὸ ἐπιεικές), and their respective relations to justice and the just. For on examination they appear to be neither absolutely the same nor generically different; and while we sometimes praise what is equitable and the equitable man (so that we 35 apply the name by way of praise even to instances of the other virtues, instead of 'good', meaning by ἐπιεικέστερον **1137ᵇ** that a thing is better[1]), at other times, when we reason it out, it seems strange if the equitable, being something different from the just, is yet praiseworthy; for either the just or the equitable is not good,[2] if they are different; or, if both are good, they are the same.

These, then, are pretty much the considerations that give 5 rise to the problem about the equitable; they are all in a sense correct and not opposed to one another; for the equitable, though it is better than one kind of justice, yet is just, and it is not as being a different class of thing that it is better than the just. The same thing, then, is just and equitable, and while both are good the equitable is superior. 10 What creates the problem is that the equitable is just, but not the legally just but a correction of legal justice. The reason is that all law is universal but about some things it is not possible to make a universal statement which shall be correct. In those cases, then, in which it is necessary to speak universally, but not possible to do so correctly, the 15 law takes the usual case, though it is not ignorant of the

---

[1] Reading τῷ ἐπιεικέστερον in l. 1.
[2] The sense requires us to omit οὐ δίκαιον (with Nᵇ Γ) or read οὐ σπουδαῖον for it in ll. 4–5.

possibility of error. And it is none the less correct; for the error is not in the law nor in the legislator but in the nature of the thing, since the matter of practical affairs is of this kind from the start. When the law speaks universally, 20 then, and a case arises on it which is not covered by the universal statement, then it is right, where the legislator fails us and has erred by over-simplicity, to correct the omission—to say what the legislator himself would have said had he been present, and would have put into his law if he had known. Hence the equitable is just, and better 25 than one kind of justice—not better than absolute justice but better than the error that arises from the absoluteness of the statement. And this is the nature of the equitable, a correction of law where it is defective owing to its universality. In fact this is the reason why all things are not determined by law, viz. that about some things it is impossible to lay down a law, so that a decree is needed. For when the thing is indefinite the rule also is indefinite, 30 like the leaden rule used in making the Lesbian moulding; the rule adapts itself to the shape of the stone and is not rigid, and so too the decree is adapted to the facts.

It is plain, then, what the equitable is, and that it is just and is better than one kind of justice. It is evident also 35 from this who the equitable man is; the man who chooses and does such acts, and is no stickler for his rights in a bad **1138**[a] sense but tends to take less than his share though he has the law on his side, is equitable, and this state of character is equity, which is a sort of justice and not a different state of character.

Whether a man can treat himself unjustly or not, is 11 5 evident from what has been said.[1] For (a) one class of just acts are those acts in accordance with any virtue which are prescribed by the law; e.g. the law does not expressly permit suicide, and what it does not expressly permit it forbids. Again, when a man in violation of the law harms another (otherwise than in retaliation) voluntarily, he acts unjustly, and a voluntary agent is one who knows both the

---

[1] Cf. 1129[a] 32–[b] 1, 1136[a] 10–1137[a] 4.

person he is affecting by his action and the instrument he is using; and he who through anger voluntarily stabs himself does this contrary to the right rule of life, and this the law does not allow; therefore he is acting unjustly. But towards whom? Surely towards the state, not towards himself. For he suffers voluntarily, but no one is voluntarily treated unjustly. This is also the reason why the state punishes; a certain loss of civil rights attaches to the man who destroys himself, on the ground that he is treating the state unjustly.

Further (*b*) in that sense of 'acting unjustly' in which the man who 'acts unjustly' is unjust only and not bad all round, it is not possible to treat oneself unjustly (this is different from the former sense; the unjust man in one sense of the term is wicked in a particularized way just as the coward is, not in the sense of being wicked all round, so that his 'unjust act' does not manifest wickedness in general). For (i) that would imply the possibility of the same thing's having been subtracted from and added to the same thing at the same time; but this is impossible— the just and the unjust always involve more than one person. Further, (ii) unjust action is voluntary and done by choice, and *takes the initiative* (for the man who because he has suffered does the same in return is not thought to act unjustly); but if a man harms himself he suffers and does the same things *at the same time*. Further, (iii) if a man could treat himself unjustly, he could be voluntarily treated unjustly. Besides, (iv) no one acts unjustly without committing particular acts of injustice; but no one can commit adultery with his own wife or housebreaking on his own house or theft on his own property.

In general, the question 'can a man treat himself unjustly?' is solved also by the distinction we applied to the question 'can a man be voluntarily treated unjustly?'[1]

(It is evident too that both are bad, being unjustly treated and acting unjustly; for the one means having less and the other having more than the intermediate amount, which plays the part here that the healthy does in the medical

[1] Cf. 1136ᵃ 31–ᵇ 5.

art, and that good condition does in the art of bodily
training.   But still acting unjustly is the worse, for it
involves vice and is blameworthy—involves vice which is
either of the complete and unqualified kind or almost so
(we must admit the latter alternative, because not all
voluntary unjust action implies injustice as a state of
character), while being unjustly treated does not involve
35 vice and injustice in oneself.   In itself, then, being unjustly
1138ᵇ treated is less bad, but there is nothing to prevent its being
incidentally a greater evil.   But theory cares nothing for
this; it calls pleurisy a more serious mischief than a
stumble; yet the latter may become incidentally the more
serious, if the fall due to it leads to your being taken
prisoner or put to death by the enemy.)

5   Metaphorically and in virtue of a certain resemblance
there is a justice, not indeed between a man and himself,
but between certain parts of him; yet not every kind of
justice but that of master and servant or that of husband
and wife.[1]   For these are the ratios in which the part of
the soul that has a rational principle stands to the irrational
part; and it is with a view to these parts that people also
10 think a man can be unjust to himself, viz. because these
parts are liable to suffer something contrary to their respective desires; there is therefore thought to be a mutual
justice between them as between ruler and ruled.

Let this be taken as our account of justice and the other,
i.e. the other moral, virtues.

[1] Cf. 1134ᵇ 15-17.

BOOK VI

I   SINCE we have previously said that one ought to choose
that which is intermediate, not the excess nor the defect,[1]
and that the intermediate is determined by the dictates
of the right rule,[2] let us discuss the nature of these dictates. 20
In all the states of character we have mentioned,[3] as in all
other matters, there is a mark to which the man who has the
rule looks, and heightens or relaxes his activity accordingly,
and there is a standard which determines the mean states
which we say are intermediate between excess and defect,
being in accordance with the right rule.   But such a state- 25
ment, though true, is by no means clear; for not only
here but in all other pursuits which are objects of knowledge
it is indeed true to say that we must not exert ourselves
nor relax our efforts too much nor too little, but to an
intermediate extent and as the right rule dictates; but if a
man had only this knowledge he would be none the wiser—
e. g. we should not know what sort of medicines to apply to 30
our body if some one were to say 'all those which the
medical art prescribes, and which agree with the practice of
one who possesses the art'.   Hence it is necessary with
regard to the states of the soul also not only that this true
statement should be made, but also that it should be
determined what is the right rule and what is the standard
that fixes it.

We divided the virtues of the soul and said that some 35
are virtues of character and others of intellect.[4]   Now we **1139ᵃ**
have discussed in detail the moral virtues;[3] with regard
to the others let us express our view as follows, beginning
with some remarks about the soul.   We said before[5] that
there are two parts of the soul—that which grasps a rule

---

[1] 1104ᵃ 11–27, 11c6ᵃ 26–1107ᵃ 27.
[2] 1107ᵃ 1, cf. 1103ᵇ 31, 1114ᵇ 29.
[3] In iii. 6–v. 11.
[4] 1103ᵃ 3–7.
[5] 1102ᵃ 26–8.

5 or rational principle, and the irrational; let us now draw a similar distinction within the part which grasps a rational principle. And let it be assumed that there are two parts which grasp a rational principle—one by which we contemplate the kind of things whose originative causes are invariable, and one by which we contemplate variable things; for where objects differ in kind the part of the soul 10 answering to each of the two is different in kind, since it is in virtue of a certain likeness and kinship with their objects that they have the knowledge they have. Let one of these parts be called the scientific and the other the calculative; for to deliberate and to calculate are the same thing, but no one deliberates about the invariable. Therefore the calculative is one part of the faculty which grasps a rational 15 principles. We must, then, learn what is the best state of each of these two parts; for this is the virtue of each.

The virtue of a thing is relative to its proper work.[1] Now 2 there are three things in the soul which control action and truth—sensation, reason, desire.

Of these sensation originates no action; this is plain 20 from the fact that the lower animals have sensation but no share in action.

What affirmation and negation are in thinking, pursuit and avoidance are in desire; so that since moral virtue is a state of character' concerned with choice, and choice is deliberate desire, therefore both the reasoning must be true 25 and the desire right, if the choice is to be good, and the latter must pursue just what the former asserts. Now this kind of intellect and of truth is practical; of the intellect which is contemplative, not practical nor productive, the good and the bad state are truth and falsity respectively (for this is the work of everything intellectual); while of the 30 part which is practical and intellectual the good state is truth in agreement with right desire.

The origin of action—its efficient, not its final cause—is choice, and that of choice is desire and reasoning with a view

[1] There should, as Greenwood observes, be a full stop after ἑκατέρου in l. 16. ἡ δ' ἀρετή, &c. is the beginning of the argument which occupies ch. 2.

to an end. This is why choice cannot exist either without
reason and intellect or without a moral state; for good
action and its opposite cannot exist without a combination
of intellect and character.   Intellect itself, however, moves 35
nothing, but only the intellect which aims at an end and is
practical; for this rules the productive intellect as well, since **1139^b**
every one who makes makes for an end, and that which is
made is not an end in the unqualified sense (but only an end
in a particular relation, and the end of a particular operation)—only that which is *done* is that; for good action is an
end, and desire aims at this.   Hence choice is either desiderative reason or ratiocinative desire, and such an origin of action
is a man. (It is to be noted that nothing that is past is an 5
object of choice, e. g. no one chooses to have sacked Troy;
for no one *deliberates* about the past, but about what is
future and capable of being otherwise, while what is past is
not capable of not having taken place; hence Agathon
is right in saying ¹

    For this alone is lacking even to God,   10
    To make undone things that have once been done.)

    The work of both the intellectual parts, then, is truth.
Therefore the states that are most strictly those in respect
of which each of these parts will reach truth are the virtues
of the two parts.

3   Let us begin, then, from the beginning, and discuss these
states once more. Let it be assumed that the states by virtue 15
of which the soul possesses truth by way of affirmation or
denial are five in number, i. e. art, scientific knowledge,
practical wisdom, philosophic wisdom, intuitive reason; we
do not include judgement and opinion because in these we
may be mistaken.

    Now what *scientific knowledge* is, if we are to speak
exactly and not follow mere similarities, is plain from what
follows. We all suppose that what we know is not even 20
capable of being otherwise; of things capable of being otherwise we do not know, when they have passed outside our observation, whether they exist or not.   Therefore the object

¹ Fr. 5, Nauck².

of scientific knowledge is of necessity. Therefore it is eternal; for things that are of necessity in the unqualified sense are all eternal;[1] and things that are eternal are ungenerated and
25 imperishable. Again, every science is thought to be capable of being taught, and its object of being learned. And all teaching starts from what is already known, as we maintain in the *Analytics*[2] also; for it proceeds sometimes through induction and sometimes by syllogism. Now induction is the starting-point which knowledge even of the universal presupposes, while syllogism proceeds *from* universals. There are therefore starting-points from which
30 syllogism proceeds, which are not reached by syllogism; it is therefore by induction that they are acquired. Scientific knowledge is, then, a state of capacity to demonstrate, and has the other limiting characteristics which we specify in the *Analytics*;[3] for it is when a man believes in a certain way and the starting-points are known to him that he has scientific knowledge, since if they are not better known to him than the conclusion; he will have his knowledge only incidentally.

35 Let this, then, be taken as our account of scientific knowledge.

1140^a In the variable are included both things made and things 4 done; making and acting are different (for their nature we treat even the discussions outside our school as reliable); so that the reasoned state of capacity to act is different from
5 the reasoned state of capacity to make. Hence too they are not included one in the other; for neither is acting making nor is making acting. Now since architecture is an art and is essentially a reasoned state of capacity to make, and there is neither any art that is not such a state nor any such state that is not an art, *art* is identical with a state of capacity to
10 make, involving a true course of reasoning. All art is concerned with coming into being, i.e. with contriving and considering how something may come into being which is capable of either being or not being, and whose origin is

---

[1] A colon is required after πάντα ἀίδια in l. 24.
[2] *An. Post.* 71^a 1. [3] Ib. ^b 9–23.

in the maker and not in the thing made; for art is concerned
neither with things that are, or come into being, by necessity,
nor with things that do so in accordance with nature (since 15
these have their origin in themselves).   Making and acting
being different, art must be a matter of making, not of acting.
And in a sense chance and art are concerned with the same
objects; as Agathon says,[1] 'art loves chance and chance
loves art'.   Art, then, as has been said,[2] is a state concerned 20
with making, involving a true course of reasoning, and lack
of art on the contrary is a state concerned with making,
involving a false course of reasoning; both are concerned
with the variable.

5   Regarding *practical wisdom* we shall get at the truth by
considering who are the persons we credit with it.   Now it 25
is thought to be the mark of a man of practical wisdom to
be able to deliberate well about what is good and expedient
for himself, not in some particular respect, e. g. about what
sorts of thing conduce to health or to strength, but about
what sorts of thing conduce to the good life in general.   This
is shown by the fact that we credit men with practical
wisdom in some particular respect when they have calcu-
lated well with a view to some good end which is one
of those that are not the object of any art.   It follows that 30
in the general sense also the man who is capable of deliberating has practical wisdom.   Now no one deliberates about
things that are invariable, nor about things that it is
impossible for him to do.   Therefore, since scientific knowledge involves demonstration, but there is no demonstration
of things whose first principles are variable (for all such
things might actually be otherwise), and since it is 35
impossible to deliberate about things that are of necessity,
practical wisdom cannot be scientific knowledge nor art; not 1140^b
science because that which can be done is capable of being
otherwise, not art because action and making are different
kinds of thing.   The remaining alternative, then, is that it is
a true and reasoned state of capacity to act with regard to 5
the things that are good or bad for man.   For while making

<hr />

[1] Fr. 6, Nauck².   [2] l. 9.

has an end other than itself, action cannot; for good action itself is its end.　It is for this reason that we think Pericles and men like him have practical wisdom, viz. because they can see what is good for themselves and what is good for

10 men in general; we consider that those can do this who are good at managing households or states.　(This is why we call temperance (σωφροσύνη) by this name; we imply that it preserves one's practical wisdom (σῴζουσα τὴν φρόνησιν). Now what it preserves is a judgement of the kind we have described.　For it is not any and every judgement that pleasant and painful objects destroy and pervert, e. g. the judgement that the triangle has or has not its angles equal

15 to two right angles, but only judgements about what is to be done.　For the originating causes of the things that are done consist in the end at which they are aimed; but the man who has been ruined by pleasure or pain forthwith fails to see any such originating cause—to see that for the sake of this or because of this he ought to choose and do whatever he chooses and does; for vice is destructive of the originating cause of action.)

20　Practical wisdom, then, must be a reasoned and true state of capacity to act with regard to human goods.　But further, while there is such a thing as excellence in art, there is no such thing as excellence in practical wisdom; and in art he who errs willingly is preferable, but in practical wisdom, as in the virtues, he is the reverse.　Plainly, then, practical wisdom

25 is a virtue and not an art.　There being two parts of the soul that can follow a course of reasoning, it must be the virtue of one of the two, i. e. of that part which forms opinions; for opinion is about the variable and so is practical wisdom.　But yet it is not only a reasoned state; this is shown by the fact that a state of that sort may be forgotten

30 but practical wisdom cannot.

Scientific knowledge is judgement about things that are 6 universal and necessary, and the conclusions of demonstration, and all scientific knowledge, follow from first principles (for scientific knowledge involves apprehension of a rational ground).　This being so, the first principle from which what

is scientifically known follows cannot be an object of scientific
knowledge, of art, or of practical wisdom ; for that which can 35
be scientifically known can be demonstrated, and art and
practical wisdom deal with things that are variable. Nor are 1141^a
these first principles the objects of philosophic wisdom, for it
is a mark of the philosopher to have *demonstration* about
some things.   If, then, the states of mind by which we have
truth and are never deceived about things invariable or
even variable are scientific knowledge, practical wisdom,
philosophic wisdom, and intuitive reason, and it cannot be 5
any of the three (i. e. practical wisdom, scientific knowledge,
or philosophic wisdom), the remaining alternative is that it is
intuitive reason that grasps the first principles.

7   *Wisdom*[1] (1) in the arts we ascribe to their most finished
exponents, e. g. to Phidias as a sculptor and to Polyclitus as 10
a maker of portrait-statues, and here we mean nothing
by wisdom except excellence in art; but (2) we think that
some people are wise in general, not in some particular
field or in any other limited respect, as Homer says in the
Margites,[2]

Him did the gods make neither a digger nor yet a 15
     ploughman
Nor wise in anything else.

Therefore wisdom must plainly be the most finished of the
forms of knowledge.   It follows that the wise man must not
only know what follows from the first principles, but must also
possess truth about the first principles.   Therefore wisdom
must be intuitive reason combined with scientific knowledge
—scientific knowledge of the highest objects which has
received as it were its proper completion.

    Of the highest objects, we say ; for it would be strange to 20
think that the art of politics, or practical wisdom, is the
best knowledge, since man is not the best thing in the
world.   Now if what is healthy or good is different for men
and for fishes, but what is white or straight is always

---

[1] In this chapter Aristotle restricts to a very definite meaning the
word σοφία, which in ordinary Greek, as the beginning of the chapter
points out, was used both of skill in a particular art or craft, and of
wisdom in general.   [2] Fr. 2, Allen.

the same, any one would say that what is wise is the same
25 but what is practically wise is different; for it is to that which
observes well the various matters concerning itself that one
ascribes practical wisdom, and it is to this that one will
entrust such matters. This is why we say that some even of
the lower animals have practical wisdom,[1] viz. those which
are found to have a power of foresight with regard to their
own life. It is evident also that philosophic wisdom and the
art of politics cannot be the same; for if the state of mind
concerned with a man's own interests is to be called
30 philosophic wisdom, there will be many philosophic
wisdoms; there will not be one concerned with the good of
all animals (any more than there is one art of medicine
for all existing things), but a different philosophic wisdom
about the good of each species.

But if the argument be that man is the best of the animals,
this makes no difference; for there are other things much
1141ᵇ more divine in their nature even than man, e. g., most con-
spicuously, the bodies of which the heavens are framed. From
what has been said it is plain, then, that philosophic wisdom
is scientific knowledge, combined with intuitive reason,
of the things that are highest by nature. This is why we say
Anaxagoras, Thales, and men like them have philosophic but
5 not practical wisdom, when we see them ignorant of what is
to their own advantage, and why we say that they know things
that are remarkable, admirable, difficult, and divine, but
useless; viz. because it is not human goods that they seek.[2]

Practical wisdom on the other hand is concerned with
things human and things about which it is possible to
deliberate; for we say this is above all the work of the
10 man of practical wisdom, to deliberate well, but no one
deliberates about things invariable, nor about things which
have not an end, and that a good that can be brought about
by action. The man who is without qualification good at
deliberating is the man who is capable of aiming in accordance with calculation at the best for man of things attainable

---

[1] We do not say this in English; but we call them 'intelligent' or
'sagacious', which comes to the same thing.
[2] Cf. Diels, *Vors.* 46 A 30.

by action. Nor is practical wisdom concerned with universals only—it must also recognize the particulars; for it is practical, 15 and practice is concerned with particulars. This is why some who do not know, and especially those who have experience, are more practical than others who know ; for if a man knew that light meats are digestible and wholesome, but did not know which sorts of meat are light, he would not produce health, but the man who knows that chicken is wholesome 20 is more likely to produce health.

Now practical wisdom is concerned with action; therefore one should have both forms of it, or the latter in preference to the former. But of practical as of philosophic wisdom there must be a controlling kind.

8   Political wisdom and practical wisdom are the same state of mind, but their essence is not the same. Of the wisdom concerned with the city, the practical wisdom which plays a controlling part is legislative wisdom, while that which 25 is related to this as particulars to their universal is known by the general name ' political wisdom ' ; this has to do with action and deliberation, for a decree is a thing to be carried out in the form of an individual act. This is why the exponents of this art are alone said to ' take part in politics ' ; for these alone ' do things ' as manual labourers ' do things '.

Practical wisdom also is identified especially with that form of it which is concerned with a man himself—with the individual ; and this is known by the general name ' practical 30 wisdom ' ; of the other kinds one is called household manage- ment, another legislation, the third politics, and of the latter one part is called deliberative and the other judicial. Now knowing what is good for oneself will be one kind of know- ledge, but it is very different from the other kinds ; and the 1142^a man who knows and concerns himself with his own interests is thought to have practical wisdom, while politicians are thought to be busybodies ; hence the words of Euripides,[1]

> But how could I be wise, who might at ease,
> Numbered among the army's multitude,
> Have had an equal share ? . . .   5
> For those who aim too high and do too much . . . .

[1] Prologue to *Philoctetes* (Fr. 787, 782. 2, Nauck²).

Those who think thus seek their own good, and consider that one ought to do so. From this opinion, then, has come the view that such men have practical wisdom; yet perhaps one's own good cannot exist without household 10 management, nor without a form of government. Further, how one should order one's own affairs is not clear and needs inquiry.

What has been said is confirmed by the fact that while young men become geometricians and mathematicians and wise in matters like these, it is thought that a young man of practical wisdom cannot be found. The cause is that such wisdom is concerned not only with universals but with particulars, which become familiar from experience, but 15 a young man has no experience, for it is length of time that gives experience; indeed one might ask this question too, why a boy may become a mathematician, but not a philosopher or a physicist. Is it because the objects of mathematics exist by abstraction, while the first principles of these other subjects come from experience, and because young men have no conviction about the latter but merely use the proper language, while the essence of mathematical objects is plain enough to them?

20 Further, error in deliberation may be either about the universal or about the particular; we may fail to know either that all water that weighs heavy is bad, or that this particular water weighs heavy.

That practical wisdom is not scientific knowledge is evident; for it is, as has been said,[1] concerned with the ultimate particular fact, since the thing to be done is of 25 this nature. It is opposed, then, to intuitive reason; for intuitive reason is of the limiting premisses, for which no reason can be given, while practical wisdom is concerned with the ultimate particular, which is the object not of scientific knowledge but of perception—not the perception of qualities peculiar to one sense but a perception akin to that by which we perceive that the particular figure before us is a triangle; for in that direction as well as in that of the major premiss there will be a limit. But this is rather

[1] 1141ᵇ 14–22.

perception than practical wisdom,¹ though it is another kind 30 of perception than that of the qualities peculiar to each sense.

9   There is a difference between inquiry and deliberation; for deliberation is inquiry into a particular kind of thing. We must grasp the nature of excellence in deliberation as well—whether it is a form of scientific knowledge, or opinion, or skill in conjecture, or some other kind of thing. *Scientific knowledge* it is not; for men do not inquire about the things they know about, but good deliberation is a kind 1142ᵇ of deliberation, and he who deliberates inquires and calculates. Nor is it *skill in conjecture*; for this both involves no reasoning and is something that is quick in its operation, while men deliberate a long time, and they say that one should carry out quickly the conclusions of one's deliberation, but should deliberate slowly. Again, *readiness of mind* 5 is different from excellence in deliberation; it is a sort of skill in conjecture. Nor again is excellence in deliberation *opinion* of any sort. But since the man who deliberates badly makes a mistake, while he who deliberates well does so correctly, excellence in deliberation is clearly a kind of correctness, but neither of knowledge nor of opinion; for there is 10 no such thing as correctness of knowledge (since there is no such thing as error of knowledge), and correctness of opinion is truth; and at the same time everything that is an object of opinion is already determined. But again excellence in deliberation involves reasoning. The remaining alternative, then, is that it is *correctness of thinking*; for this is not yet assertion, since, while even opinion is not inquiry but has reached the stage of assertion, the man who is deliberating, whether he does so well or ill, is searching 15 for something and calculating.

But excellence in deliberation is a certain correctness of deliberation; hence we must first inquire what deliberation is and what it is about. And, there being more than one kind of correctness, plainly excellence in deliberation is not

---

¹ I should prefer to read in l. 30 ἢ ἡ φρόνησις, 'this is more truly perception than practical wisdom is'.

any and every kind; for (1) the incontinent man and the bad man, if he is clever,[1] will reach as a result of his calculation what he sets before himself, so that he will have deliberated correctly, but he will have got for himself a great
20 evil. Now to have deliberated well is thought to be a good thing; for it is this kind of correctness of deliberation that is excellence in deliberation, viz. that which tends to attain what is good. But (2) it is possible to attain even good by a false syllogism, and to attain what one ought to do but not by the right means, the middle term being false; so
25 that this too is not yet excellence in deliberation—this state in virtue of which one attains what one ought but not by the right means. Again (3) it is possible to attain it by long deliberation while another man attains it quickly. Therefore in the former case we have not yet got excellence in delibera-tion, which is rightness with regard to the expedient—right-ness in respect both of the end, the manner, and the time. (4) Further it is possible to have deliberated well either in the unqualified sense or with reference to a particular end. Excellence in deliberation in the unqualified sense, then, is that which succeeds with reference to what is the end in the
30 unqualified sense, and excellence in deliberation in a par-ticular sense is that which succeeds relatively to a particular end. If, then, it is characteristic of men of practical wisdom to have deliberated well, excellence in deliberation will be correctness with regard to what conduces to the end of which practical wisdom is the true apprehension.

Understanding, also, and goodness of understanding, in 10 virtue of which men are said to be men of understanding or
1143^a of good understanding, are neither entirely the same as opinion or scientific knowledge (for at that rate all men would have been men of understanding), nor are they one of the particular sciences, such as medicine, the science of things connected with health, or geometry, the science of spatial magnitudes. For understanding is neither about
5 things that are always and are unchangeable, nor about any and every one of the things that come into being, but

---

[1] Reading εἰ δεινός for ἰδεῖν in l. 19 as suggested by Apelt.

about things which may become subjects of questioning
and deliberation. Hence it is about the same objects as
practical wisdom; but understanding and practical wisdom
are not the same. For practical wisdom issues commands,
since its end is what ought to be done or not to be done;
but understanding only judges. (Understanding is identical 10
with goodness of understanding, men of understanding with
men of good understanding.) Now understanding is neither
the having nor the acquiring of practical wisdom; but as
learning is called understanding when it means the exercise
of the faculty of knowledge,[1] so ' understanding ' is applicable
to the exercise of the faculty of opinion for the purpose of
judging of what some one else says about matters with
which practical wisdom is concerned—and of judging
soundly; for ' well ' and ' soundly ' are the same thing. And 15
from this has come the use of the name ' understanding ' in
virtue of which men are said to be ' of good understanding ',
viz. from the application of the word to the grasping of
scientific truth; for we often call such grasping understanding.

11   What is called judgement, in virtue of which men are said
to ' be sympathetic judges ' and to ' have judgement ', is the 20
right discrimination of the equitable. This is shown by the
fact that we say the equitable man is above all others a man
of sympathetic judgement, and identify equity with sympathetic judgement about certain facts. And sympathetic
judgement is judgement which discriminates what is equitable and does so correctly; and correct judgement is that
which judges what is true.

Now all the states we have considered converge, as might 25
be expected, to the same point; for when we speak of judgement and understanding and practical wisdom and intuitive
reason we credit the same people with possessing judgement
and having reached years of reason and with having practical wisdom and understanding. For all these faculties
deal with ultimates, i. e. with particulars; and being a man

---

[1] For this use of μανθάνειν (which is not shared by the English
' learn ') cf. *Soph. El.* 165^b 32, and L. and S.⁸ *s.v.* IV.

of understanding and of good or sympathetic judgement
30 consists in being able to judge about the things with which
practical wisdom is concerned ; for the equities are common
to all good men in relation to other men.   Now all things
which have to be done are included among particulars or
ultimates ; for not only must the man of practical wisdom
know particular facts, but understanding and judgement
are also concerned with things to be done, and these are
35 ultimates.   And intuitive reason is concerned with the
ultimates in both directions ; for both the first terms and
the last are objects of intuitive reason and not of argument,
1143^b and the intuitive reason which is presupposed by demonstrations grasps the unchangeable and first terms, while the
intuitive reason involved in practical reasonings grasps
the last and variable fact, i. e. the minor premiss.   For these
variable facts are the starting-points for the apprehension
of the end, since the universals are reached from the par-
5 ticulars ; of these therefore we must have perception, and
this perception is intuitive reason.

This is why these states are thought to be natural endow-
ments—why, while no one is thought to be a philosopher by
nature, people are thought to have by nature judgement,
understanding, and intuitive reason.   This is shown by the
fact that we think our powers correspond to our time of life,
and that a particular age brings with it intuitive reason and
judgement ; this implies that nature is the cause.   [Hence
10 intuitive reason is both beginning and end ; for demonstrations are from these and about these.[1]]   Therefore we
ought to attend to the undemonstrated sayings and opinions
of experienced and older people or of people of practical
wisdom not less than to demonstrations ; for because
experience has given them an eye they see aright.

We have stated, then, what practical and philosophic
15 wisdom are, and with what each of them is concerned, and
we have said that each is the virtue of a different part of
the soul.

---

[1] This sentence should probably be read, as Bywater suggests, at
the end of the previous paragraph.

2   Difficulties might be raised as to the utility of these
qualities of mind.   For (1) philosophic wisdom will contemplate none of the things that will make a man happy
(for it is not concerned with any coming into being), and 20
though practical wisdom has *this* merit, for what purpose
do we need it?   Practical wisdom is the quality of mind
concerned with things just and noble and good for man,
but these are the things which it is the mark of a *good* man
to do, and we are none the more able to act for *knowing*
them if the virtues are states of *character*, just as we are 25
none the better able to act for knowing the things that are
healthy and sound, in the sense not of producing but of
issuing from the state of health; for we are none the more
able to act for having the art of medicine or of gymnastics.
But (2) if we are to say that a man should have practical
wisdom not for the sake of knowing moral truths but for
the sake of becoming good, practical wisdom will be of no
use to those who *are* good; but again it is of no use to 30
those who have *not* virtue; for it will make no difference
whether they have practical wisdom themselves or obey
others who have it, and it would be enough for us to do
what we do in the case of health; though we wish to
become healthy, yet we do not learn the art of medicine.
(3) Besides this, it would be thought strange if practical
wisdom, being inferior to philosophic wisdom, is to be
put in authority over it, as seems to be implied by the
fact that the art which produces anything rules and issues
commands about that thing.

These, then, are the questions we must discuss; so far 35
we have only stated the difficulties.

(1) Now first let us say that in themselves these states 1144^a
must be worthy of choice because they are the virtues of
the two parts of the soul respectively, even if neither
of them produce anything.

(2) Secondly, they do produce something, not as the art of
medicine produces health, however, but as health produces
health;¹ so does philosophic wisdom produce happiness;

¹ i. e. as health, as an inner state, produces the activities which we
know as constituting health.

5 for, being a part of virtue entire, by being possessed and by actualizing itself it makes a man happy.

(3) Again, the work of man is achieved only in accordance with practical wisdom as well as with moral virtue; for virtue makes us aim at the right mark, and practical wisdom makes us take the right means. (Of the fourth part of the soul—the nutritive[1]—there is no such virtue; 10 for there is nothing which it is in its power to do or not to do.)

(4) With regard to our being none the more able to do because of our practical wisdom what is noble and just, let us begin a little further back, starting with the following principle. As we say that some people who do just acts are not necessarily just, i. e. those who do the acts ordained 15 by the laws either unwillingly or owing to ignorance or for some other reason and not for the sake of the acts themselves (though, to be sure, they do what they should and all the things that the good man ought), so is it, it seems, that in order to be good one must be in a certain state when one does the several acts, i. e. one must do them as a result of 20 choice and for the sake of the acts themselves. Now virtue makes the choice right, but the question of the things which should naturally be done to carry out our choice belongs not to virtue but to another faculty. We must devote our attention to these matters and give a clearer statement about them. There is a faculty which is called cleverness; and this 25 is such as to be able to do the things that tend towards the mark we have set before ourselves, and to hit it. Now if the mark be noble, the cleverness is laudable, but if the mark be bad, the cleverness is mere smartness; hence we call even men of practical wisdom clever or smart. Practical wisdom is not the faculty, but it does not exist without this faculty. And this eye of the soul acquires its 30 formed state not without the aid of virtue, as has been said[2] and is plain; for the syllogisms which deal with acts to be done are things which involve a starting-point, viz. ' since the

---

[1] The other three being the scientific (τὸ ἐπιστημονικόν), the calculative (τὸ λογιστικόν), and the desiderative (τὸ ὀρεκτικόν).
[2] ll. 6–26.

end, i. e. what is best, is of such and such a nature ', whatever
it may be (let it for the sake of argument be what we please) ;
and this is not evident except to the good man ; for wickedness perverts us and causes us to be deceived about the 35
starting-points of action.   Therefore it is evident that it is
impossible to be practically wise without being good.

13   We must therefore consider virtue also once more ; for 1144^b
virtue too is similarly related ; as practical wisdom is to
cleverness—not the same, but like it—so is natural virtue
to virtue in the strict sense.   For all men think that each
type of character belongs to its possessors in some sense by
nature ; for from the very moment of birth we are just or 5
fitted for self-control or brave or have the other moral
qualities ; but yet we seek something else as that which is
good in the strict sense—we seek for the presence of such
qualities in another way.   For both children and brutes
have the natural dispositions to these qualities, but without
reason these are evidently hurtful.   Only we seem to see 10
this much, that, while one may be led astray by them, as
a strong body which moves without sight may stumble
badly because of its lack of sight, still, if a man once
acquires reason, that makes a difference in action ; and his
state, while still like what it was, will then be virtue in the
strict sense.   Therefore, as in the part of us which forms
opinions there are two types, cleverness and practical
wisdom, so too in the moral part there are two types, 15
natural virtue and virtue in the strict sense, and of these
the latter involves practical wisdom.   This is why some
say that all the virtues are forms of practical wisdom, and
why Socrates in one respect was on the right track while in
another he went astray ; in thinking that all the virtues
were forms of practical wisdom he was wrong, but in saying 20
they implied practical wisdom he was right.   This is confirmed by the fact that even now all men, when they define
virtue, after naming the state of character and its objects
add 'that (state) which is in accordance with the right
rule ; now the right rule is that which is in accordance
with practical wisdom.   All men, then, seem somehow to

divine that this kind of state is virtue, viz. that which is in
25 accordance with practical wisdom. But we must go a little
further. For it is not merely the state in accordance with
the right rule, but the state that implies the *presence* of the
right rule, that is virtue; and practical wisdom is a right
rule about such matters. Socrates, then, thought the virtues
were rules or rational principles (for he thought they were,
all of them, forms of scientific knowledge), while we think
they *involve* a rational principle.

30 It is clear, then, from what has been said, that it is not
possible to be good in the strict sense without practical
wisdom, nor practically wise without moral virtue. But in
this way we may also refute the dialectical argument
whereby it might be contended that the virtues exist in
separation from each other; the same man, it might be
said, is not best equipped by nature for all the virtues, so
that he will have already acquired one when he has not yet
35 acquired another. This is possible in respect of the natural
virtues, but not in respect of those in respect of which a man
1145^a is called without qualification good; for with the presence
of the one quality, practical wisdom, will be given all the
virtues. And it is plain that, even if it were of no practical
value, we should have needed it because it is the virtue of
the part of us in question; plain too that the choice will not
be right without practical wisdom any more than without
5 virtue; for the one determines the end and the other
makes us do the things that lead to the end.

But again it is not *supreme* over philosophic wisdom,
i. e. over the superior part of us, any more than the art of
medicine is over health; for it does not use it but provides
for its coming into being; it issues orders, then, for its sake,
10 but not to it. Further, to maintain its supremacy would be
like saying that the art of politics rules the gods because it
issues orders about all the affairs of the state.

BOOK VII

1 LET us now make a fresh beginning and point out that 15 of moral states to be avoided there are three kinds—vice, incontinence, brutishness. The contraries of two of these are evident—one we call virtue, the other continence; to brutishness it would be most fitting to oppose superhuman virtue, a heroic and divine kind of virtue, as Homer has 20 represented Priam saying of Hector that he was very good,

> For he seemed not, he,
> The child of a mortal man, but as one that of God's
>   seed came.[1]

Therefore if, as they say, men become gods by excess of virtue, of this kind must evidently be the state opposed to the brutish state; for as a brute has no vice or virtue, so 25 neither has a god; his state is higher than virtue, and that of a brute is a different kind of state from vice.

Now, since it is rarely that a godlike man is found—to use the epithet of the Spartans, who when they admire any one highly call him a 'godlike man'—so too the brutish type is rarely found among men; it is found chiefly 30 among barbarians, but some brutish qualities are also produced by disease or deformity; and we also call by this evil name those men who go beyond all ordinary standards by reason of vice. Of this kind of disposition, however, we must later make some mention,[2] while we have discussed vice before;[3] we must now discuss incontinence and soft- 35 ness (or effeminacy), and continence and endurance; for we must treat each of the two neither as identical with virtue 1145[b] or wickedness, nor as a different genus. We must, as in all other cases, set the observed facts before us and, after first discussing the difficulties, go on to prove, if possible, the truth of all the common opinions about these affections

---

[1] *Il.* xxiv. 258 f.   [2] Ch. 5.   [3] Bks. II–V.

5 of the mind, or, failing this, of the greater number and the most authoritative; for if we both refute the objections and leave the common opinions undisturbed, we shall have proved the case sufficiently.

Now (1) both continence and endurance are thought to be included among things good and praiseworthy, and both incontinence and softness among things bad and 10 blameworthy; and the same man is thought to be continent and ready to abide by the result of his calculations, or incontinent and ready to abandon them. And (2) the incontinent man, knowing that what he does is bad, does it as a result of passion, while the continent man, knowing that his appetites are bad, refuses on account of his rational principle to follow them. (3) The temperate man all men 15 call continent and disposed to endurance, while the continent man some maintain to be always temperate but others do not; and some call the self-indulgent man incontinent and the incontinent man self-indulgent indiscriminately, while others distinguish them. (4) The man of practical wisdom, they sometimes say, cannot be incontinent, while sometimes they say that some who are practically wise and clever *are* incontinent. Again (5) men are said to be 20 incontinent even with respect to anger, honour, and gain.— These, then, are the things that are said.

Now we may ask (1) how a man who judges rightly can **2** behave incontinently. That he should behave so when he has knowledge, some say is impossible; for it would be strange—so Socrates[1] thought—if when knowledge was in a man something else could master it and drag it about 25 like a slave. For *Socrates* was entirely opposed to the view in question, holding that there is no such thing as incontinence; no one, he said, when he judges acts against what he judges best—people act so only by reason of ignorance. Now this view plainly contradicts the observed facts, and we must inquire about what happens to such a man; if he acts by reason of ignorance, what is the 30 manner of his ignorance? For that the man who behaves incontinently does not, before he gets into this state, *think* he ought to act so, is evident.　But there are *some* who concede certain of Socrates' contentions but not others; that nothing is stronger than knowledge they admit, but not that no one acts contrary to what has seemed to him the better course, and therefore they say that the incontinent man has not knowledge when he is mastered by his pleasures, but opinion.　But *if* it is opinion and not know- 35 ledge, if it is not a strong conviction that resists but a weak one, as in men who hesitate, we sympathize with their 1146^a failure to stand by such convictions against strong appetites; but we do not sympathize with wickedness, nor with any of the other blameworthy states.　Is it then *practical wisdom* whose resistance is mastered?　That is the strongest of all states.　But this is absurd; the same man 5 will be at once practically wise and incontinent, but *no one* would say that it is the part of a practically wise man to do willingly the basest acts.　Besides, it has been shown before that the man of practical wisdom is one who will *act* [1] (for he is a man concerned with the individual facts) [2] and who has the other virtues. [3]

(2) Further, if continence involves having strong and bad appetites, the temperate man will not be continent 10 nor the continent man temperate; for a temperate man will have neither excessive nor bad appetites.　But the continent man *must*; for if the appetites are good, the state of character that restrains us from following them is bad, so that not all continence will be good; while if 15 they are weak and not bad, there is nothing admirable in resisting them, and if they are weak and bad, there is nothing great in resisting these either.

(3) Further, if continence makes a man ready to stand by any and every opinion, it is bad, i. e. if it makes him stand even by a false opinion; and if incontinence makes a man apt to abandon any and every opinion, there will be a good incontinence, of which Sophocles' Neoptolemus in the *Philoctetes* [4] will be an instance; for he is to be 20

---

[1] 1140^b 4–6.　　[2] 1141^b 16, 1142^a 24.
[3] 1144^b 30–1145^a 2.　　[4] ll. 895–916.

praised for not standing by what Odysseus persuaded him to do, because he is pained at telling a lie.

(4) Further, the sophistic argument presents a difficulty; the syllogism arising from men's wish to expose para-doxical results arising from an opponent's view, in order that they may be admired when they succeed, is one that 25 puts us in a difficulty (for thought is bound fast when it will not rest because the conclusion does not satisfy it, and cannot advance because it cannot refute the argument). There is an argument from which it follows that folly coupled with incontinence is virtue; for a man does the opposite of what he judges, owing to incontinence, but judges what is good to be evil and something that he 30 should not do, and in consequence he will do what is good and not what is evil.

(5) Further, he who on conviction does and pursues and chooses what is pleasant would be thought to be better than one who does so as a result not of calculation but of incontinence; for he is easier to cure since he may be persuaded to change his mind. But to the incontinent man may be applied the proverb 'when water chokes, 35 what is one to wash it down with?' If he had been persuaded of the rightness of what he does, he would have desisted 1146ᵇ when he was persuaded to change his mind; but now he acts in spite of his being persuaded of something quite different.

(6) Further, if incontinence and continence are concerned with any and every kind of object, who is it that is incon-tinent in the unqualified sense? No one has all the forms of incontinence, but we say some people are incontinent 5 without qualification.

Of some such kind are the difficulties that arise; some of these points must be refuted and the others left in possession of the field; for the solution of the difficulty is the discovery of the truth. (1) We must consider first, then, whether incontinent people act knowingly or not, and in what sense knowingly; then (2) with what sorts of object the incontinent and the continent man may be

said to be concerned (i. e. whether with any and every 10
pleasure and pain or with certain determinate kinds), and
whether the continent man and the man of endurance are
the same or different; and similarly with regard to the
other matters germane to this inquiry. The starting-point
of our investigation is (a) the question whether the continent man and the incontinent are differentiated by their 15
objects or by their attitude, i. e. whether the incontinent
man is incontinent simply by being concerned with such
and such objects, or, instead, by his attitude, or, instead of
that, by both these things; (b) the second question is
whether incontinence and continence are concerned with
any and every object or not. The man who is incontinent
in the unqualified sense is neither concerned with any and
every object, but with precisely those with which the self-
indulgent man is concerned, nor is he characterized by being 20
simply related to these (for then his state would be the
same as self-indulgence), but by being related to them in
a certain way. For the one is led on in accordance with
his own choice, thinking that he ought always to pursue
the present pleasure; while the other does not think so,
but yet pursues it.

(1) As for the suggestion that it is true opinion and
not knowledge against which we act incontinently, that
makes no difference to the argument; for some people 25
when in a state of opinion do not hesitate, but think they
know exactly. If, then, the notion is that owing to their
weak conviction those who have opinion are more likely
to act against their judgement than those who know, we
answer that there need be no difference between knowledge
and opinion in this respect; for some men are no less
convinced of what they think than others of what they
know; as is shown by the case of Heraclitus. But (a), 30
since we use the word 'know' in two senses (for both the
man who has knowledge but is not using it and he who
is using it are said to know), it *will* make a difference
whether, when a man does what he should not, he has
the knowledge but is not exercising it, or *is* exercising it;
for the latter seems strange, but not the former.

35   (b) Further, since there are two kinds of premisses, there
1147ᵃ is nothing to prevent a man's having both premisses and
acting against his knowledge, provided that he is using
only the universal premiss and not the particular; for it is
particular acts that have to be done.   And there are also
two kinds of universal term; one ,is predicable of the
5 agent, the other of the object; e. g. 'dry food is good
for every man', and 'I am a man', or 'such and such food
is dry'; but whether 'this food is such and such', of this
the incontinent man either has not or is not exercising the
knowledge.[1]   There will, then, be, firstly, an enormous
difference between these manners of knowing, so that to
know in one way when we act incontinently would not
seem anything strange, while to know in the other way
would be extraordinary.

10   And further (c) the possession of knowledge in another
sense than those just named is something that happens
to men; for within the case of having knowledge but not
using it we see a difference of state, admitting of the
possibility of having knowledge in a sense and yet not
having it, as in the instance of a man asleep, mad, or drunk.
But now this is just the condition of men under the
15 influence of passions; for outbursts of anger and sexual
appetites and some other such passions, it is evident,
actually alter our bodily condition, and in some men even
produce fits of madness.   It is plain, then, that incontinent
people must be said to be in a similar condition to men
asleep, mad, or drunk.   The fact that men use the language
that flows from knowledge proves nothing; for even men
20 under the influence of these passions utter scientific proofs
and verses of Empedocles, and those who have just begun
to learn a science can string together its phrases, but do
not yet know it; for it has to become part of themselves,
and that takes time; so that we must suppose that the

---

[1] i.e., if I am to be able to deduce from (a) 'dry food is good for
all men' that 'this food is good for me', I must have (b) the premiss
'I am a man' and (c) the premisses (i) 'x food is dry', (ii) 'this food
is x'.   I cannot fail to know (b), and I may know (c i); but if I do
not know (c ii), or know it only 'at the back of my mind', I shall not
draw the conclusion.

use of language by men in an incontinent state means no
more than its utterance by actors on the stage.

(d) Again, we may also view the cause as follows with 25
reference to the facts of human nature. The one opinion
is universal, the other is concerned with the particular
facts, and here we come to something within the sphere
of perception; when a single opinion results from the two,
the soul must in one type of case[1] affirm the conclusion,
while in the case of opinions concerned with production
it must immediately act (e. g. if 'everything sweet ought
to be tasted', and 'this is sweet', in the sense of being one
of the particular sweet things, the man who can act and 30
is not prevented must at the same time actually act accordingly). When, then, the universal opinion is present in
us forbidding us to taste, and there is also the opinion that
'everything sweet is pleasant', and that 'this is sweet'
(now this is the opinion that is active),[2] and when appetite
happens to be present in us, the one opinion bids us avoid
the object, but appetite leads us towards it (for it can move 35
each of our bodily parts); so that it turns out that a man
behaves incontinently under the influence (in a sense) of
a rule and an opinion, and of one not contrary in itself, 1147^b
but only incidentally—for the appetite is contrary, not the
opinion—to the right rule. It also follows that this is
the reason why the lower animals are not incontinent, viz.
because they have no universal judgement but only imagina- 5
tion and memory of particulars.

The explanation of how the ignorance is dissolved and
the incontinent man regains his knowledge, is the same as
in the case of the man drunk or asleep and is not peculiar
to this condition; we must go to the students of natural
science for it. Now, the last premiss both being an opinion
about a perceptible object, and being what determines our
actions, this a man either has not when he is in the state 10
of passion, or has it in the sense in which having knowledge
did not mean knowing but only talking, as a drunken man
may mutter the verses of Empedocles.[3] And because the

---

[1] I. e. in scientific reasoning.   [2] I. e. determines action (cf. ^b10).
[3] Cf. ^a10–24.

last term is not universal nor equally an object of scientific knowledge with the universal term, the position that 15 Socrates sought to establish[1] actually seems to result; for it is not in the presence of what is thought to be knowledge proper that the affection of incontinence arises (nor is it this that is 'dragged about' as a result of the state of passion), but in that of perceptual knowledge.[2]

This must suffice as our answer to the question of action with and without knowledge, and how it is possible to behave incontinently with knowledge.

20   (2) We must next discuss whether there is any one who **4** is incontinent without qualification, or all men who are incontinent are so in a particular sense, and if there is, with what sort of objects he is concerned. That both continent persons and persons of endurance, and incontinent and soft persons, are concerned with pleasures and pains, is evident.

Now of the things that produce pleasure some are necessary, while others are worthy of choice in themselves but 25 admit of excess, the bodily causes of pleasure being necessary (by such I mean both those concerned with food and those concerned with sexual intercourse, i.e. the bodily matters with which we defined[3] self-indulgence and temperance as being concerned), while the others are not necessary but worthy of choice in themselves (e.g. victory, honour, 30 wealth, and good and pleasant things of this sort). This being so, (a) those who go to excess with reference to the latter, contrary to the right rule which is in themselves, are not called incontinent simply, but incontinent with the qualification 'in respect of money, gain, honour, or anger', —not simply incontinent, on the ground that they are different from incontinent people and are called incontinent 35 by reason of a resemblance. (Compare the case of Anthropos (Man), who won a contest at the Olympic games;

---

[1] 1145ᵇ 22–24.
[2] Even before the minor premiss of the practical syllogism has been obscured by passion, the incontinent man has not scientific knowledge in the strict sense, since his minor premiss is not universal but has for its subject a sensible particular, e. g. 'this glass of wine'.
[3] III. 10.

in his case the general definition of man differed little 1148ᵃ
from the definition peculiar to *him*, but yet it *was* different.[1]) This is shown by the fact that incontinence either
without qualification or in respect of some particular bodily
pleasure is blamed not only as a fault but as a kind of
vice, while none of the people who are incontinent in these
other respects is so blamed.

But (*b*) of the people who are incontinent with respect
to bodily enjoyments, with which we say the temperate 5
and the self-indulgent man are concerned, he who pursues
the excesses of things pleasant—and shuns those of things
painful, of hunger and thirst and heat and cold and all the
objects of touch and taste—not by choice but contrary to
his choice and his judgement, is called incontinent, not 10
with the qualification 'in respect of this or that', e.g. of
anger, but just simply. This is confirmed by the fact that
men are called 'soft' with regard to these pleasures, but
not with regard to any of the others. And for this reason
we group together the incontinent and the self-indulgent,
the continent and the temperate man—but not any of these
other types—because they are concerned somehow with the 15
same pleasures and pains; but though these are concerned
with the same objects, they are not similarly related to
them, but some of them make a deliberate choice while the
others do not.[2]

This is why we should describe as self-indulgent rather
the man who without appetite or with but a slight appetite
pursues the excesses of pleasure and avoids moderate
pains, than the man who does so because of his strong
appetites; for what would the former do, if he had in 20
addition a vigorous appetite, and a violent pain at the lack
of the 'necessary' objects?

Now of appetites and pleasures some belong to the class

---

[1] I.e. the definition appropriate to him was not 'rational animal'
but 'rational animal who won the boxing contest at Olympia in 456 B.C.'
The reading ῎Ανθρωπος in l. 35 is confirmed not only by Alexander but
by an Oxyrhynchus papyrus giving a list of Olympian victors; cf.
Class. Rev. XIII (1899), 290 f.

[2] I.e. the temperate and the self-indulgent, not the continent and
the incontinent.

of things generically noble and good—for some pleasant things are by nature worthy of choice, while others are contrary to these, and others are intermediate, to adopt our
25 previous distinction [1]—e. g. wealth, gain, victory, honour. And with reference to all objects whether of this or of the intermediate kind men are not blamed for being affected by them, for desiring and loving them, but for doing so in a certain way, i. e. for going to excess. (This is why all those who contrary to the rule either are mastered by or pursue one of the objects which are
30 naturally noble and good, e. g. those who busy themselves more than they ought about honour or about children and parents, ⟨are not wicked⟩; for these too are goods, and those who busy themselves about them are praised; but yet there is an excess even in them—if like Niobe one were to fight even against the gods, or were to be as much
1148ᵇ devoted to one's father as Satyrus nicknamed 'the filial', who was thought to be very silly on this point.[2]) There is no wickedness, then, with regard to these objects, for the reason named, viz. because each of them is by nature a thing worthy of choice for its own sake; yet excesses in respect of them are bad and to be avoided. Similarly
5 there is no incontinence with regard to them; for incontinence is not only to be avoided but is also a thing worthy of blame; but owing to a similarity in the state of feeling people apply the name incontinence, adding in each case what it is in respect of, as we may describe as a bad doctor or a bad actor one whom we should not call bad, simply. As, then, in this case we do not apply the term without qualification because each of these conditions is not badness
10 but only analogous to it, so it is clear that in the other case also that alone must be taken to be incontinence and continence which is concerned with the same objects as temperance and self-indulgence, but we apply the term to

---

[1] 1147ᵇ 23–31, where, however, the 'contraries' are not mentioned. It is better to end the parenthesis at πρότερον, l. 25, than at αἱρετά, l. 24, since χρήματα κτλ are instances of τὰ τῷ γένει καλὰ καὶ σπουδαῖα.

[2] Nothing is really known about the Satyrus referred to, but Prof. Burnet's suggestion that he was a king of Bosporus who deified his father seems probable.

anger by virtue of a resemblance; and this is why we say with a qualification 'incontinent in respect of anger' as we say 'incontinent in respect of honour, or of gain'.

5   (1) Some things are pleasant by nature, and of these 15 (*a*) some are so without qualification, and (*b*) others are so with reference to particular classes either of animals or of men; while (2) others are not pleasant by nature, but (*a*) some of them become so by reason of injuries to the system, and (*b*) others by reason of acquired habits, and (*c*) others by reason of originally bad natures. This being so, it is possible with regard to each of the latter kinds to discover similar states of character to those recognized with regard to the former; I mean (A) the brutish states,[1] as in 20 the case of the female who, they say, rips open pregnant women and devours the infants, or of the things in which some of the tribes about the Black Sea that have gone savage are said to delight—in raw meat or in human flesh, or in lending their children to one another to feast upon— or of the story told of Phalaris.[2]

These states are brutish, but (B) others arise as a result of disease[3] (or, in some cases, of madness, as with the man 25 who sacrificed and ate his mother, or with the slave who ate the liver of his fellow), and others are morbid states (C) resulting from custom,[4] e. g. the habit of plucking out the hair or of gnawing the nails, or even coals or earth, and in addition to these paederasty; for these arise in some by nature and in others, as in those who have been the victims 30 of lust from childhood, from habit.

Now those in whom nature is the cause of such a state no one would call incontinent, any more than one would apply the epithet to women because of the passive part they play in copulation; nor would one apply it to those who are in a morbid condition as a result of habit. To have these various types of habit is beyond the limits of vice, as brutishness is too; for a man who has them to 1149ᵃ master or be mastered by them is not simple ⟨continence

---

[1] Answering to (2 *c*).   [2] Sc. and the bull.   But cf. 1149ᵃ 14.
[3] Answering to (2 *a*).
[4] Answering to (2 *b*).   Omit ἤ in l. 27, with Kᵇ.

or) incontinence but that which is so by analogy, as the man who is in this condition in respect of fits of anger is to be called incontinent in respect of that feeling, but not incontinent simply.

5   For every excessive state whether of folly, of cowardice, of self-indulgence, or of bad temper, is either brutish or morbid; the man who is by nature apt to fear everything, even the squeak of a mouse, is cowardly with a brutish cowardice, while the man who feared a weasel did so in consequence of disease; and of foolish people those who by nature are thoughtless and live by their senses alone 10 are brutish, like some races of the distant barbarians, while those who are so as a result of disease (e. g. of epilepsy) or of madness are morbid. Of these characteristics it is possible to have some only at times, and not to be mastered by them, e. g. Phalaris may have restrained a desire to eat the flesh of a child or an appetite for 15 unnatural sexual pleasure; but it is also possible to be mastered, not merely to have the feelings. Thus, as the wickedness which is on the human level is called wickedness simply, while that which is not is called wickedness not simply but with the qualification 'brutish' or 'morbid', in the same way it is plain that some incontinence is brutish 20 and some morbid, while only that which corresponds to *human* self-indulgence is incontinence simply.

That incontinence and continence, then, are concerned only with the same objects as self-indulgence and temperance and that what is concerned with other objects is a type distinct from incontinence, and called incontinence by a metaphor and not simply, is plain.

That incontinence in respect of anger is less disgraceful **6** than that in respect of the appetites is what we will now 25 proceed to see. (1) Anger seems to listen to argument to some extent, but to mishear it, as do hasty servants who run out before they have heard the whole of what one says, and then muddle the order, or as dogs bark if there is but a knock at the door, before looking to see if it is a friend; 30 so anger by reason of the warmth and hastiness of its

nature, though it hears, does not hear an order, and springs
to take revenge. For argument or imagination informs us
that we have been insulted or slighted, and anger, reasoning
as it were that anything like this must be fought against,
boils up straightway; while appetite, if argument or perception merely says that an object is pleasant, springs to 35
the enjoyment of it. Therefore anger obeys the argument 1149^{b}
in a sense, but appetite does not. It is therefore more
disgraceful; for the man who is incontinent in respect of
anger is in a sense conquered by argument, while the other
is conquered by appetite and not by argument.

(2) Further, we pardon people more easily for following
natural desires, since we pardon them more easily for 5
following such appetites as are common to all men, and in
so far as they are common; now anger and bad temper are
more natural than the appetites for excess, i. e. for unnecessary objects. Take for instance the man who defended
himself on the charge of striking his father by saying 'yes,
but *he* struck *his* father, and *he* struck *his*, and' (pointing 10
to his child) 'this boy will strike *me* when he is a man;
it runs in the family'; or the man who when he was being
dragged along by his son bade him stop at the doorway,
since he himself had dragged his father only as far as that.

(3) Further, those who are more given to plotting against
others are more criminal. Now a passionate man is not
given to plotting, nor is anger itself—it is open; but the 15
nature of appetite is illustrated by what the poets call
Aphrodite, 'guile-weaving daughter of Cyprus',[1] and by
Homer's words about her 'embroidered girdle':

> And the whisper of wooing is there,
> Whose subtlety stealeth the wits of the wise, how pru-
> dent soe'er.[2]

Therefore if this form of incontinence is more criminal and
disgraceful than that in respect of anger, it is both incontinence without qualification and in a sense vice.

(4) Further, no one commits wanton outrage with a 20
feeling of pain, but every one who acts in anger acts with

---

[1] Author unknown.   [2] *Il.* xiv. 214, 217.

pain, while the man who commits outrage acts with pleasure. If, then, those acts at which it is most just to be angry are more criminal than others, the incontinence which is due to appetite is the more criminal; for there is no wanton outrage involved in anger.

Plainly, then, the incontinence concerned with appetite is
25 more disgraceful than that concerned with anger, and continence and incontinence are concerned with bodily appetites and pleasures; but we must grasp the differences among the latter themselves. For, as has been said at the beginning,[1] some are human and natural both in kind and in magnitude, others are brutish, and others are due to organic
30 injuries and diseases. Only with the first of these are temperance and self-indulgence concerned; this is why we call the lower animals neither temperate nor self-indulgent except by a metaphor, and only if some one[2] race of animals exceeds another as a whole in wantonness, destructiveness, and omnivorous greed; these have no power of choice or
35 calculation, but they *are* departures from the natural norm,[3]
1150^a as, among men, madmen are. Now brutishness is a less evil than vice, though more alarming; for it is not that the better part has been perverted, as in man,—they *have* no better part. Thus it is like comparing a lifeless thing with a living in respect of badness; for the badness of that which has no originative source of movement is always less
5 hurtful, and reason is an originative source. Thus it is like comparing injustice in the abstract with an unjust man. Each is in some sense worse; for a bad man will do ten thousand times as much evil as a brute.[4]

---

[1] 1148^b 15–31.   [2] Reading τι in l. 32 as suggested by Bywater.
[3] And therefore cannot be called self-indulgent properly, but *can* be so called by a metaphor.
[4] The comparison between the badness of a brute and that of a bad man is illustrated (1) by a comparison between the badness of a lifeless and that of a living thing; a living thing can do more harm than a lifeless because it has in ψυχή an ἀρχὴ κινήσεως which the other has not; and a man can do more harm than a brute because he has in νοῦς an ἀρχὴ κινήσεως which the brute has not; (2) by a comparison between injustice in the abstract and an unjust man; injustice is in a sense worse—more terrible—because it is what makes the unjust man unjust; and in a sense less bad because it cannot operate except as realized in an unjust man; and a brute is more alarming than a bad man, but (owing to its lack of νοῦς) does much less harm. The

7 With regard to the pleasures and pains and appetites
and aversions arising through touch and taste, to which 10
both self-indulgence and temperance were formerly nar-
rowed down,[1] it is possible to be in such a state as to be
defeated even by those of them which most people master,
or to master even those by which most people are defeated ;
among these possibilities, those relating to pleasures are
incontinence and continence, those relating to pains softness
and endurance. The state of most people is intermediate, 15
even if they lean more towards the worse states.

Now, since some pleasures are necessary while others are
not, and are necessary up to a point while the excesses of
them are not, nor the deficiencies, and this is equally true
of appetites and pains, the man who pursues the excesses of
things pleasant, or pursues to excess necessary objects, and [2]
does so by choice, for their own sake and not at all for the 20
sake of any result distinct from them, is self-indulgent ; for
such a man is of necessity unlikely to repent, and therefore
incurable, since a man who cannot repent cannot be cured.[3]
The man who is deficient in his pursuit of them is the
opposite of self-indulgent ; the man who is intermediate is
temperate. Similarly, there is the man who avoids bodily
pains not because he is defeated by them but by choice.
(Of those who do not *choose* such acts, one kind of man 25
is led to them as a result of the pleasure involved, another
because he avoids the pain arising from the appetite, so
that these types differ from one another. Now any one
would think worse of a man if with no appetite or with
weak appetite he were to do something disgraceful, than if
he did it under the influence of powerful appetite, and
worse of him if he struck a blow not in anger than if he
did it in anger ; for what would he have done if he *had* been
strongly affected? This is why the self-indulgent man is worse 30
than the incontinent.) Of the states named, then,[4] the latter

second illustration is very far-fetched, and corruption may be suspected
in l. 6.

  [1] III. 10.
  [2] Reading ἢ καθ' ὑπερβολὴν καί, with Mᵇ and Aspasius, in ll. 19, 20.
  [3] ἀνάγκη . . . ἀνίατος ll. 21–22 is a note to defend the use of the word
ὅλαστος, lit. incorrigible.
  [4] In ll. 19–25.

is rather a kind of softness;[1] the former is self-indulgence. While to the incontinent man is opposed the continent, to the soft is opposed the man of endurance; for endurance consists in resisting, while continence consists in conquer-
35 ing, and resisting and conquering are different, as not being beaten is different from winning; this is why continence
1150^b is also more worthy of choice than endurance. Now the man who is defective in respect of resistance to the things which most men both resist and resist successfully is soft and effeminate; for effeminacy too is a kind of softness; such a man trails his cloak to avoid the pain of lifting it, and plays the invalid without thinking himself wretched, though the man he imitates is a wretched man.

5 The case is similar with regard to continence and incontinence. For if a man is defeated by violent and excessive pleasures or pains, there is nothing wonderful in that; indeed we are ready to pardon him if he has resisted, as Theodectes' Philoctetes does when bitten by the snake,[2]
10 or Carcinus' Cercyon in the *Alope*,[3] and as people who try to restrain their laughter burst out in a guffaw, as happened to Xenophantus.[4] But it is surprising if a man is defeated by and cannot resist pleasures or pains which most men can hold out against, when this is not due to heredity or disease, like the softness that is hereditary with the kings
15 of the Scythians, or that which distinguishes the female sex from the male.

The lover of amusement, too, is thought to be self-indulgent, but is really soft. For amusement is a relaxation, since it is a rest from work; and the lover of amusement is one of the people who go to excess in this.

Of incontinence one kind is impetuosity, another weak-
20 ness. For some men after deliberating fail, owing to their emotion, to stand by the conclusions of their deliberation, others because they have not deliberated are led by their emotion; since some men (just as people who first tickle others are not tickled themselves), if they have first per-

---

[1] Not softness proper, which is non-deliberate avoidance of pain (ll. 13–15).
[2] Cf. Nauck², p. 803.   [3] Cf. ib. p. 797.
[4] Apparently a musician at Alexander's court.

ceived and seen what is coming and have first roused
themselves and their calculative faculty, are not defeated
by their emotion, whether it be pleasant or painful.   It is 25
keen and excitable people that suffer especially from the
impetuous form of incontinence ; for the former by reason
of their quickness and the latter by reason of the violence
of their passions do not await the argument, because they
are apt to follow their imagination.

8   The self-indulgent man, as was said,[1] is not apt to repent ;
for he stands by his choice ; but any incontinent man is likely 30
to repent.   This is why the position is not as it was expressed
in the formulation of the problem,[2] but the self-indulgent man
is incurable and the incontinent man curable ; for wickedness is like a disease such as dropsy or consumption, while
incontinence is like epilepsy ; the former is a permanent,
the latter an intermittent badness.   And generally inconti- 35
nence and vice are different in kind ; vice is unconscious of
itself, incontinence is not (of incontinent men themselves, 1151^a
those who become temporarily beside themselves are better
than those who have the rational principle but do not abide
by it, since the latter are defeated by a weaker passion, and
do not act without previous deliberation like the others) ;
for the incontinent man is like the people who get drunk
quickly and on little wine,[3] i. e. on less than most people.

Evidently, then, incontinence is not vice (though perhaps 5
it is so in a qualified sense) ; for incontinence is contrary to
choice while vice is in accordance with choice ; not but
what they are similar in respect of the actions they lead to ;
as in the saying of Demodocus about the Milesians, ' the
Milesians are not without sense, but they do the things that
senseless people do ', so too incontinent people are not 10
criminal, but they will do criminal acts.

Now, since the incontinent man is apt to pursue, not on
conviction, bodily pleasures that are excessive and contrary
to the right rule, while the self-indulgent man is convinced
because he is the sort of man to pursue them, it is on the

---

[1] a 21.   [2] 1146^a 31–^b 2.
[3] To get a proper sense for this clause it seems necessary to treat
ll. 1–3 as parenthetical.

contrary the former that is easily persuaded to change his
15 mind, while the latter is not. For virtue and vice respectively
preserve and destroy the first principle, and in actions the
final cause is the first principle, as the hypotheses[1] are in
mathematics; neither in that case is it argument that
teaches the first principles, nor is it so here—virtue either
natural or produced by habituation is what teaches right
opinion about the first principle. Such a man as this, then,
is temperate; his contrary is the self-indulgent.

20 But there is a sort of man who is carried away as a
result of passion and contrary to the right rule—a man whom
passion masters so that he does not act according to the
right rule, but does not master to the extent of making him
ready to believe that he ought to pursue such pleasures
without reserve; this is the incontinent man, who is better
25 than the self-indulgent man, and not bad without qualification; for the best thing in him, the first principle, is preserved. And contrary to him is another kind of man, he who
abides by his convictions and is not carried away, at least as
a result of passion. It is evident from these considerations
that the latter is a good state and the former a bad one.

Is the man continent who abides by any and every rule **9**
and any and every choice, or the man who abides by the
30 right choice, and is he incontinent who abandons any and
every choice and any and every rule, or he who abandons
the rule that is not false and the choice that is right; this is
how we put it before in our statement of the problem.[2] Or is
it incidentally any and every choice but *per se* the true rule
and the right choice by which the one abides and the other
35 does not? If any one chooses or pursues this for the sake
1151ᵇ of that, *per se* he pursues and chooses the latter, but
incidentally the former. But when we speak without
qualification we mean what is *per se*. Therefore in a sense
the one abides by, and the other abandons, any and every
opinion; but without qualification, the true opinion.

There are some who are apt to abide by their opinion,

---

[1] i.e. the assumptions of the existence of the primary objects of
mathematics, such as the straight line or the unit.
[2] 1146ᵃ 16–31.

who are called strong-headed, viz. those who are hard to 5
persuade in the first instance and are not easily persuaded
to change ; these have in them something like the continent
man, as the prodigal is in a way like the liberal man and
the rash man like the confident man ; but they are different
in many respects. For it is to passion and appetite that
the one will not yield, since on occasion the continent man
will be easy to persuade ; but it is to argument that the 10
others refuse to yield, for they do form appetites and many
of them are led by their pleasures. Now the people who
are strong-headed are the opinionated, the ignorant, and the
boorish—the opinionated being influenced by pleasure and
pain ; for they delight in the victory they gain if they are
not persuaded to change, and are pained if their decisions 15
become null and void as decrees sometimes do ; so that
they are liker the incontinent than the continent man.

But there are some who fail to abide by their resolutions, not as a result of incontinence, e. g. Neoptolemus
in Sophocles' *Philoctetes* ;[1] yet it was for the sake of
pleasure that he did not stand fast—but a noble pleasure ;
for telling the truth was noble to him, but he had been 20
persuaded by Odysseus to tell the lie. For not every one
who does anything for the sake of pleasure is either
self-indulgent or bad or incontinent, but he who does it for
a disgraceful pleasure.

Since there is also a sort of man who takes less delight
than he should in bodily things, and does not abide by the
rule, he who is intermediate between him and the incontinent man is the continent man ; for the incontinent man 25
fails to abide by the rule because he delights too much in
them, and this man because he delights in them too little ;
while the continent man abides by the rule and does
not change on either account. Now if continence is good,
both the contrary states must be bad, as they actually
appear to be ; but because the other extreme is seen in few 30
people and seldom, as temperance is thought to be contrary
only to self-indulgence, so is continence to incontinence.

Since many names are applied analogically, it is by

[1] ll. 895–916.

analogy that we have come to speak of the 'continence' of
the temperate man; for both the continent man and the
35 temperate man are such as to do nothing contrary to the
1152^a rule for the sake of the bodily pleasures, but the former
has and the latter has not bad appetites, and the latter is
such as not to feel pleasure contrary to the rule, while the
former is such as to feel pleasure but not to be led by it.
And the incontinent and the self-indulgent man are also
5 like another; they are different, but both pursue bodily
pleasures—the latter, however, also thinking that he ought
to do so, while the former does not think this.

Nor can the same man have practical wisdom and be 10
incontinent; for it has been shown[1] that a man is at the
same time practically wise, and good in respect of character.
Further, a man has practical wisdom not by knowing only
but by being able to act; but the incontinent man is unable
to act—there is, however, nothing to prevent a *clever* man
10 from being incontinent; this is why it is sometimes actually
thought that some people have practical wisdom but are
incontinent, viz. because cleverness and practical wisdom
differ in the way we have described in our first discussions,[2]
and are near together in respect of their reasoning, but
differ in respect of their purpose—nor yet is the incontinent
man like the man who knows and is contemplating a truth,
15 but like the man who is asleep or drunk. And he acts
willingly (for he acts in a sense with knowledge both of
what he does and of the end to which he does it), but is
not wicked, since his purpose is good; so that he is half-
wicked. And he is not a criminal; for he does not act of
malice aforethought; of the two types of incontinent man
the one does not abide by the conclusions of his deliberation, while the excitable man does not deliberate at all.
20 And thus the incontinent man is like a city which passes
all the right decrees and has good laws, but makes no
use of them, as in Anaxandrides' jesting remark,[3]

'The city willed it, that cares nought for laws';

---

[1] 1144^a 11–^b 32.   [2] 1144^a 23–^b4.

[3] Fr. 67 Kock.

but the wicked man is like a city that uses its laws, but has wicked laws to use.

Now incontinence and continence are concerned with 25 that which is in excess of the state characteristic of most men ; for the continent man abides by his resolutions more and the incontinent man less than most men can.

Of the forms of incontinence, that of excitable people is more curable than that of those who deliberate but do not abide by their decisions, and those who are incontinent through habituation are more curable than those in whom incontinence is innate ; for it is easier to change a habit than to change one's nature ; even habit is hard to change 30 just because it is like nature, as Evenus says :[1]

> I say that habit's but long practice, friend,
> And this becomes men's nature in the end.

We have now stated what continence, incontinence, endurance, and softness are, and how these states are related 35 to each other.

11   The study of pleasure and pain belongs to the province 1152ᵇ of the political philosopher ; for he is the architect of the end, with a view to which we call one thing bad and another good without qualification.   Further, it is one of our necessary tasks to consider them ; for not only did we lay it down that moral virtue and vice are concerned with pains and 5 pleasures,[2] but most people say that happiness involves pleasure ; this is why the blessed man is called by a name derived from a word meaning enjoyment.[3]

Now (1) some people think that no pleasure is a good, either in itself or incidentally, since the good and pleasure are not the same ; (2) others think that some pleasures are 10 good but that most are bad.   (3) Again there is a third view, that even if all pleasures are goods, yet the best thing in the world cannot be pleasure.   (1) The reasons given for the view that pleasure is not a good at all are (a) that every pleasure is a perceptible process to a natural state, and that no process is of the same kind as its end, e.g. no process

---

[1] Fr. 9 Diehl.   [2] 1104ᵇ 8-1105ᵃ 13.
[3] μακάριος from μάλα χαίρειν !

15 of building of the same kind as a house. (*b*) A temperate man avoids pleasures. (*c*) A man of practical wisdom pursues what is free from pain, not what is pleasant. (*d*) The pleasures are a hindrance to thought, and the more so the more one delights in them, e.g. in sexual pleasure; for no one could think of anything while absorbed in this. (*e*) There is no art of pleasure; but every good is the product of some art. (*f*) Children and the brutes 20 pursue pleasures. (2) The reasons for the view that not all pleasures are good are that (*a*) there are pleasures that are actually base and objects of reproach, and (*b*) there are harmful pleasures; for some pleasant things are unhealthy. (3) The reason for the view that the best thing in the world is not pleasure is that pleasure is not an end but a process.

25   These are pretty much the things that are said. That it 12 does not follow from these grounds that pleasure is not a good, or even the chief good, is plain from the following considerations. (A)¹ (*a*) First, since that which is good may be so in either of two senses (one thing good simply and another good for a particular person), natural constitutions and states of being, and therefore also the corresponding movements and processes, will be correspondingly divisible. Of those which are thought to be bad some will be bad if taken without qualification but not bad for 30 a particular person, but worthy of his choice, and some will not be worthy of choice even for a particular person, but only at a particular time and for a short period, though not without qualification; while others are not even pleasures, but seem to be so, viz. all those which involve pain and whose end is curative, e.g. the processes that go on in sick persons.

(*b*) Further, one kind of good being activity and another being state, the processes that restore us to our natural 35 state are only incidentally pleasant; for that matter the activity at work in the appetites for them is the activity of so much of our state and nature as has remained unimpaired; for there are actually pleasures that involve *no*

¹ (A) is the answer to (1 *a*) and (3).

pain or appetite (e. g. those of contemplation), the nature in 1153ᵃ
such a case not being defective at all.   That the others are
incidental is indicated by the fact that men do not enjoy
the same pleasant objects when their nature is in its settled
state as they do when it is being replenished, but in the
former case they enjoy the things that are pleasant without
qualification, in the latter the contraries of these as well ;
for then they enjoy even sharp and bitter things, none of 5
which is pleasant either by nature or without qualification.
The states they produce, therefore, are not pleasures
naturally or without qualification; for as pleasant things
differ, so do the pleasures arising from them.

(c) Again, it is not necessary that there should be something else better than pleasure, as some say the end is better
than the process ; for pleasures are not processes nor do
they all involve process—they are activities and ends ; nor 10
do they arise when we are becoming something, but when
we are exercising some faculty ; and not all pleasures have
an end different from themselves, but only the pleasures of
persons who are being led to the perfecting of their nature.
This is why it is not right to say that pleasure is perceptible
process, but it should rather be called activity of the natural
state, and instead of 'perceptible' 'unimpeded'.   It is 15
thought by *some* people to be process just because they
think it is in the strict sense *good* ; for they think that
activity is process, which it is not.

(B)¹ The view that pleasures are bad because some
pleasant things are unhealthy is like saying that healthy
things are bad because some healthy things are bad for
money-making ; both are bad in the respect mentioned, but
they are not *bad* for *that* reason—indeed, thinking itself is 20
sometimes injurious to health.

Neither practical wisdom nor any state of being is
impeded by the pleasure arising from it ; it is foreign
pleasures that impede, for the pleasures arising from
thinking and learning will make us think and learn all
the more.

(C)² The fact that no pleasure is the product of any art

¹ Answer to (2 *b*) and (1 *d*).   ² Answer to (1 *e*).

arises naturally enough; there is no art of any other
25 activity either, but only of the corresponding faculty;
though for that matter the arts of the perfumer and the
cook *are* thought to be arts of pleasure.

(D)[1] The arguments based on the grounds that the
temperate man avoids pleasure and that the man of
practical wisdom pursues the painless life, and that children
and the brutes pursue pleasure, are all refuted by the same
consideration. We have pointed out[2] in what sense pleasures
are good without qualification and in what sense some are not
30 good; now both the brutes and children pursue pleasures
of the latter kind (and the man of practical wisdom pursues
tranquil freedom from that kind), viz. those which imply
appetite and pain, i. e. the bodily pleasures (for it is these
that are of this nature) and the excesses of them, in respect
of which the self-indulgent man is self-indulgent. This is
35 why the temperate man avoids these pleasures; for even he
has pleasures of his own.

1153ᵇ But further (E) it is agreed that pain is bad and to be 13
avoided; for some pain is without qualification bad, and
other pain is bad because it is in some respect an impediment
to us. Now the contrary of that which is to be avoided,
qua something to be avoided and bad, is good. Pleasure,
then, is necessarily a good. For the answer of Speusippus,
5 that pleasure is contrary both to pain and to good, as the
greater is contrary both to the less and to the equal, is not
successful; since he would not say that pleasure is essentially
just a species of evil.

And (F)[3] if certain pleasures are bad, that does not prevent the chief good from being some pleasure, just as the
chief good may be some form of knowledge though certain
kinds of knowledge are bad. Perhaps it is even necessary,
10 if each disposition has unimpeded activities, that, whether
the activity (if unimpeded) of all our dispositions or that of
some one of them is happiness, this should be the thing
most worthy of our choice; and this activity is pleasure.

---

[1] Answer to (1 *b*), (1 *c*), (1 *f*).   [2] 1152ᵇ 26–1153ᵃ 7.
[3] Answer to (2 *a*).

Thus the chief good would be some pleasure, though most pleasures might perhaps be bad without qualification. And for this reason all men think that the happy life is pleasant and weave pleasure into their ideal of happiness—and 15 reasonably too; for no activity is perfect when it is impeded, and happiness is a perfect thing; this is why the happy man needs the goods of the body and external goods, i. e. those of fortune, viz. in order that he may not be impeded in these ways. Those who say that the victim on the rack or the man who falls into great misfortunes is happy if he is good, are, whether they mean to or not, 20 talking nonsense. Now because we need fortune as well as other things, some people think good fortune the same thing as happiness; but it is not that, for even good fortune itself when in excess is an impediment, and perhaps should then be no longer called good fortune; for its limit is fixed by reference to happiness.

And indeed the fact that all things, both brutes and men, 25 pursue pleasure is an indication of its being somehow the chief good:

No voice is wholly lost that many peoples¹...

But since no one nature or state either is or is thought the best for all, neither do all pursue the same pleasure; yet 30 all pursue pleasure. And perhaps they actually pursue not the pleasure they think they pursue nor that which they would say they pursue, but the same pleasure; for all things have by nature something divine in them. But the bodily pleasures have appropriated the name both because we oftenest steer our course for them and because all men share in them; thus because they alone are familiar, men 35 think there are no others.

It is evident also that if pleasure, i. e. the activity of our 1154ª faculties, is not a good, it will not be the case that the happy man lives a pleasant life; for to what end should he need pleasure, if it is not a good but the happy man may even live a painful life? For pain is neither an evil nor a good, if pleasure is not; why then should he avoid it?

¹ Hes. *Op.* 763.

5 Therefore, too, the life of the good man will not be pleasanter than that of any one else, if his activities are not more pleasant.

(G)[1] With regard to the bodily pleasures, those who say **14** that *some* pleasures are very much to be chosen, viz. the noble pleasures, but not the bodily pleasures, i. e. those with
10 which the self-indulgent man is concerned, must consider why,[2] then, the contrary pains are bad. For the contrary of bad is good. Are the necessary pleasures good in the sense in which even that which is not bad is good? Or are they good up to a point? Is it that where you have states and processes of which there cannot be too much, there cannot be too much of the corresponding pleasure, and that where there can be too much of the one there can be too much of
15 the other also? Now there can be too much of bodily goods, and the bad man is bad by virtue of pursuing the excess, not by virtue of pursuing the necessary pleasures (for *all* men enjoy in some way or other both dainty foods and wines and sexual intercourse, but not all men do so as they ought). The contrary is the case with pain; for he does not avoid the excess of it, he avoids it altogether;
20 and this is peculiar to him, for the alternative to excess of pleasure is not pain, except to the man who pursues this excess.[3]

Since we should state not only the truth, but also the cause of error—for this contributes towards producing conviction, since when a reasonable explanation is given of why the false view appears true, this tends to produce belief in
25 the true view—therefore we must state why the bodily pleasures appear the more worthy of choice. (*a*) Firstly, then, it is because they expel pain; owing to the excesses of pain that men experience, they pursue excessive and in general bodily pleasure as being a cure for the pain. Now
30 curative agencies produce intense feeling—which is the

---

[1] Answer to (2).
[2] Reading a comma after ἀκόλαστος in l. 10.
[3] I have expanded this sentence slightly to bring out the rather obscure connexion of thought. To the voluptuary, and to him alone, pain and violent bodily pleasure appear exhaustive alternatives, and because he always pursues the latter he always shuns the former.

reason why they are pursued—because they show up against the contrary pain. (Indeed pleasure is thought not to be good for these two reasons, as has been said,[1] viz. that (α) some of them are activities belonging to a bad nature—either congenital, as in the case of a brute, or due to habit, i. e. those of bad men ; while (β) others are meant to cure a defective nature, and it is better to be in a healthy state than to be getting into it, but these arise during the **1154^b** process of being made perfect and are therefore only incidentally good.) (b) Further, they are pursued because of their violence by those who cannot enjoy other pleasures. (At all events they go out of their way to manufacture thirsts somehow for themselves. When these are harmless, the practice is irreproachable; when they are hurtful, it is bad.) For they have nothing else to enjoy, and, besides, 5 a neutral state is painful to many people because of their nature. For the animal nature is always in travail, as the students of natural science also testify, saying that sight and hearing are painful ; but we have become used to this, as they maintain. Similarly, while, in youth, people are, owing to the growth that is going on, in a situation like that of drunken men, and youth is pleasant,[2] on the other 10 hand people of excitable nature[3] always need relief ; for even their body is ever in torment owing to its special composition, and they are always under the influence of violent desire ; but pain is driven out both by the contrary pleasure, and by any chance pleasure if it be strong ; and for these reasons they become self-indulgent and bad. But the pleasures 15 that do not involve pains do not admit of excess ; and these are among the things pleasant by nature and not incidentally. By things pleasant incidentally I mean those that act as cures (for because as a result people are cured, through some action of the part that remains healthy, for this reason the process is thought pleasant) ; by things naturally pleasant I mean those that stimulate the action of the healthy nature.

---

[1] 1152^b 26–33.

[2] i. e. the growth or replenishment that is going on produces exhilaration and pleasure. Read a comma after νεότης.

[3] Lit., melancholic people, those characterized by an excess of black bile.

20 There is no one thing that is always pleasant, because our nature is not simple but there is another element in us as well, inasmuch as we are perishable creatures, so that if the one element does something, this is unnatural to the other nature, and when the two elements are evenly balanced, what is done seems neither painful nor pleasant; for if the 25 nature of anything were simple, the same action would always be most pleasant to it. This is why God always enjoys a single and simple pleasure; for there is not only an activity of movement but an activity of immobility, and pleasure is found more in rest than in movement. But 'change in all things is sweet', as the poet says,[1] because of some vice; for as it is the vicious man that is changeable, 30 so the nature that needs change is vicious; for it is not simple nor good.

We have now discussed continence and incontinence, and pleasure and pain, both what each is and in what sense some of them are good and others bad; it remains to speak of friendship.

[1] Eur. *Or.* 234.

BOOK VIII

1   AFTER what we have said, a discussion of friendship 1155^a
would naturally follow, since it is a virtue or implies virtue,
and is besides most necessary with a view to living.   For 5
without friends no one would choose to live, though he had
all other goods; even rich men and those in possession of
office and of dominating power are thought to need friends
most of all; for what is the use of such prosperity without
the opportunity of beneficence, which is exercised chiefly
and in its most laudable form towards friends?   Or how
can prosperity be guarded and preserved without friends?
The greater it is, the more exposed is it to risk.   And in 10
poverty and in other misfortunes men think friends are the
only refuge.   It helps the young, too, to keep from error;
it aids [1] older people by ministering to their needs and
supplementing the activities that are failing from weakness;
those in the prime of life it stimulates to noble actions—
'two going together' [2]—for with friends men are more able 15
both to think and to act.   Again, parent seems by nature
to feel it for offspring and offspring for parent, not only
among men but among birds and among most animals;
it is felt mutually by members of the same race, and 20
especially by men, whence we praise lovers of their fellow-
men.   We may see even in our travels how near and dear
every man is to every other.   Friendship seems too to
hold states together, and lawgivers to care more for it than
for justice; for unanimity seems to be something like
friendship, and this they aim at most of all, and expel 25
faction as their worst enemy; and when men are friends
they have no need of justice, while when they are just they
need friendship as well, and the truest form of justice is
thought to be a friendly quality.

But it is not only necessary but also noble; for we praise
those who love their friends, and it is thought to be a fine 30

---

[1] Reading βοήθεια in l. 14 with M^b.   [2] *Il.* x. 224.

thing to have many friends; and again we think it is the same people that are good men and are friends.

Not a few things about friendship are matters of debate. Some define it as a kind of likeness and say like people are friends, whence come the sayings 'like to like',[1] 'birds
35 of a feather flock together',[2] and so on; others on the
1155ᵇ contrary say 'two of a trade never agree'.[3] On this very question they inquire for deeper and more physical causes, Euripides saying that 'parched earth loves the rain, and stately heaven when filled with rain loves to fall to earth',[4]
5 and Heraclitus that 'it is what opposes that helps' and 'from different tones comes the fairest tune' and 'all things are produced through strife';[5] while Empedocles, as well as others, expresses the opposite view that like aims at like.[6] The physical problems we may leave alone (for they do not belong to the present inquiry); let us examine those which are human and involve character and feeling,
10 e.g. whether friendship can arise between any two people or people cannot be friends if they are wicked, and whether there is one species of friendship or more than one. Those who think there is only one because it admits of degrees have relied on an inadequate indication; for even things
15 different in species admit of degree. We have discussed this matter previously.[7]

The kinds of friendship may perhaps be cleared up if 2 we first come to know the object of love. For not everything seems to be loved but only the lovable, and this is good, pleasant, or useful; but it would seem to be that by which some good or pleasure is produced that is useful,
20 so that it is the good and the useful that are lovable as ends. Do men love, then, *the* good, or what is good for *them*? These sometimes clash. So too with regard to the pleasant. Now it is thought that each loves what is

---

[1] *Od.* xvii. 218.

[2] Lit. 'jackdaw to jackdaw'. The source is unknown.

[3] Lit. 'all such men (i. e. all those who resemble one another) are potters to one another', an allusion to Hes. *Op.* 25, καὶ κεραμεὺς κεραμεῖ κοτέει καὶ τέκτονι τέκτων.

[4] Fr. 898. 7–10 Nauck².

[5] Fr. 8 Diels.

[6] Fr. 22. 5, 62. 6, 90. 1–2 Diels.

[7] Place unknown.

good for himself, and that the good is without qualification
lovable, and what is good for each man is lovable for him;
but each man loves not what is good for him but what 25
seems good. This however will make no difference; we
shall just have to say that this is 'that which seems lovable'.
Now there are three grounds on which people love; of
the love of lifeless objects we do not use the word 'friendship'; for it is not mutual love, nor is there a wishing
of good to the other (for it would surely be ridiculous to
wish wine well; if one wishes anything for it, it is that 30
it may keep, so that one may have it oneself); but to a
friend we say we ought to wish what is good for his sake.
But to those who thus wish good we ascribe only goodwill,
if the wish is not reciprocated; goodwill when it *is* reciprocal being friendship. Or must we add 'when it is recognized'? For many people have goodwill to those whom
they have not seen but judge to be good or useful; and 35
one of these might return this feeling. These people seem 1156^a
to bear goodwill to each other; but how could one call
them friends when they do not know their mutual feelings?
To be friends, then, they must be mutually recognized as
bearing goodwill and wishing well to each other for one of 5
the aforesaid reasons.

3　　Now these reasons differ from each other in kind; so, therefore, do the corresponding forms of love and friendship. There
are therefore three kinds of friendship, equal in number to
the things that are lovable; for with respect to each there
is a mutual and recognized love, and those who love each
other wish well to each other in that respect in which they
love one another. Now those who love each other for their 10
utility do not love each other for themselves but in virtue
of some good which they get from each other. So too
with those who love for the sake of pleasure; it is not for
their character that men love ready-witted people, but
because they find them pleasant. Therefore those who love
for the sake of utility love for the sake of what is good for
themselves, and those who love for the sake of pleasure
do so for the sake of what is pleasant to *themselves*, and 15

not in so far as the other is the person loved[1] but in so far as he is useful or pleasant. And thus these friendships are only incidental; for it is not as being the man he is that the loved person is loved, but as providing some good or pleasure. Such friendships, then, are easily dissolved, if 20 the parties do not remain like themselves; for if the one party is no longer pleasant or useful the other ceases to love him.

Now the useful is not permanent but is always changing. Thus when the motive of the friendship is done away, the friendship is dissolved, inasmuch as it existed only for the ends in question. This kind of friendship seems to exist 25 chiefly between old people (for at that age people pursue not the pleasant but the useful) and, of those who are in their prime or young, between those who pursue utility. And such people do not live much with each other either; for sometimes they do not even find each other pleasant; therefore they do not need such companionship unless they are useful to each other; for they are pleasant to each other only in so far as they rouse in each other 30 hopes of something good to come. Among such friendships people also class the friendship of host and guest. On the other hand the friendship of young people seems to aim at pleasure; for they live under the guidance of emotion, and pursue above all what is pleasant to themselves and what is immediately before them; but with increasing age their pleasures become different. This is why they quickly become 35 friends and quickly cease to be so; their friendship changes with the object that is found pleasant, and such pleasure alters 1156ᵇ quickly. Young people are amorous too; for the greater part of the friendship of love depends on emotion and aims at pleasure; this is why they fall in love and quickly fall out of love, changing often within a single day. But these people do wish to spend their days and lives together; 5 for it is thus that they attain the purpose of their friendship.

Perfect friendship is the friendship of men who are good, and alike in virtue; for these wish well alike to each other *qua* good, and they are good in themselves. Now those

[1] The MS. reading seems to be sufficiently supported by *E.E.* 1237ᵇ 1.

who wish well to their friends for their sake are most truly
friends; for they do this by reason of their own nature 10
and not incidentally; therefore their friendship lasts as
long as they are good—and goodness is an enduring thing.
And each is good without qualification and to his friend,
for the good are both good without qualification and useful
to each other. So too they are pleasant; for the good are 15
pleasant both without qualification and to each other, since
to each his own activities and others like them are plea-
surable, and the actions of the good *are* the same or like.
And such a friendship is as might be expected permanent,
since there meet in it all the qualities that friends should
have. For all friendship is for the sake of good or of
pleasure—good or pleasure either in the abstract or such 20
as will be enjoyed by him who has the friendly feeling—and
is based on a certain resemblance; and to a friendship of
good men all the qualities we have named belong in virtue
of the nature of the friends themselves; for in the case of
this kind of friendship the other qualities also[1] are alike in
both friends, and that which is good without qualification
is also without qualification pleasant, and these are the
most lovable qualities. Love and friendship therefore are
found most and in their best form between such men.

But it is natural that such friendships should be infre-
quent; for such men are rare. Further, such friendship 25
requires time and familiarity; as the proverb says, men
cannot know each other till they have 'eaten salt together';
nor can they admit each other to friendship or be friends
till each has been found lovable and been trusted by each.
Those who quickly show the marks of friendship to each
other wish to be friends, but are not friends unless they 30
both are lovable and know the fact; for a wish for friendship may arise quickly, but friendship does not.

4   This kind of friendship, then, is perfect both in respect
of duration and in all other respects, and in it each gets
from each in all respects the same as, or something like

---

[1] i. e. absolute pleasantness, relative goodness, and relative pleasantness, as well as absolute goodness.

what, he gives; which is what ought to happen between
35 friends. Friendship for the sake of pleasure bears a resem-
1157^a blance to this kind; for good people too *are* pleasant to
each other. So too does friendship for the sake of utility;
for the good are also useful to each other. Among men
of these inferior sorts too, friendships are most permanent
when the friends get the same thing from each other (e. g.
5 pleasure), and not only that but also from the same source,
as happens between ready-witted people, not as happens
between lover and beloved. For these do not take pleasure
in the same things, but the one in seeing the beloved and the
other in receiving attentions from his lover; and when
the bloom of youth is passing the friendship sometimes
passes too (for the one finds no pleasure in the sight of
the other, and the other gets no attentions from the first);
10 but many lovers on the other hand are constant, if familiarity has led them to love each other's characters, these
being alike. But those who exchange not pleasure but
utility in their amour are both less truly friends and less
constant. Those who are friends for the sake of utility part
15 when the advantage is at an end; for they were lovers not
of each other but of profit.

For the sake of pleasure or utility, then, even bad men
may be friends of each other, or good men of bad, or one
who is neither good nor bad may be a friend to any sort
of person, but for their own sake clearly only good men
can be friends; for bad men do not delight in each other
unless some advantage come of the relation.

20 The friendship of the good too and this alone is proof
against slander; for it is not easy to trust any one's talk
about a man who has long been tested by oneself; and
it is among good men that trust and the feeling that
'he would never wrong me' and all the other things that
are demanded in true friendship are found. In the other
kinds of friendship, however, there is nothing to prevent
these evils arising.

25 For men apply the name of friends even to those
whose motive is utility, in which sense states are said to be
friendly (for the alliances of states seem to aim at advantage),

and to those who love each other for the sake of pleasure,
in which sense children are called friends.   Therefore we
too ought perhaps to call such people friends, and say that 30
there are several kinds of friendship—firstly and in the proper
sense that of good men *qua* good, and by analogy the other
kinds ; for it is in virtue of something good and something
akin to what is found in true friendship that they are
friends, since even the pleasant is good for the lovers of
pleasure.   But these two kinds of friendship are not often
united, nor do the same people become friends for the sake
of utility and of pleasure ; for things that are only inci- 35
dentally connected are not often coupled together.

Friendship being divided into these kinds, bad men will 1157^b
be friends for the sake of pleasure or of utility, being in this
respect like each other, but good men will be friends for
their own sake, i. e. in virtue of their goodness.   These,
then, are friends without qualification ; the others are
friends incidentally and through a resemblance to these.

5   As in regard to the virtues some men are called good 5
in respect of a state of character, others in respect of an
activity, so too in the case of friendship ; for those who
live together delight in each other and confer benefits on
each other, but those who are asleep or locally separated
are not performing, but are disposed to perform, the activities of friendship ; distance does not break off the friendship 10
absolutely, but only the activity of it.   But if the absence
is lasting, it seems actually to make men forget their
friendship ; hence the saying ' out of sight, out of mind '.[1]
Neither old people nor sour people seem to make friends
easily ; for there is little that is pleasant in them, and no 15
one can spend his days with one whose company is painful, or not pleasant, since nature seems above all to avoid
the painful and to aim at the pleasant.   Those, however,
who approve of each other but do not live together seem
to be well-disposed rather than actual friends.   For there
is nothing so characteristic of friends as living together

---

[1] Lit. ' many a friendship has lack of converse broken '.   The source
is unknown.

20 (since while it is people who are in need that desire benefits, even those who are supremely happy desire to spend their days together; for solitude suits such people least of all); but people cannot live together if they are not pleasant and do not enjoy the same things, as friends who are companions seem to do.

25 The truest friendship, then, is that of the good, as we have frequently said;[1] for that which is without qualification good or pleasant seems to be lovable and desirable, and for each person that which is good or pleasant to him; and the good man is lovable and desirable to the good man for both these reasons. Now it looks as if love were a feeling, friendship a state of character; for love 30 may be felt just as much towards lifeless things, but mutual love involves choice and choice springs from a state of character; and men wish well to those whom they love, for their sake, not as a result of feeling but as a result of a state of character. And in loving a friend men love what is good for themselves; for the good man in becoming a friend becomes a good to his friend. Each, then, both loves what 35 is good for himself, and makes an equal return in goodwill and in pleasantness; for friendship is said to be equality, and both of these are found most in the friendship of the good.

1158^a Between sour and elderly people friendship arises less 6 readily, inasmuch as they are less good-tempered and enjoy companionship less; for these are thought to be the greatest marks of friendship and most productive of it. This is why, while young men become friends quickly, old 5 men do not; it is because men do not become friends with those in whom they do not delight; and similarly sour people do not quickly make friends either. But such men may bear goodwill to each other; for they wish one another well and aid one another in need; but they are hardly *friends* because they do not spend their days together nor delight in each other, and these are thought the greatest marks of friendship.

10 One cannot be a friend to many people in the sense of

[1] 1156^b 7, 23, 33, 1157^a 30, ^b 4.

having friendship of the perfect type with them, just as one cannot be in love with many people at once (for love is a sort of excess of feeling, and it is the nature of such only to be felt towards one person); and it is not easy for many people at the same time to please the same person very greatly, or perhaps even to be good in his eyes. One must, too, acquire some experience of the other person and become familiar with him, and that is very hard. But with 15 a view to utility or pleasure it is possible that many people should please one; for many people are useful or pleasant, and these services take little time.

Of these two kinds that which is for the sake of pleasure is the more like friendship, when both parties get the same things from each other and delight in each other or in the same things, as in the friendships of the young; for gene- 20 rosity is more found in such friendships. Friendship based on utility is for the commercially minded. People who are supremely happy, too, have no need of useful friends, but do need pleasant friends; for they wish to live with *some one* and, though they can endure for a short time what is painful, no one could put up with it continuously, nor even with the Good itself if it were painful to him; this is why 25 they look out for friends who are pleasant. Perhaps they should look out for friends who, being pleasant, are also good, and good for them too; for so they will have all the characteristics that friends should have.

People in positions of authority seem to have friends who fall into distinct classes; some people are useful to them and others are pleasant, but the same people are rarely both; for they seek neither those whose pleasantness 30 is accompanied by virtue nor those whose utility is with a view to noble objects, but in their desire for pleasure they seek for ready-witted people, and their other friends they choose as being clever at doing what they are told, and these characteristics are rarely combined. Now we have said that the *good* man *is* at the same time pleasant and useful; [1] but such a man does not become the friend of one who surpasses him in station, unless he is surpassed also in

[1] 1156^b 13-15, 1157^a 1-3.

35 virtue; if this is not so, he does not establish equality by being proportionally exceeded in both respects. But people who surpass him in both respects are not so easy to find.

1158ᵇ However that may be, the aforesaid friendships involve equality; for the friends get the same things from one another and wish the same things for one another, or exchange one thing for another, e. g. pleasure for utility; we have said,[1] however, that they are both less truly

5 friendships and less permanent. But it is from their likeness and their unlikeness to the same thing that they are thought both to be and not to be friendships. It is by their likeness to the friendship of virtue that they seem to be friendships (for one of them involves pleasure and the other utility, and these characteristics belong to the friendship of virtue as well); while it is because the friendship of virtue is proof against slander and permanent, while these quickly change (besides differing from the former in

10 many other respects), that they appear *not* to be friendships; i. e. it is because of their unlikeness to the friendship of virtue.

But there is another kind of friendship, viz. that which **7** involves an inequality between the parties, e. g. that of father to son and in general of elder to younger, that of man to wife and in general that of ruler to subject. And

15 these friendships differ also from each other; for it is not the same that exists between parents and children and between rulers and subjects, nor is even that of father to son the same as that of son to father, nor that of husband to wife the same as that of wife to husband. For the virtue and the function of each of these is different, and so are the reasons for which they love; the love and

20 the friendship are therefore different also. Each party, then, neither gets the same from the other, nor ought to seek it; but when children render to parents what they ought to render to those who brought them into the world, and parents render what they should to their children, the friendship of such persons will be abiding and excellent.

[1] 1156ᵃ 16–24, 1157ᵃ 20–33.

In all friendships implying inequality the love also should
be proportional, i. e. the better should be more loved than 25
he loves, and so should the more useful, and similarly in
each of the other cases; for when the love is in proportion
to the merit of the parties, then in a sense arises equality,
which is certainly held to be characteristic of friendship.

But equality does not seem to take the same form in acts
of justice and in friendship; for in acts of justice what is 30
equal in the primary sense is that which is in proportion
to merit, while quantitative equality is secondary, but in
friendship quantitative equality is primary and proportion
to merit secondary. This becomes clear if there is a great
interval in respect of virtue or vice or wealth or anything
else between the parties; for then they are no longer
friends, and do not even expect to be so. And this is most 35
manifest in the case of the gods; for they surpass us most
decisively in all good things. But it is clear also in the
case of kings; for with them, too, men who are much their **1159^a**
inferiors do not expect to be friends; nor do men of no
account expect to be friends with the best or wisest men.
In such cases it is not possible to define exactly up to what
point friends can remain friends; for much can be taken
away and friendship remain, but when one party is removed
to a great distance, as God is, the possibility of friendship
ceases. This is in fact the origin of the question whether 5
friends really wish for their friends the greatest goods,
e. g. that of being gods; since in that case their friends will
no longer be friends to them, and therefore will not be
good things for them (for friends *are* good things). The
answer is that if we were right in saying that friend wishes
good to friend for his sake,[1] his friend must remain the sort
of being he is, whatever that may be; therefore it is for 10
him only so long as he remains a man that he will wish the
greatest goods. But perhaps not *all* the greatest goods;
for it is for himself most of all that each man wishes what is
good.

8   Most people seem, owing to ambition, to wish to be
loved rather than to love; which is why most men love

[1] 1155^b 31.

flattery; for the flatterer is a friend in an inferior position,
15 or pretends to be such and to love more than he is loved;
and being loved seems to be akin to being honoured, and
this is what most people aim at. But it seems to be
not for its own sake that people choose honour, but incidentally. For most people enjoy being honoured by those
20 in positions of authority because of their hopes (for they
think that if they want anything they will get it from
them; and therefore they delight in honour as a token of
favour to come); while those who desire honour from good
men, and men who know, are aiming at confirming their
own opinion of themselves; they delight in honour, therefore, because they believe in their own goodness on the
strength of the judgement of those who speak about them.
In being loved, on the other hand, people delight for its
25 own sake; whence it would seem to be better than being
honoured, and friendship to be desirable in itself. But it
seems to lie in loving rather than in being loved, as is
indicated by the delight mothers take in loving; for some
mothers hand over their children to be brought up, and so
30 long as they know their fate they love them and do not
seek to be loved in return (if they cannot have both), but
seem to be satisfied if they see them prospering; and they
themselves love their children even if these owing to their
ignorance give them nothing of a mother's due. Now
since friendship depends more on loving, and it is those
who love their friends that are praised, loving seems to be
35 the characteristic virtue of friends, so that it is only those
in whom this is found in due measure that are lasting
friends, and only their friendship that endures.

1159ᵇ It is in this way more than any other that even unequals
can be friends; they can be equalized. Now equality and
likeness are friendship, and especially the likeness of those
who are like in virtue; for being steadfast in themselves
5 they hold fast to each other, and neither ask nor give base
services, but (one may say) even prevent them; for it is
characteristic of good men neither to go wrong themselves
nor to let their friends do so. But wicked men have no
steadfastness (for they do not remain even like to them-

selves), but become friends for a short time because they delight in each other's wickedness. Friends who are useful 10 or pleasant last longer; i. e. as long as they provide each other with enjoyments or advantages. Friendship for utility's sake seems to be that which most easily exists between contraries, e.g. between poor and rich, between ignorant and learned; for what a man actually lacks he aims at, and one gives something else in return. But under this head, 15 too, might bring lover and beloved, beautiful and ugly. This is why lovers sometimes seem ridiculous, when they demand to be loved as they love; if they are equally lovable their claim can perhaps be justified, but when they have nothing lovable about them it is ridiculous. Perhaps, however, contrary does not even aim at contrary by its own nature, but only incidentally, the desire being for what is inter- 20 mediate; for that is what is good, e.g. it is good for the dry not to become wet[1] but to come to the intermediate state, and similarly with the hot and in all other cases. These subjects we may dismiss; for they are indeed some-what foreign to our inquiry.

9 Friendship and justice seem, as we have said at the 25 outset of our discussion,[2] to be concerned with the same objects and exhibited between the same persons. For in every community there is thought to be some form of justice, and friendship too; at least men address as friends their fellow-voyagers and fellow-soldiers, and so too those associated with them in any other kind of community. And the extent of their association is the extent of their friendship, as it is the extent to which justice exists between 30 them. And the proverb 'what friends have is common property' expresses the truth; for friendship depends on community. Now brothers and comrades have all things in common, but the others to whom we have referred have definite things in common—some more things, others fewer; for of friendships, too, some are more and others less truly friendships. And the claims of justice differ too; the 35 duties of parents to children and those of brothers to **1160ᵃ**

---

[1] Cf. 1155ᵇ 3.   [2] 1155ᵃ 22–28.

each other are not the same, nor those of comrades and those of fellow-citizens, and so, too, with the other kinds of friendship. There is a difference, therefore, also between the acts that are unjust towards each of these classes of associates, and the injustice increases by being exhibited towards those who are friends in a fuller sense; e.g. it is a more terrible thing to defraud a comrade than a fellow-
5 citizen, more terrible not to help a brother than a stranger, and more terrible to wound a father than any one else. And the demands of justice also seem to increase with the intensity of the friendship, which implies that friendship and justice exist between the same persons and have an equal extension.

Now all forms of community are like parts of the political community; for men journey together with a view
10 to some particular advantage, and to provide something that they need for the purposes of life; and it is for the sake of advantage that the political community too seems both to have come together originally and to endure, for this is what legislators aim at, and they call just that which is to the common advantage. Now the other communities aim
15 at advantage bit by bit, e.g. sailors at what is advantageous on a voyage with a view to making money or something of the kind, fellow-soldiers at what is advantageous in war, whether it is wealth or victory or the taking of a city that they seek, and members of tribes and demes act similarly [Some communities seem to arise for the sake of pleasure,
20 viz. religious guilds and social clubs; for these exist respectively for the sake of offering sacrifice and of companionship. But all these seem to fall under the political community; for it aims not at present advantage but at what is advantageous for life as a whole],[1] offering sacrifices and arranging gatherings for the purpose, and assigning honours to the gods, and providing pleasant relaxations
25 for themselves. For the ancient sacrifices and gatherings seem to take place after the harvest as a sort of firstfruits, because it was at these seasons that people had most

---

[1] It seems best to treat ll. 19-23 as an insertion from an alternative version. So J. Cook Wilson in *Class. Rev.* xvi. (1902), 28.

leisure. All the communities, then, seem to be parts of the political community; and the particular kinds of friendship will correspond to the particular kinds of community. 30

10 There are three kinds of constitution, and an equal number of deviation-forms—perversions, as it were, of them. The constitutions are monarchy, aristocracy, and thirdly that which is based on a property qualification, which it seems appropriate to call timocratic, though most people are wont to call it polity. The best of these is monarchy, the 35 worst timocracy. The deviation from monarchy is tyranny; for both are forms of one-man rule, but there is the greatest 1160^b difference between them; the tyrant looks to his own advantage, the king to that of his subjects. For a man is not a king unless he is sufficient to himself and excels his subjects in all good things; and such a man needs nothing further; therefore he will not look to his own interests but 5 to those of his subjects; for a king who is not like that would be a mere titular king. Now tyranny is the very contrary of this; the tyrant pursues his own good. And it is clearer in the case of tyranny that it is the worst deviation-form;[1] but it is the contrary of the best that is worst.[2] Monarchy passes over into tyranny; for tyranny is the evil 10 form of one-man rule and the bad king becomes a tyrant. Aristocracy passes over into oligarchy by the badness of the rulers, who distribute contrary to equity what belongs to the city—all or most of the good things to themselves, and office always to the same people, paying most regard to wealth; thus the rulers are few and are bad men instead 15 of the most worthy. Timocracy passes over into democracy; for these are coterminous, since it is the ideal even of timocracy to be the rule of the majority, and all who have the property qualification count as equal. Democracy is the least bad of the deviations; for in its case the form 20 of constitution is but a slight deviation. These then are the changes to which constitutions are most subject; for these are the smallest and easiest transitions.

[1] Than it is that monarchy is the best genuine form (^{a} 35).
[2] Therefore monarchy must be the best.

One may find resemblances to the constitutions and, as it were, patterns of them even in households. For the association of a father with his sons bears the form of monarchy, 25 since the father cares for his children; and this is why Homer calls Zeus 'father';[1] it is the ideal of monarchy to be paternal rule. But among the Persians the rule of the father is tyrannical; they use their sons as slaves. Tyrannical too is the rule of a master over slaves; for it is the ad- 30 vantage of the master that is brought about in it. Now this seems to be a correct form of government, but the Persian type is perverted; for the modes of rule appropriate to different relations are diverse. The association of man and wife seems to be aristocratic; for the man rules in accordance with his worth, and in those matters in which a man should rule, but the matters that befit a woman he hands 35 over to her. If the man rules in everything the relation passes over into oligarchy; for in doing so he is not acting in accordance with their respective worth, and not ruling in virtue of his superiority. Sometimes, however, women rule, **1161ᵃ** because they are heiresses; so their rule is not in virtue of excellence but due to wealth and power, as in oligarchies. The association of brothers is like timocracy; for they are 5 equal, except in so far as they differ in age; hence if they differ *much* in age, the friendship is no longer of the fraternal type. Democracy is found chiefly in masterless dwellings (for here every one is on an equality), and in those in which the ruler is weak and every one has licence to do as he pleases.

10 Each of the constitutions may be seen to involve friend- **11** ship just in so far as it involves justice. The friendship between a king and his subjects depends on an excess of benefits conferred; for he confers benefits on his subjects if being a good man he cares for them with a view to their well-being, as a shepherd does for his sheep (whence Homer called Agamemnon 'shepherd of the 15 peoples ').[2] Such too is the friendship of a father, though this exceeds the other in the greatness of the benefits conferred; for he is responsible for the existence of his

[1] E.g. *Il.* i. 503.   [2] E.g. *Il.* ii. 243.

children, which is thought the greatest good, and for their
nurture and upbringing. These things are ascribed to
ancestors as well. Further, by nature a father tends to rule
over his sons, ancestors over descendants, a king over his
subjects. These friendships imply superiority of one party 20
over the other, which is why ancestors are honoured. The
justice therefore that exists between persons so related is
not the same on both sides but is in every case propor-
tioned to merit; for that is true of the friendship as well.
The friendship of man and wife, again, is the same that is
found in an aristocracy; for it is in accordance with virtue
—the better gets more of what is good, and each gets what
befits him; and so, too, with the justice in these relations.
The friendship of brothers is like that of comrades; for they 25
are equal and of like age, and such persons are for the most
part like in their feelings and their character. Like this,
too, is the friendship appropriate to timocratic government;
for in such a constitution the ideal is for the citizens to be
equal and fair; therefore rule is taken in turn, and on equal
terms; and the friendship appropriate here will correspond.

But in the deviation-forms, as justice hardly exists, so too 30
does friendship. It exists least in the worst form; in
tyranny there is little or no friendship. For where there
is nothing common to ruler and ruled, there is not friendship either, since there is not justice; e.g. between crafts-
man and tool, soul and body, master and slave; the latter 35
in each case is benefited by that which uses it, but there is 1161^b
no friendship nor justice towards lifeless things. But neither
is there friendship towards a horse or an ox, nor to a slave
qua slave. For there is nothing common to the two parties;
the slave is a living tool and the tool a lifeless slave. *Qua* 5
slave then, one cannot be friends with him. But *qua* man
one can; for there seems to be some justice between any
man and any other who can share in a system of law or be
a party to an agreement; therefore there can also be friendship with him in so far as he is a man. Therefore while in
tyrannies friendship and justice hardly exist, in democracies
they exist more fully; for where the citizens are equal they 10
have much in common.

Every form of friendship, then, involves association, as **12** has been said.[1] One might, however, mark off from the rest both the friendship of kindred and that of comrades. Those of fellow-citizens, fellow-tribesmen, fellow-voyagers, and the like are more like mere friendships of association;
15 for they seem to rest on a sort of compact. With them we might class the friendship of host and guest.

The friendship of kinsmen itself, while it seems to be of many kinds, appears to depend in every case on parental friendship ; for parents love their children as being a part of themselves, and children their parents as being something originating from them. Now (1) parents know their off-
20 spring better than their children know that they are their children, and (2) the originator feels his offspring to be his own more than the offspring do their begetter ; for the product belongs to the producer (e.g. a tooth or hair or anything else to him whose it is), but the producer does not belong to the product, or belongs in a less degree. And (3) the length of time produces the same result ; parents
25 love their children as soon as these are born, but children love their parents only after time has elapsed and they have acquired understanding or the power of discrimination by the senses. From these considerations it is also plain why mothers love more than fathers do. Parents, then, love their children as themselves (for their issue are by virtue of their separate existence a sort of other selves), while children love their parents as being born of them, and
30 brothers love each other as being born of the same parents; for their identity with them makes them identical with each other (which is the reason why people talk of ' the same blood ', ' the same stock ', and so on). They are, there-fore, in a sense the same thing, though in separate individuals. Two things that contribute greatly to friendship are a common upbringing and similarity of age; for ' two of an age take to each other ',[2] and people brought up together
35 tend to be comrades; whence the friendship of brothers is
1162ᵃ akin to that of comrades. And cousins and other kinsmen are bound up together by derivation from brothers, viz. by

---

[1] 1159ᵇ 29-32.　　　[2] Source unknown.

being derived from the same parents. They come to be closer together or farther apart by virtue of the nearness or distance of the original ancestor

The friendship of children to parents, and of men to gods, is a relation to them as to something good and 5 superior; for they have conferred the greatest benefits, since they are the causes of their being and of their nourishment, and of their education from their birth; and this kind of friendship possesses pleasantness and utility also, more than that of strangers, inasmuch as their life is lived more in common. The friendship of brothers has the characteristics found in that of comrades (and especially when these 10 are good), and in general between people who are like each other, inasmuch as they belong more to each other and start with a love for each other from their very birth, and inasmuch as those born of the same parents and brought up together and similarly educated are more akin in character; and the test of time has been applied most fully and convincingly in their case.

Between other kinsmen friendly relations are found in 15 due proportion. Between man and wife friendship seems to exist by nature; for man is naturally inclined to form couples—even more than to form cities, inasmuch as the household is earlier and more necessary than the city, and reproduction is more common to man with the animals. With the other animals the union extends only to this point, but human beings live together not only for the sake 20 of reproduction but also for the various purposes of life; for from the start the functions are divided, and those of man and woman are different; so they help each other by throwing their peculiar gifts into the common stock. It is for these reasons that both utility and pleasure seem to be 25 found in this kind of friendship. But this friendship may be based also on virtue, if the parties are good; for each has its own virtue and they will delight in the fact. And children seem to be a bond of union (which is the reason why childless people part more easily); for children are a good common to both and what is common holds them together.

How man and wife and in general friend and friend ought

30 mutually to behave seems to be the same question as how it is just for them to behave; for a man does not seem to have the same duties to a friend, a stranger, a comrade, and a schoolfellow.

There are three kinds of friendship, as we said at the 13 35 outset of our inquiry,[1] and in respect of each some are friends on an equality and others by virtue of a superiority (for not only can equally good men become friends but 1162ᵇ a better man can make friends with a worse, and similarly in friendships of pleasure or utility the friends may be equal or unequal in the benefits they confer). This being so, equals must effect the required equalization on a basis of equality in love and in all other respects, while unequals must render what is in proportion to their superiority or inferiority.

5 Complaints and reproaches arise either only or chiefly in the friendship of utility, and this is only to be expected. For those who are friends on the ground of virtue are anxious to do well by each other (since that is a mark of virtue and of friendship), and between men who are emulating each other in this there cannot be complaints or quarrels; no one is offended by a man who loves him and 10 does well by him—if he is a person of nice feeling he takes his revenge by doing well by the other. And the man who excels the other in the services he renders will not complain of his friend, since he gets what he aims at; for each man desires what is good. Nor do complaints arise much even in friendships of pleasure; for both get at the same time what they desire, if they enjoy spending their time together; and even a man who complained of another 15 for *not* affording him pleasure would seem ridiculous, since it is in his power not to spend his days with him.

But the friendship of utility is full of complaints; for as they use each other for their own interests they always want to get the better of the bargain, and think they have got less than they should, and blame their partners because they do not get all they ' want and deserve '; and those who 20 do well by others cannot help them as much as those whom they benefit want.

[1] 1156ᵃ 7.

Now it seems that, as justice is of two kinds, one un-written and the other legal, one kind of friendship of utility is moral and the other legal. And so complaints arise most of all when men do not dissolve the relation in the spirit of the same type of friendship in which they contracted it. The *legal* type is that which is on fixed terms; its purely 25 commercial variety is on the basis of immediate payment, while the more liberal variety allows time but stipulates for a definite *quid pro quo*. In this variety the debt is clear and not ambiguous, but in the postponement it contains an ele-ment of friendliness; and so some states do not allow suits arising out of such agreements, but think men who 30 have bargained on a basis of credit ought to accept the consequences. The *moral* type is not on fixed terms; it makes a gift, or does whatever it does, as to a friend; but one expects to receive as much or more, as having not given but lent; and if a man is worse off when the relation is dissolved than he was when it was contracted he will com-plain. This happens because all or most men, while they 35 wish for what is noble, choose what is advantageous; now it is noble to do well by another without a view to repayment, but it is the receiving of benefits that is advantageous.

Therefore if we can we should return the equivalent of **1163**^a what we have received (for we must not make a man our friend against his will; we must recognize that we were mistaken at the first and took a benefit from a person we should not have taken it from—since it was not from a friend, nor from one who did it just for the sake of acting so—and we must settle up just as if we had been benefited 5 on fixed terms). Indeed, one would agree to repay [1] if one could (if one could not, even the giver would not have expected one to do so); therefore if it is possible we must repay. But at the outset we must consider the man by whom we are being benefited and on what terms he is acting, in order that we may accept the benefit on these terms, or else decline it.

---

[1] It seems possible to keep the MS. reading, and suppose Aristotle to mean that in such a case, though we made no promise when we got the service, we should be willing, if we were asked, to promise to repay if we could.

10   It is disputable whether we ought to measure a service by its utility to the receiver and make the return with a view to that, or by the benevolence of the giver. For those who have received say they have received from their benefactors what meant little to the latter and what they might have got from others—minimizing the service; while the givers, on the contrary, say it was the biggest thing they 15 had, and what could not have been got from others, and that it was given in times of danger or similar need. Now if the friendship is one that aims at *utility*, surely the advantage to the receiver is the measure. For it is he that asks for the service, and the other man helps him on the assumption that he will receive the equivalent; so the assistance has been precisely as great as the advantage to 20 the receiver, and therefore he must return as much as he has received, or even more (for that would be nobler). In friendships based on *virtue* on the other hand, complaints do not arise, but the purpose of the doer is a sort of measure; for in purpose lies the essential element of virtue and character.

Differences arise also in friendships based on superiority; 14 25 for each expects to get more out of them, but when this happens the friendship is dissolved. Not only does the better man think he ought to get more, since more should be assigned to a good man, but the more useful similarly expects this; they say a useless man should not get as much as they should, since it becomes an act of public service and not a friendship if the proceeds of the friendship 30 do not answer to the worth of the benefits conferred. For they think that, as in a commercial partnership those who put more in get more out, so it should be in friendship. But the man who is in a state of need and inferiority makes the opposite claim; they think it is the part of a good friend to help those who are in need; what, they say, is the 35 use of being the friend of a good man or a powerful man, if one is to get nothing out of it?

1163ᵇ   At all events it seems that each party is justified in his claim, and that each should get more out of the friendship than the other—not more of the same thing, however, but the superior more honour and the inferior more gain; for honour is the prize of virtue and of beneficence, while gain is the assistance required by inferiority.

It seems to be so in constitutional arrangements also.; 5 the man who contributes nothing good to the common stock is not honoured; for what belongs to the public is given to the man who benefits the public, and honour does belong to the public. It is not possible to get wealth from the common stock and at the same time honour. For no one puts up with the smaller share in *all* things; therefore 10 to the man who loses in wealth they assign honour and to the man who is willing to be paid, wealth, since the proportion to merit equalizes the parties and preserves the friendship, as we have said.[1]

This then is also the way in which we should associate with unequals; the man who is benefited in respect of wealth or virtue must give honour in return, repaying what he can. For friendship asks a man to do what he can, not what is proportional to the merits of the case; since that cannot always 15 be done, e. g. in honours paid to the gods or to parents; for no one could ever return to them the equivalent of what he gets, but the man who serves them to the utmost of his power is thought to be a good man.

This is why it would not seem open to a man to disown his father (though a father may disown his son); being 20 in debt, he should repay, but there is nothing by doing which a son will have done the equivalent of what he has received, so that he is always in debt. But creditors can remit a debt; and a father can therefore do so too. At the same time it is thought that presumably no one would repudiate a son who was not far gone in wickedness; for apart from the natural friendship of father and son it is human nature not to reject a son's assistance. But the son, if he *is* wicked, 25 will naturally avoid aiding his father, or not be zealous about it; for most people wish to get benefits, but avoid doing them, as a thing unprofitable.—So much for these questions.

[1] 1162^a 34–^b 4, cf. 1158^b 27, 1159^a 35–^b 3.

BOOK IX

IN all friendships between dissimilars it is, as we have **1** said,[1] proportion that equalizes the parties and preserves the friendship; e. g. in the political form of friendship the shoe-
35 maker gets a return for his shoes in proportion to his worth,
1164ᵃ and the weaver and all other craftsmen do the same. Now here a common measure has been provided in the form of money, and therefore everything is referred to this and measured by this; but in the friendship of lovers some-times the lover complains that his excess of love is not met by love in return (though perhaps there is nothing lovable
5 about him), while often the beloved complains that the lover who formerly promised everything now performs nothing. Such incidents happen when the lover loves the beloved for the sake of pleasure while the beloved loves the lover for the sake of utility, and they do not both possess the qualities expected of them. If these be the objects of the friendship it is dissolved when they do not get the things that formed
10 the motives of their love; for each did not love the other person himself but the qualities he had, and these were not enduring; that is why the friendships also are transient. But the love of characters, as has been said, endures because it is self-dependent.[2] Differences arise when what they get is something different and not what they desire; for it is like getting nothing at all when we do not get
15 what we aim at; compare the story of the person who made promises to a lyre-player, promising him the more, the better he sang, but in the morning, when the other demanded the fulfilment of his promises, said that he had given pleasure [3] for pleasure. Now if this had been what each wanted, all would have been well; but if the one wanted enjoyment but the other gain, and the one has

---

[1] This has not been said precisely of friendship between dissimilars, but cf. 1132ᵇ 31–33, 1158ᵇ 27, 1159ᵃ 35–ᵇ 3, 1162ᵃ 34–ᵇ 4, 1163ᵇ 11.
[2] 1156ᵇ 9–12.   [3] i. e. the pleasure of expectation.

what he wants while the other has not, the terms of the association will not have been properly fulfilled; for what 20 each in fact wants is what he attends to, and it is for the sake of that that he will give what he has.

But who is to fix the worth of the service; he who makes the sacrifice or he who has got the advantage? At any rate the other seems to leave it to him. This is what they say Protagoras used to do;[1] whenever he taught anything 25 whatsoever, he bade the learner assess the value of the knowledge, and accepted the amount so fixed. But in such matters some men approve of the saying 'let a man have his fixed reward'.[2]

Those who get the money first and then do none of the things they said they would, owing to the extravagance of their promises, naturally find themselves the objects of complaint; for they do not fulfil what they agreed to. The 30 sophists are perhaps compelled to do this because no one would give money for the things they *do* know. These people then, if they do not do what they have been paid for, are naturally made the objects of complaint.

But where there is *no* contract of service, those who give up something for the sake of the other party cannot (as we have said[3]) be complained of (for that is the nature of the 35 friendship of virtue), and the return to them must be made 1164ᵇ on the basis of their purpose (for it is purpose that is the characteristic thing in a friend and in virtue). And so too, it seems, should one make a return to those with whom one has studied philosophy; for their worth cannot be measured against money, and they can get no honour which will balance their services, but still it is perhaps enough, as it is 5 with the gods and with one's parents, to give them what one can.

If the gift was not of this sort, but was made with a view to a return, it is no doubt preferable that the return made should be one that seems fair to both parties, but if this cannot be achieved, it would seem not only necessary that the person who gets the first service should fix the reward,

---

[1] Cf. Pl. *Prot.* 328 B, C.   [2] Hes. *Op.* 370 Rzach.
[3] 1162ᵇ 6–13.

10 but also just; for if the other gets in return the equivalent of the advantage the beneficiary has received, or the price he would have paid for the pleasure, he will have got what is fair as from the other.

We see this happening too with things put up for sale, and in some places there are laws providing that no actions shall arise out of voluntary contracts, on the assumption that one should settle with a person to whom one has given 15 credit, in the spirit in which one bargained with him. The law holds that it is more just that the person to whom credit was given should fix the terms than that the person who gave credit should do so. For most things are not assessed at the same value by those who have them and those who want them; each class values highly what is its own and what it is offering; yet the return is made on the 20 terms fixed by the receiver. But no doubt the receiver should assess a thing not at what it seems worth when he has it, but at what he assessed it at before he had it.

A further problem is set by such questions as, whether **2** one should in all things give the preference to one's father and obey him, or whether when one is ill one should trust a doctor, and when one has to elect a general should elect 25 a man of military skill; and similarly whether one should render a service by preference to a friend or to a good man, and should show gratitude to a benefactor or oblige a friend, if one cannot do both.

All such questions are hard, are they not, to decide with precision? For they admit of many variations of all sorts in respect both of the magnitude of the service and of its 30 nobility and necessity. But that we should not give the preference in all things to the same person is plain enough; and we must for the most part return benefits rather than oblige friends, as we must pay back a loan to a creditor rather than make one to a friend. But perhaps even this is not always true; e. g. should a man who has been ransomed out of the hands of brigands ransom his ransomer in return, 35 whoever he may be (or pay him if he has not been captured **1165**[a] but demands payment), or should he ransom his father? It

would seem that he should ransom his father in preference
even to himself. As we have said,[1] then, generally the debt
should be paid, but if the gift is exceedingly noble or
exceedingly necessary, one should defer to these considerations. For sometimes it is not even fair to return the equi- 5
valent of what one has received, when the one man has
done a service to one whom he knows to be good, while the
other makes a return to one whom he believes to be bad.
For that matter, one should sometimes not lend in return
to one who has lent to oneself; for the one person lent to
a good man, expecting to recover his loan, while the other
has no hope of recovering from one who is believed to be
bad. Therefore if the facts really are so, the demand is not 10
fair; and if they are not, but people think they are, they would
be held to be doing nothing strange in refusing. As we
have often pointed out,[2] then, discussions about feelings and
actions have just as much definiteness as their subject-matter.

That we should not make the same return to every one,
nor give a father the preference in everything, as one does 15
not sacrifice everything to Zeus,[3] is plain enough; but since
we ought to render different things to parents, brothers,
comrades, and benefactors, we ought to render to each class
what is appropriate and becoming. And this is what people
seem in fact to do; to marriages they invite their kinsfolk;
for these have a part in the family and therefore in the
doings that affect the family; and at funerals also they 20
think that kinsfolk, before all others, should meet, for the
same reason. And it would be thought that in the matter
of food we should help our parents before all others, since
we owe our own nourishment to them, and it is more
honourable to help in this respect the authors of our being
even before ourselves; and honour too one should give to
one's parents as one does to the gods, but not any and
every honour; for that matter one should not give the same 25
honour to one's father and one's mother, nor again should
one give them the honour due to a philosopher or to a

---

[1] 1164ᵇ 31–1165ᵃ 2.
[2] 1094ᵇ 11–27, 1098ᵃ 26–29, 1103ᵇ 34–1104ᵃ 5.
[3] Cf. 1134ᵇ 18–24.

general, but the honour due to a father, or again to a mother.
To all older persons, too, one should give honour appropriate
to their age, by rising to receive them and finding seats for
them and so on ; while to comrades and brothers one should
30 allow freedom of speech and common use of all things.   To
kinsmen, too, and fellow-tribesmen and fellow-citizens and
to every other class one should always try to assign what is
appropriate, and to compare the claims of each class with
respect to nearness of relation and to virtue or usefulness.
The comparison is easier when the persons belong to the
same class, and more laborious when they are different.   Yet
35 we must not on *that* account shrink from the task, but decide
the question as best we can.

Another question that arises is whether friendships should **3**
or should not be broken off when the other party does not
1165ᵇ remain the same.   Perhaps we may say that there is nothing
strange in breaking off a friendship based on utility or
pleasure, when our friends no longer have these attributes.
For it was of these attributes that we were the friends ; and
when these have failed it is reasonable to love no longer.
5 But one might complain of another if, when he loved us for
our usefulness or pleasantness, he pretended to love us for
our character.   For, as we said at the outset,[1] most differences
arise between friends when they are not friends in the spirit
in which they think they are.   So when a man has deceived
himself and has thought he was being loved for his character,
when the other person was doing nothing of the kind, he
10 must blame himself ; but when he has been deceived by the
pretences of the other person, it is just that he should complain against his deceiver ; he will complain with more
justice than one does against people who counterfeit the
currency, inasmuch as the wrongdoing is concerned with
something more valuable.

But if one accepts another man as good, and he turns out
badly and is seen to do so, must one still love him?   Surely
it is impossible, since not everything can be loved, but only
15 what is good.   What is evil neither can nor should be loved ;

[1] 1162ᵇ 23–25.

for it is not one's duty to be a lover of evil, nor to become like what is bad; and we have said[1] that like is dear to like. Must the friendship, then, be forthwith broken off? Or is this not so in all cases, but only when one's friends are incurable in their wickedness? If they are capable of being reformed one should rather come to the assistance of their character or their property, inasmuch as this is better and more characteristic of friendship. But a man who breaks 20 off such a friendship would seem to be doing nothing strange; for it was not to a man of this sort that he was a friend; when his friend has changed, therefore, and he is unable to save him, he gives him up.

But if one friend remained the same while the other became better and far outstripped him in virtue, should the latter treat the former as a friend? Surely he cannot. When the interval is great this becomes most plain, e. g. in 25 the case of childish friendships; if one friend remained a child in intellect while the other became a fully developed man, how could they be friends when they neither approved of the same things nor delighted in and were pained by the same things? For not even with regard to each other will their tastes agree, and without this (as we saw[2]) they cannot be friends; for they cannot live together. But we have 30 discussed these matters.[3]

Should he, then, behave no otherwise towards him than he would if he had never been his friend? Surely he should keep a remembrance of their former intimacy, and as we think we ought to oblige friends rather than strangers, so to those who have been our friends we ought to make some 35 allowance for our former friendship, when the breach has not been due to excess of wickedness.

4   Friendly relations with one's neighbours, and the marks **1166ᵃ** by which friendships are defined, seem to have proceeded from a man's relations to himself. For (1) we define a friend as one who wishes and does what is good, or seems so, for the sake of his friend, or (2) as one who wishes his

---

[1] 1156ᵇ 19-21, 1159ᵇ 1.   [2] 1157ᵇ 22-24.
[3] Ib. 17-24, 1158ᵇ 33-35.

5 friend to exist and live, for his sake; which mothers do to their children, and friends do who have come into conflict. And (3) others define him as one who lives with and (4) has the same tastes as another, or (5) one who grieves and rejoices with his friend; and this too is found in mothers most of all. It is by some one of these characteristics that friendship too is defined.

10 Now each of these is true of the good man's relation to himself (and of all other men in so far as they think themselves good; virtue and the good man seem, as has been said,[1] to be the measure of every class of things). For[2] his opinions are harmonious, and he desires the same things with all his soul; and therefore[3] he wishes for himself what 15 is good and what seems so, and does it (for it is characteristic of the good man to work out the good), and does so for his own sake (for he does it for the sake of the intellectual element in him, which is thought to be the man himself); and[4] he wishes himself to live and be preserved, and especially the element by virtue of which he thinks. For existence is good to the virtuous man, and each man wishes 20 himself what is good, while no one chooses to possess the whole world if he has first to become some one else (for that matter, even now God possesses the good[5]); he wishes for this only on condition of being whatever he is; and the element that thinks would seem to be the individual man, or to be so more than any other element in him. And[6] such a man wishes to live with himself; for he does so with pleasure, since the memories of his past acts are delightful 25 and his hopes for the future are good, and therefore pleasant. His mind is well stored too with subjects of contemplation. And[7] he grieves and rejoices, more than any other, with himself; for the same thing is always painful, and the same thing always pleasant, and not one thing at one time and another at another; he has, so to speak, nothing to repent of.

---

[1] 1113ª 22–33, cf. 1099ª 13.   [2] (4) above.
[3] (1) above.   [4] (2) above.
[5] Sc. but as no one gains by God's now having the good, he would not gain if a new person which was no longer himself were to possess it. Cf. 1159ª 5–11.   [6] (3) above.   [7] (5) above.

Therefore, since each of these characteristics belongs to the good man in relation to himself, and he is related to 30 his friend as to himself (for his friend is another self), friendship too is thought to be one of these attributes, and those who have these attributes to be friends. Whether there is or is not friendship between a man and himself is a question we may dismiss for the present ;[1] there would seem to be friendship in so far as he is two or more, to 35 judge from the afore-mentioned attributes of friendship, and **1166ᵇ** from the fact that the extreme of friendship is likened to one's love for oneself.

But the attributes named seem to belong even to the majority of men, poor creatures though they may be. Are we to say then that in so far as they are satisfied with themselves and think they are good, they share in these attributes? Certainly no one who is thoroughly bad and 5 impious has these attributes, or even seems to do so. They hardly belong even to inferior people; for they[2] are at variance with themselves, and have appetites for some things and rational desires for others. This is true, for instance, of incontinent people; for they choose, instead of the things they themselves think good, things that are pleasant but hurtful; while others again, through cowardice 10 and laziness, shrink from doing what they think best for themselves. And[3] those who have done many terrible deeds and are hated for their wickedness even shrink from life and destroy themselves. And[4] wicked men seek for people with whom to spend their days, and shun themselves; for they remember many a grievous deed, and anticipate others 15 like them, when they are by themselves, but when they are with others they forget. And[5] having nothing lovable in them they have no feeling of love to themselves. Therefore[6] also such men do not rejoice or grieve with themselves; for their soul is rent by faction, and one element in it by reason of its wickedness grieves when it abstains from certain 20 acts, while the other part is pleased, and one draws them this way and the other that, as if they were pulling them in

---

[1] Cf. 1168ᵃ 28–1169ᵇ 2. 　　[2] (4) above. 　　[3] (2) above.
[4] (3) above. 　　　　　　　　[5] (1) above. 　　[6] (5) above.

pieces. If a man cannot at the same time be pained and pleased, at all events after a short time he is pained *because* he was pleased, and he could have wished that these things had not been pleasant to him ; for bad men are laden with repentance.

25   Therefore the bad man does not seem to be amicably disposed even to himself, because there is nothing in him to love ; so that if to be thus is the height of wretchedness, we should strain every nerve to avoid wickedness and should endeavour to be good ; for so and only so can one be either friendly to oneself or a friend to another.

30   Goodwill is a friendly sort of relation, but is not *identical* 5 with friendship ; for one may have goodwill both towards people whom one does not know, and without their knowing it, but not friendship. This has indeed been said already.[1] But goodwill is not even friendly feeling. For it does not involve intensity or desire, whereas these accompany friendly feeling ; and friendly feeling implies intimacy while goodwill 35 may arise of a sudden, as it does towards competitors in 1167ᵃ a contest ; we come to feel goodwill for them and to share in their wishes, but we would not *do* anything with them ; for, as we said, we feel goodwill suddenly and love them only superficially.

Goodwill seems, then, to be a beginning of friendship, as the pleasure of the eye is the beginning of love. For no one loves if he has not first been delighted by the form of the 5 beloved, but he who delights in the form of another does not, for all that, love him, but only does so when he also longs for him when absent and craves for his presence ; so too it is not possible for people to be friends if they have not come to feel goodwill for each other, but those who feel goodwill are not for all that friends ; for they only *wish* well to those for whom they feel goodwill, and would not do anything with them nor take trouble for them. 10 And so one might by an extension of the term friendship say that goodwill is inactive friendship, though when it is prolonged and reaches the point of intimacy it becomes

[1] 1155ᵇ 32-1156ᵃ 5.

friendship—not the friendship based on utility nor that based on pleasure; for goodwill too does not arise on those terms. The man who has received a benefit bestows goodwill in return for what has been done to him, but in doing so is only doing what is just; while he who wishes some 15 one to prosper because he hopes for enrichment through him seems to have goodwill not to him but rather to himself, just as a man is not a friend to another if he cherishes him for the sake of some use to be made of him. In general, goodwill arises on account of some excellence and worth, when one man seems to another beautiful or brave or something of the sort, as we pointed out in the 20 case of competitors in a contest.

6 Unanimity also seems to be a friendly relation. For this reason it is not identity of opinion; for that might occur even with people who do not know each other; nor do we say that people who have the same views on any and every subject are unanimous, e. g. those who agree about the heavenly bodies (for unanimity about these is 25 not a friendly relation), but we do say that a city is unanimous when men have the same opinion about what is to their interest, and choose the same actions, and do what they have resolved in common. It is about things to be done, therefore, that people are said to be unanimous, and, among these, about matters of consequence and in which it is possible for both or all parties to get what they want; e. g. a city is unanimous when all its citizens think 30 that the offices in it should be elective, or that they should form an alliance with Sparta, or that Pittacus should be their ruler—at a time when he himself was also willing to rule. But when each of two people wishes himself to have the thing in question, like the captains in the *Phoenissae*,[1] they are in a state of faction; for it is not unanimity when each of two parties thinks of the same thing, whatever that may be, but only when they think of the same thing in the 35 same hands, e. g. when both the common people and those of the better class wish the best men to rule; for thus 1167ᵇ

¹ Eteocles and Polynices (Eur. *Phoen.* 588 ff.).

and thus alone do all get what they aim at. Unanimity seems, then, to be political friendship, as indeed it is commonly said to be; for it is concerned with things that are to our interest and have an influence on our life.

5   Now such unanimity is found among good men; for they are unanimous both in themselves and with one another, being, so to say, of one mind (for the wishes of such men are constant and not at the mercy of opposing currents like a strait of the sea), and they wish for what is just and what is advantageous, and these are the objects of their common endeavour as well. But bad men cannot be unanimous except to a small extent, any more than they 10 can be friends, since they aim at getting more than their share of advantages, while in labour and public service they fall short of their share; and each man wishing for advantage to himself criticizes his neighbour and stands in his way; for if people do not watch it carefully the common weal is soon destroyed. The result is that they are in a state of 15 faction, putting compulsion on each other but unwilling themselves to do what is just.

Benefactors are thought to love those they have benefited, 7 more than those who have been well treated love those that have treated them well, and this is discussed as though it were paradoxical. Most people think it is because the latter are in the position of debtors and the former of 20 creditors; and therefore as, in the case of loans, debtors wish their creditors did not exist, while creditors actually take care of the safety of their debtors, so it is thought that benefactors wish the objects of their action to exist since they will then get their gratitude, while the beneficiaries 25 take no interest in making this return. Epicharmus would perhaps declare that they say this because they 'look at things on their bad side',[1] but it is quite like human nature; for most people are forgetful, and are more anxious to be well treated than to treat others well. But the cause would seem to be more deeply rooted in the nature of things; the case of those who have lent money is not even analogous.

[1] Fr. 146 Kaibel.

For they have no friendly feeling to their debtors, but only 30 a wish that they may be kept safe with a view to what is to be got from them; while those who have done a service to others feel friendship and love for those they have served even if these are not of any use to them and never will be. This is what happens with craftsmen too; every man loves his own handiwork better than he would be loved by it 35 if it came alive; and this happens perhaps most of all with 1168^a poets; for they have an excessive love for their own poems, doting on them as if they were their children. This is what the position of benefactors is like; for that which they have treated well is their handiwork, and therefore they love this more than the handiwork does its maker. The cause 5 of this is that existence is to all men a thing to be chosen and loved, and that we exist by virtue of activity (i. e. by living and acting), and that the handiwork *is* in a sense, the producer in activity; he loves his handiwork, therefore, because he loves existence. And this is rooted in the nature of things; for what he is in potentiality, his handiwork manifests in activity.

At the same time to the benefactor that is noble which depends on his action, so that he delights in the object of 10 his action, whereas to the patient there is nothing noble in the agent, but at most something advantageous, and this is less pleasant and lovable. What *is* pleasant is the activity of the present, the hope of the future, the memory of the past; but most pleasant is that which depends on activity, and similarly this is most lovable. Now for a man who 15 has made something his work remains (for the noble is lasting), but for the person acted on the utility passes away. And the memory of noble things is pleasant, but that of useful things is not likely to be pleasant, or is less so; though the reverse seems true of expectation.

Further, love is like activity, being loved like passivity; and loving and its concomitants are attributes of those who 20 are the more active.[1]

Again, all men love more what they have won by labour; e. g. those who have made their money love it more than

---

[1] I. e. benefactors.

those who have inherited it; and to be well treated seems to involve no labour, while to treat others well is a laborious task. These are the reasons, too, why mothers are fonder ²⁵ of their children than fathers; bringing them into the world costs them more pains, and they know better that the children are their own. This last point, too, would seem to apply to benefactors.

The question is also debated, whether a man should love **8** himself most, or some one else. People criticize those who love themselves most, and call them self-lovers, using this ³₀ as an epithet of disgrace, and a bad man seems to do everything for his own sake, and the more so the more wicked he is—and so men reproach him, for instance, with doing nothing of his own accord—while the good man acts for honour's sake, and the more so the better he is, and acts for his friend's sake, and sacrifices his own interest.

³⁵ But the facts clash with these arguments, and this is not **1168ᵇ** surprising. For men say that one ought to love best one's best friend, and a man's best friend is one who wishes well to the object of his wish for his sake, even if no one is to know of it; and these attributes are found most of all in a man's attitude towards himself, and so are all the other ⁵ attributes by which a friend is defined; for, as we have said,[1] it is from this relation that all the characteristics of friendship have extended to our neighbours. All the proverbs, too, agree with this, e. g. 'a single soul',[2] and 'what friends have is common property', and 'friendship is equality', and 'charity begins at home';[3] for all these marks will be found most in a man's relation to himself; he is his own best friend and therefore ought to love himself ¹₀ best. It is therefore a reasonable question, which of the two views we should follow; for both are plausible.

Perhaps we ought to mark off such arguments from each other and determine how far and in what respects each view is right. Now if we grasp the sense in which each school uses the phrase 'lover of self', the truth may become ¹⁵ evident. Those who use the term as one of reproach

[1] Ch. 4.   [2] Eur. *Or.* 1046.
[3] Lit. 'the knee is nearer than the shin'.

ascribe self-love to people who assign to themselves the greater share of wealth, honours, and bodily pleasures; for these are what most people desire, and busy themselves about as though they were the best of all things, which is the reason, too, why they become objects of competition. So those who are grasping with regard to these things gratify their appetites and in general their feelings and the 20 irrational element of the soul; and most men are of this nature (which is the reason why the epithet has come to be used as it is—it takes its meaning from the prevailing type of self-love, which is a bad one); it is just, therefore, that men who are lovers of self in this way are reproached for being so. That it is those who give themselves the preference in regard to objects of this sort that most people usually call lovers of self is plain; for if a man were always 25 anxious that he himself, above all things, should act justly, temperately, or in accordance with any other of the virtues, and in general were always to try to secure for himself the honourable course, no one will call such a man a lover of self or blame him.

But such a man would seem more than the other a lover of self; at all events he assigns to himself the things that are noblest and best, and gratifies the most authoritative 30 element in himself and in all things obeys this; and just as a city or any other systematic whole is most properly identified with the most authoritative element in it, so is a man; and therefore the man who loves this and gratifies it is most of all a lover of self. Besides, a man is said to have or not to have self-control according as his reason has or has not the control, on the assumption that this is the man himself; and the things men have done on 35 a rational principle are thought most properly their own 1169^a acts and voluntary acts. That this is the man himself, then, or is so more than anything else, is plain, and also that the good man loves most this part of him. Whence it follows that he is most truly a lover of self, of another type than that which is a matter of reproach, and as different from that as living according to a rational principle is from living as passion dictates, and desiring what is noble 5 from desiring what seems advantageous. Those, then, who busy themselves in an exceptional degree with noble actions all men approve and praise; and if *all* were to strive towards what is noble and strain every nerve to do the noblest deeds, everything would be as it should be for the common weal, and every one would secure for himself the goods that are greatest, since virtue is the greatest of goods.

Therefore the good man should be a lover of self (for he will both himself profit by doing noble acts, and will benefit his fellows), but the wicked man should not; for he will hurt both himself and his neighbours, following as he does evil passions. For the wicked man, what he does clashes with what he ought to do, but what the good man ought to do he does; for reason in each of its possessors chooses what is best for itself, and the good man obeys his reason. It is true of the good man too that he does many acts for the sake of his friends and his country, and if necessary dies for them; for he will throw away both wealth and honours and in general the goods that are objects of competition, gaining for himself nobility; since he would prefer a short period of intense pleasure to a long one of mild enjoyment, a twelvemonth of noble life to many years of humdrum existence, and one great and noble action to many trivial ones. Now those who die for others doubtless attain this result; it is therefore a great prize that they choose for themselves. They will throw away wealth too on condition that their friends will gain more; for while a man's friend gains wealth he himself achieves nobility; he is therefore assigning the greater good to himself. The same too is true of honour and office; all these things he will sacrifice to his friend; for this is noble and laudable for himself. Rightly then is he thought to be good, since he chooses nobility before all else. But he may even give up actions to his friend; it may be nobler to become the cause of his friend's acting than to act himself. In all the actions, therefore, that men are praised for, the good man is seen to assign to himself the greater share 1169ᵇ in what is noble. In this sense, then, as has been said, a man should be a lover of self; but in the sense in which most men are so, he ought not.

9   It is also disputed whether the happy man will need friends or not. It is said that those who are supremely happy and self-sufficient have no need of friends; for they 5 have the things that are good, and therefore being self-sufficient they need nothing further, while a friend, being another self, furnishes what a man cannot provide by his own effort; whence the saying 'when fortune is kind, what need of friends?'[1] But it seems strange, when one assigns all good things to the happy man, not to assign friends, who are thought the greatest of external goods. And if it is 10 more characteristic of a friend to do well by another than to be well done by, and to confer benefits is characteristic of the good man and of virtue, and it is nobler to do well by friends than by strangers, the good man will need people to do well by. This is why the question is asked whether we need friends more in prosperity or in adversity, on the 15 assumption that not only does a man in adversity need people to confer benefits on him, but also those who are prospering need people to do well by. Surely it is strange, too, to make the supremely happy man a solitary; for no one would choose the whole world on condition of being alone, since man is a political creature and one whose nature is to live with others. Therefore even the happy man lives with others; for he has the things that are by nature good. And plainly it is better to spend his 20 days with friends and good men than with strangers or any chance persons. Therefore the happy man needs friends.

  What then is it that the first school means, and in what respect is it right? Is it that most men identify friends with useful people? Of such friends indeed the supremely happy man will have no need, since he already has the things that are good; nor will he need those whom one 25 makes one's friends because of their pleasantness, or he will need them only to a small extent (for his life, being

---

[1] Eur. *Or.* 667.

pleasant, has no need of adventitious pleasure); and because he does not need *such* friends he is thought not to need friends.

But that is surely not true. For we have said at the outset [1] that happiness is an activity; and activity plainly comes into being and is not present at the start like a piece 30 of property. If (1) happiness lies in living and being active, and the good man's activity is virtuous and pleasant in itself, as we have said at the outset,[2] and (2) a thing's being one's own is one of the attributes that make it pleasant, and (3) we can contemplate our neighbours better 35 than ourselves and their actions better than our own, and if the actions of virtuous men who are their friends are 1170^a pleasant to good men (since these have both the attributes that are naturally pleasant [3]),—if this be so, the supremely happy man will need friends of this sort, since his purpose is to contemplate worthy actions and actions that are his own, and the actions of a good man who is his friend have both these qualities.

Further, men think that the happy man ought to live 5 pleasantly. Now if he were a solitary, life would be hard for him; for by oneself it is not easy to be continuously active; but with others and towards others it is easier. With others therefore his activity will be more continuous, and it is in itself pleasant, as it ought to be for the man who is supremely happy; for a good man *qua* good delights 10 in virtuous actions and is vexed at vicious ones, as a musical man enjoys beautiful tunes but is pained at bad ones. A certain training in virtue arises also from the company of the good, as Theognis has said before us.[4]

If we look deeper into the nature of things, a virtuous friend seems to be naturally desirable for a virtuous man. 15 For that which is good by nature, we have said,[5] is for the virtuous man good and pleasant in itself. Now life is defined in the case of animals by the power of perception, in that of man by the power of perception or thought; and

---

[1] 1098^a 16^b, 31–1099^a 7.   [2] 1099^a 14, 21.
[3] I. e. the attribute of goodness and that of being their own.
[4] Theog. 35.   [5] 1099^a 7–11, 1113^a 25- 33.

a power is defined by reference to the corresponding activity,
which is the essential thing; therefore life seems to be
essentially the act of perceiving or thinking. And life
is among the things that are good and pleasant in themselves, since it is determinate and the determinate is of the 20
nature of the good; and that which is good by nature is
also good for the virtuous man (which is the reason why
life seems pleasant to all men); but we must not apply this
to a wicked and corrupt life nor to a life spent in pain; for
such a life is indeterminate, as are its attributes. The nature
of pain will become plainer in what follows.[1] But if life 25
itself is good and pleasant (which it seems to be, from the
very fact that all men desire it, and particularly those who
are good and supremely happy; for to such men life is
most desirable, and their existence is the most supremely
happy); and if he who sees perceives that he sees, and he
who hears, that he hears, and he who walks, that he walks,
and in the case of all other activities similarly there is 30
something which perceives that we are active, so that if we
perceive, we perceive that we perceive, and if we think, that
we think; and if to perceive that we perceive or think is
to perceive that we exist (for existence was defined as
perceiving or thinking); and if perceiving that one lives 1170^b
is in itself one of the things that are pleasant (for life
is by nature good, and to perceive what is good present
in oneself is pleasant); and if life is desirable, and particularly so for good men, because to them existence is good
and pleasant (for they are pleased at the consciousness of
the presence in them of what is in itself good); and if as 5
the virtuous man is to himself, he is to his friend also (for
his friend is another self):—if all this be true, as his own
being is desirable for each man, so, or almost so, is that of
his friend. Now his being was seen to be desirable because
he perceived his own goodness, and such perception is
pleasant in itself. He needs, therefore, to be conscious of 10
the existence of his friend as well, and this will be realized
in their living together and sharing in discussion and
thought; for this is what living together would seem to

[1] x. 1–5.

mean in the case of man, and not, as in the case of cattle, feeding in the same place.

If, then, being is in itself desirable for the supremely happy
15 man (since it is by its nature good and pleasant), and that of his friend is very much the same, a friend will be one of the things that are desirable.　Now that which is desirable for him he must have, or he will be deficient in this respect. The man who is to be happy will therefore need virtuous friends.[1]

---

[1] The argument in 1170^a 14-^b 19 is admirably analysed by Prof. Burnet, whom I follow, with variations :—

Pro-syllogism A (1170^a 16–19) :
    Capacity is defined by reference to activity.
    Human life is defined by the capacity of perception or thought.
    ∴ Human life is defined by the activity of perception or thought.

Pro-syllogism B (^a 19–21) :
    The determinate is good by nature.
    Life is determinate.
    ∴ Life is good by nature.

Pro-syllogism C (implied) :
    What is good by nature is good and pleasant for the good man
        (^a 14-16, 21–22).
    Life is good by nature (conclusion of B).
    ∴ Life is good and pleasant for the good man.

Pro-syllogism D (implied) :
    Life is good and pleasant for the good man (conclusion of C).
    Perception and thought are life (conclusion of A).
    ∴ Perception and thought are good and pleasant for the good man.

Pro-syllogism E (^a 25–29) :
    What is desired by all men and particularly by the good and
        supremely happy man is good in itself.
    Life is so desired.
    ∴ Life is good in itself.

Lemma (^a 29–32) :
    Perception and thought are accompanied by consciousness of
        themselves.

Argument F (^a 32–^b 1) ;
    Perception and thought are life (conclusion of A).
    ∴ Consciousness of perception and thought is consciousness of life.

Argument G (^b 1–3) :
    Consciousness of having something good is pleasant.
    Life is good in itself (conclusion of B and E).
    ∴ Consciousness of life is pleasant.

Argument H (implied):
    Consciousness of life is pleasant (conclusion of G).
    Consciousness of perception and thought is consciousness of life
        (conclusion of F).
    ∴ Consciousness of perception and thought is pleasant.

Lemma (^b 3–5) :
    The existence of the good man is specially desirable because the
        activities of which he is conscious are good.

10   Should we, then, make as many friends as possible, or— 20
as in the case of hospitality it is thought to be suitable
advice, that one should be 'neither a man of many guests
nor a man with none¹'—will that apply to friendship
as well; should a man neither be friendless nor have an
excessive number of friends?

To friends made with a view to *utility* this saying would
seem thoroughly applicable; for to do services to many
people in return is a laborious task and life is not long 25
enough for its performance. Therefore friends in excess of
those who are sufficient for our own life are superfluous, and
hindrances to the noble life; so that we have no need
of them. Of friends made with a view to *pleasure*, also,
few are enough, as a little seasoning in food is enough.

But as regards *good* friends, should we have as many as
possible, or is there a limit to the number of one's friends, 30
as there is to the size of a city? You cannot make a city
of ten men, and if there are a hundred thousand it is a city no
longer. But the proper number is presumably not a single
number, but anything that falls between certain fixed points.
So for friends too there is a fixed number—perhaps 1171ᵃ
the largest number with whom one can live together (for
that, we found,² is thought to be very characteristic of
friendship); and that one cannot live with many people and
divide oneself up among them is plain. Further, they too
must be friends of one another, if they are all to spend their
days together; and it is a hard business for this condition to 5

Argument I (ᵇ 5-8):
    The good man is related to his friend as he is to himself (con-
        clusion of ch. 4).
    His own existence is desirable to him (conclusion of C).
    ∴ That of his friend is desirable to him.
Argument K (ᵇ 8-11):
    His own existence is desirable because of his consciousness of his
        good activities (stated in ᵇ 3-5).
    ∴ Consciousness of his friend's good activities is also desirable
        to him.
Summary (ᵇ 14-17).
Argument L (ᵇ 17-19):
    If a man is to be happy, he must have all that is desirable for him.
    Friends are desirable for a man (conclusion of I).
    ∴ If a man is to be happy, he must have friends.
¹ Hes. *Op.* 715 Rzach.   ² 1157ᵇ 19, 1158ᵃ 3, 10.

be fulfilled with a large number. It is found difficult, too, to rejoice and to grieve in an intimate way with many people, for it may likely happen that one has at once to be happy with one friend and to mourn with another. Presumably, then, it is well not to seek to have as many friends as possible, but as many as are enough for the purpose of living
10 together ; for it would seem actually impossible to be a great friend to many people. This is why one cannot love several people ; love is ideally a sort of excess of friendship, and that can only be felt towards one person ; therefore great friendship too can only be felt towards a few people. This seems to be confirmed in practice ; for we do not find many people who are friends in the comradely way of friendship, and the famous friendships of this sort are always
15 between two people. Those who have many friends and mix intimately with them all are thought to be no one's friend, except in the way proper to fellow-citizens, and such people are also called obsequious. In the way proper to fellow-citizens, indeed, it is possible to be the friend of many and yet not be obsequious but a genuinely good man ; but one cannot have with many people the friendship based on virtue and on the character of our friends themselves,
20 and we must be content if we find even a few such.

Do we need friends more in good fortune or in bad? 11 They are sought after in both ; for while men in adversity need help, in prosperity they need people to live with and to make the objects of their beneficence ; for they wish to do well by others. Friendship, then, is more necessary in bad fortune, and so it is useful friends that one wants in
25 this case ; but it is more noble in good fortune, and so we also seek for good men as our friends, since it is more desirable to confer benefits on these and to live with these. For the very presence of friends is pleasant both in good fortune and also in bad, since grief is lightened when friends
30 sorrow with us. Hence one might ask whether they share as it were our burden, or—without that happening—their presence by its pleasantness, and the thought of their grieving with us, make our pain less. Whether it is for

these reasons or for some other that our grief is lightened,
is a question that may be dismissed ; at all events what we
have described appears to take place.

But their presence seems to contain a mixture of various
factors.   The very seeing of one's friends is pleasant, espe- 35
cially if one is in adversity, and becomes a safeguard against 1171ᵇ
grief (for a friend tends to comfort us both by the sight of
him and by his words, if he is tactful, since he knows our
character and the things that please or pain us) ; but to see 5
him pained at our misfortunes is painful ; for every one
shuns being a cause of pain to his friends.   For this reason
people of a manly nature guard against making their friends
grieve with them, and, unless he be exceptionally insensible
to pain, such a man cannot stand the pain that ensues
for his friends, and in general does not admit fellow-mourners
because he is not himself given to mourning ; but women 10
and womanly men enjoy sympathisers in their grief, and
love them as friends and companions in sorrow.   But in all
things one obviously ought to imitate the better type of
person.

On the other hand, the presence of friends in our
prosperity implies both a pleasant passing of our time and
the pleasant thought of their pleasure at our own good
fortune.   For this cause it would seem that we ought to 15
summon our friends readily to share our good fortunes (for
the beneficent character is a noble one), but summon them
to our bad fortunes with hesitation ; for we ought to give
them as little a share as possible in our evils—whence the
saying ' enough is *my* misfortune '.[1]   We should summon
friends to us most of all when they are likely by suffering
a few inconveniences to do us a great service.

Conversely, it is fitting to go unasked and readily to the 20
aid of those in adversity (for it is characteristic of a friend
to render services, and especially to those who are in need
and have not demanded them ; such action is nobler
and pleasanter for both persons) ; but when our friends are
prosperous we should join readily in their activities (for
they need friends for these too), but be tardy in coming

[1] Fr. adesp. 76 Nauck².

forward to be the objects of their kindness; for it is not
25 noble to be keen to receive benefits. Still, we must no
doubt avoid getting the reputation of kill-joys by repulsing
them; for that sometimes happens.

The presence of friends, then, seems desirable in all
circumstances.

Does it not follow, then, that, as for lovers the sight of the **12**
30 beloved is the thing they love most, and they prefer this
sense to the others because on it love depends most for its
being and for its origin, so for friends the most desirable
thing is living together? For friendship is a partnership,
and as a man is to himself, so is he to his friend; now in his
own case the consciousness of his being is desirable, and so
35 therefore is the consciousness of his friend's being, and the
1172^a activity of this consciousness is produced when they live
together, so that it is natural that they aim at this. And
whatever existence means for each class of men, whatever it
is for whose sake they value life, in *that* they wish to occupy
themselves with their friends; and so some drink together,
others dice together, others join in athletic exercises and
5 hunting, or in the study of philosophy, each class spending
their days together in whatever they love most in life; for
since they wish to live with their friends, they do and share
in those things which give them the sense of living together.
Thus the friendship of bad men turns out an evil thing (for
10 because of their instability they unite in bad pursuits, and
besides they become evil by becoming like each other), while
the friendship of good men is good, being augmented by
their companionship; and they are thought to become better
too by their activities and by improving each other; for
from each other they take the mould of the characteristics
they approve—whence the saying 'noble deeds from noble
15 men'.[1]—So much, then, for friendship; our next task must
be to discuss pleasure.

[1] Theog. 35.

BOOK X

1 AFTER these matters we ought perhaps next to discuss
pleasure. For it is thought to be most intimately connected
with our human nature, which is the reason why in educating 20
the young we steer them by the rudders of pleasure and
pain; it is thought, too, that to enjoy the things we ought
and to hate the things we ought has the greatest bearing on
virtue of character. For these things extend right through
life, with a weight and power of their own in respect both
to virtue and to the happy life, since men choose what 25
is pleasant and avoid what is painful; and such things, it
will be thought, we should least of all omit to discuss,
especially since they admit of much dispute. For some[1]
say pleasure is the good, while others,[2] on the contrary, say
it is thoroughly bad—some no doubt being persuaded that
the facts are so, and others thinking it has a better effect on
our life to exhibit pleasure as a bad thing even if it is not; 30
for most people (they think) incline towards it and are the
slaves of their pleasures, for which reason they ought to
lead them in the opposite direction, since thus they
will reach the middle state. But surely this is not correct.
For arguments about matters concerned with feelings and
actions are less reliable than facts: and so when they clash 35
with the facts of perception they are despised, and discredit
the truth as well; if a man who runs down pleasure is once 1172^b
seen to be aiming at it, his inclining towards it is thought
to imply that it is all worthy of being aimed at; for most
people are not good at drawing distinctions. True arguments seem, then, most useful, not only with a view to
knowledge, but with a view to life also; for since they 5
harmonize with the facts they are believed, and so they
stimulate those who understand them to live according to

[1] The school of Eudoxus, cf. ^b 9. Aristippus is perhaps also
referred to.
[2] The school of Speusippus, cf. 1153^b 5.

them.—Enough of such questions; let us proceed to review
the opinions that have been expressed about pleasure.

Eudoxus thought pleasure was the good because he saw all 2
10 things, both rational and irrational, aiming at it, and because
in all things that which is the object of choice is what is excellent, and that which is most the object of choice the greatest
good; thus the fact that all things moved towards the same
object indicated that this was for all things the chief good (for
each thing, he argued, finds its own good, as it finds its own
nourishment); and that which is good for all things and at
15 which all aim was *the* good. His arguments were credited
more because of the excellence of his character than for their
own sake; he was thought to be remarkably self-controlled,
and therefore it was thought that he was not saying what he
did say as a friend of pleasure, but that the facts really were so.
He believed that the same conclusion followed no less plainly
from a study of the contrary of pleasure; pain was in itself
an object of aversion to all things, and therefore its
20 contrary must be similarly an object of choice. And again
that is most an object of choice which we choose not because
or for the sake of something else, and pleasure is admittedly
of this nature; for no one asks to what end he is pleased;
thus implying that pleasure is in itself an object of choice.
Further, he argued that pleasure when added to any good,
e. g. to just or temperate action, makes it more worthy
25 of choice, and that it is only by itself that the good can be
increased.

This argument seems to show it to be one of the goods,
and no more a good than any other; for every good is more
worthy of choice along with another good than taken alone.
And so it is by an argument of this kind that Plato[1] proves
the good *not* to be pleasure; he argues that the pleasant
30 life is more desirable with wisdom than without, and
that if the mixture is better, pleasure is not the good; for
the good cannot become more desirable by the addition
of anything to it. Now it is clear that nothing else, any
more than pleasure, can be the good if it is made more

[1] *Phil.* 60 B–E.

desirable by the addition of any of the things that are good
in themselves. What, then, is there that satisfies this
criterion, which at the same time we can participate in?
It is something of this sort that we are looking for.

Those who object that that at which all things aim is not 35
necessarily good are, we may surmise, talking nonsense. For
we say that that which every one thinks really is so ; and the 1173^a
man who attacks this belief will hardly have anything more
credible to maintain instead. If it is senseless creatures
that desire the things in question, there might be something
in what they say ; but if intelligent creatures do so as well,
what sense can there be in this view? But perhaps even
in inferior creatures there is some natural good stronger than
themselves which aims at their proper good.

Nor does the argument about the contrary of pleasure 5
seem to be correct. They say that if pain is an evil it does
not follow that pleasure is a good ; for evil is opposed to evil
and at the same time both are opposed to the neutral state—
which is correct enough but does not apply to the things
in question. For if both pleasure and pain belonged to 10
the class of evils they ought both to be objects of aversion,
while if they belonged to the class of neutrals neither should
be an object of aversion or they should both be equally so ;
but in fact people evidently avoid the one as evil and choose
the other as good ; that then must be the nature of the
opposition between them.

3   Nor again, if pleasure is not a quality, does it follow that
it is not a good ; for the activities of virtue are not qualities
either, nor is happiness.

They say,[1] however, that the good is determinate, while 15
pleasure is indeterminate, because it admits of degrees.
Now if it is from the feeling of pleasure that they judge
thus, the same will be true of justice and the other virtues,
in respect of which we plainly say that people of a certain
character are so more or less, and act more or less in accordance with these virtues ; for people may be more just 20
or brave, and it is possible also to act justly or temperately

---

[1] Ib. 24 E–25 A, 31 A.

more or less. But if their judgement is based on the various pleasures, surely they are not stating the real cause,[1] if in fact some pleasures are unmixed and others mixed. Again, just as health admits of degrees without being 25 indeterminate, why should not pleasure? The same proportion is not found in all things, nor a single proportion always in the same thing, but it may be relaxed and yet persist up to a point, and it may differ in degree. The case of pleasure also may therefore be of this kind.

Again, they assume [2] that the good is perfect while move-30 ments and comings into being are imperfect, and try to exhibit pleasure as being a movement and a coming into being. But they do not seem to be right even in saying that it is a movement. For speed and slowness are thought to be proper to every movement, and if a movement, e. g. that of the heavens, has not speed or slowness in itself, it has it in relation to something else; but of pleasure neither of these things is true. For while we may *become* pleased quickly as **1173ᵇ** we may become angry quickly, we cannot *be* pleased quickly, not even in relation to some one else, while we *can* walk, or grow, or the like, quickly. While, then, we can change quickly or slowly into a state of pleasure, we cannot quickly exhibit the activity of pleasure, i. e. be pleased. Again, how can it be a coming into being? It is not thought that any chance thing can come out of any chance thing, 5 but that a thing is dissolved into that out of which it comes into being; and pain would be the destruction of that of which pleasure is the coming into being.

They say, too,[3] that pain is the lack of that which is according to nature, and pleasure is replenishment. But these experiences are bodily. If then pleasure is replenishment with that which is according to nature, that which feels pleasure will be that in which the replenishment takes 10 place, i. e. the body; but that is not thought to be the case; therefore the replenishment is not pleasure, though one would be pleased when replenishment was taking place,

---

[1] *Sc.*, of the badness of (some) pleasures.   [2] Pl. *Phil.* 53 C–54 D.
[3] Ib. 31 E–32 B, 42 C D.

just as one would be pained if one was being operated on.[1]
This opinion seems to be based on the pains and pleasures
connected with nutrition; on the fact that when people
have been short of food and have felt pain beforehand they
are pleased by the replenishment. But this does not happen 15
with all pleasures; for the pleasures of learning and, among
the sensuous pleasures, those of smell, and also many
sounds and sights, and memories and hopes, do not
presuppose pain. Of what then will these be the coming
into being? There has not been lack of anything of which
they could be the supplying anew.

In reply to those who bring forward the disgraceful 20
pleasures one may say that these are not pleasant; if things
are pleasant to people of vicious constitution, we must
not suppose that they are also pleasant to others than these,
just as we do not reason so about the things that are
wholesome or sweet or bitter to sick people, or ascribe
whiteness to the things that seem white to those suffering
from a disease of the eye. Or one might answer thus— 25
that the pleasures are desirable, but not from *these* sources,
as wealth is desirable, but not as the reward of betrayal, and
health, but not at the cost of eating anything and everything. Or perhaps pleasures differ in kind; for those derived
from noble sources are different from those derived from
base sources, and one cannot get the pleasure of the just
man without being just, nor that of the musical man without 30
being musical, and so on.

The fact, too, that a friend is different from a flatterer
seems to make it plain that pleasure is not a good or that
pleasures are different in kind; for the one is thought to
consort with us with a view to the good, the other with
a view to our pleasure, and the one is reproached for his
conduct while the other is praised on the ground that he
consorts with us for different ends. And no one would 1174[a]
choose to live with the intellect of a child throughout his
life, however much he were to be pleased at the things that
children are pleased at, nor to get enjoyment by doing

---

[1] The point being that the being replenished no more *is* pleasure
than the being operated on *is* pain. For the instance, cf. Pl. *Tim.* 65 B.

some most disgraceful deed, though he were never to feel any
pain in consequence.   And there are many things we should
5 be keen about even if they brought no pleasure, e.g. seeing,
remembering, knowing, possessing the virtues.   If pleasures
necessarily do accompany these, that makes no odds; we
should choose these even if no pleasure resulted.   It seems
to be clear, then, that neither is pleasure the good nor is all
pleasure desirable, and that some pleasures *are* desirable in
10 themselves, differing in kind or in their sources from the
others.   So much for the things that are said about pleasure
and pain.

What pleasure is, or what kind of thing it is, will become 4
plainer if we take up the question again from the beginning.
15 Seeing seems to be at any moment complete, for it does
not lack anything which coming into being later will complete its form; and pleasure also seems to be of this nature.
For it is a whole, and at no time can one find a pleasure
whose form will be completed if the pleasure lasts longer.
For this reason, too, it is not a movement.   For every
movement (e.g. that of building) takes time and is for the
20 sake of an end, and is complete when it has made what it
aims at.   It is complete, therefore, only in the whole time
or at that final moment.   In their parts and during the
time they occupy, all movements are incomplete, and are
different in kind from the whole movement and from each
other.   For the fitting together of the stones is different
from the fluting of the column, and these are both different
from the making of the temple; and the making of the
25 temple is complete (for it lacks nothing with a view to the
end proposed), but the making of the base or of the triglyph
is incomplete; for each is the making of only a part.   They
differ in kind, then, and it is not possible to find at any
and every time a movement complete in form, but if at all,
only in the whole time.   So, too, in the case of walking and
all other movements.   For if locomotion is a movement
30 from here to there, it, too, has differences in kind—flying,
walking, leaping, and so on.   And not only so, but in
walking itself there are such differences; for the whence

and whither are not the same in the whole racecourse and
in a part of it, nor in one part and in another, nor is it the
same thing to traverse this line and that; for one traverses 1174^b
not only a line but one which is in a place, and this one is in
a different place from that. We have discussed movement
with precision in another work,[1] but it seems that it is not
complete at any and every time, but that the many movements are incomplete and different in kind, since the whence
and whither give them their form. But of pleasure the 5
form is complete at any and every time. Plainly, then,
pleasure and movement must be different from each other,
and pleasure must be one of the things that are whole and
complete. This would seem to be the case, too, from the
fact that it is not possible to move otherwise than in time,
but it *is* possible to be pleased; for that which takes place
in a moment is a whole.

From these considerations it is clear, too, that these
thinkers are not right in saying there is a movement or
a coming into being *of* pleasure.[2] For these cannot be 10
ascribed to all things, but only to those that are divisible
and not wholes; there is no coming into being of seeing nor
of a point nor of a unit, nor is any of these a movement
or coming into being; therefore there is no movement
or coming into being of pleasure either; for it is a whole.

Since every sense is active in relation to its object, and 15
a sense which is in good condition acts perfectly in relation
to the most beautiful of its objects (for perfect activity
seems to be ideally of this nature; whether we say that
it is active, or the organ in which it resides, may be assumed
to be immaterial), it follows that in the case of each sense
the best activity is that of the best-conditioned organ in
relation to the finest of its objects. And this activity will
be the most complete and pleasant. For, while there is 20
pleasure in respect of any sense, and in respect of thought
and contemplation no less, the most complete is pleasantest,
and that of a well-conditioned organ in relation to the
worthiest of its objects is the most complete; and the

---

[1] *Phys.* vi–viii.
[2] Reading τῆς ἡδονῆς in l. 10 with Ramsauer.

pleasure completes the activity. But the pleasure does not complete it in the same way as the combination of 25 object and sense, both good, just as health and the doctor are not in the same way the cause of a man's being healthy. (That pleasure is produced in respect to each sense is plain; for we speak of sights and sounds as pleasant. It is also plain that it arises most of all when both the sense is at its best and it is active in reference to an object which corresponds; when both object and 30 perceiver are of the best there will always be pleasure, since the requisite agent and patient are both present.) Pleasure completes the activity not as the corresponding permanent state does, by its immanence, but as an end which supervenes as the bloom of youth does on those in the flower of their age. So long, then, as both the intelligible or sensible object and the discriminating or contemplative faculty are as they should be, the pleasure will be **1175^a** involved in the activity; for when both the passive and the active factor are unchanged and are related to each other in the same way, the same result naturally follows.

How, then, is it that no one is continuously pleased? Is it that we grow weary? Certainly all human things are 5 incapable of continuous activity. Therefore pleasure also is not continuous; for it accompanies activity. Some things delight us when they are new, but later do so less, for the same reason; for at first the mind is in a state of stimulation and intensely active about them, as people are with respect to their vision when they look hard at a thing, but afterwards our activity is not of this kind, but has grown relaxed; for which reason the pleasure also is dulled.

10 One might think that all men desire pleasure because they all aim at life; life is an activity, and each man is active about those things and with those faculties that he loves most; e. g. the musician is active with his hearing in reference to tunes, the student with his mind in reference to theoretical 15 questions, and so on in each case; now pleasure completes the activities, and therefore life, which they desire. It is with good reason, then, that they aim at pleasure too, since for every one it completes life, which is desirable.

But whether we choose life for the sake of pleasure or pleasure for the sake of life is a question we may dismiss for the present. For they seem to be bound up together and not to admit of separation, since without activity plea- 20 sure does not arise, and every activity is completed by the attendant pleasure.

5 For this reason pleasures seem, too, to differ in kind. For things different in kind are, we think, completed by different things (we see this to be true both of natural objects and of things produced by art, e.g. animals, trees, a painting, a sculpture, a house, an implement); and, 25 similarly, we think that activities differing in kind are completed by things differing in kind. Now the activities of thought differ from those of the senses, and both differ among themselves, in kind; so, therefore, do the pleasures that complete them.

This may be seen, too, from the fact that each of the pleasures is bound up with the activity it completes. For 30 an activity is intensified by its proper pleasure, since each class of things is better judged of and brought to precision by those who engage in the activity with pleasure; e. g. it is those who enjoy geometrical thinking that become geometers and grasp the various propositions better, and, similarly, those who are fond of music or of building, and so on, make progress in their proper function by enjoying 35 it; so¹ the pleasures intensify the activities, and what intensifies a thing is proper to it, but things different in kind have properties different in kind.

This will be even more apparent from the fact that **1175ᵇ** activities are hindered by pleasures arising from other sources. For people who are fond of playing the flute are incapable of attending to arguments if they over-hear some one playing the flute, since they enjoy flute-playing more than the activity in hand; so the pleasure 5 connected with flute-playing destroys the activity concerned with argument. This happens, similarly, in all other cases, when one is active about two things at once; the more

¹ Reading συναύξουσι δή in l. 36 with Par. 1417.

pleasant activity drives out the other, and if it is much
more pleasant does so all the more, so that one even ceases
10 from the other. This is why when we enjoy anything very
much we do not throw ourselves into anything else, and do
one thing only when we are not much pleased by another ;
e. g. in the theatre the people who eat sweets do so
most when the actors are poor. Now since activities are
made precise and more enduring and better by their proper
15 pleasure, and injured by alien pleasures, evidently the two
kinds of pleasure are far apart. For alien pleasures do
pretty much what proper pains do, since activities are
destroyed by their proper pains ; e.g. if a man finds writing
or doing sums unpleasant and painful, he does not write, or
does not do sums, because the activity is painful. So an
20 activity suffers contrary effects from its proper pleasures
and pains, i. e. from those that supervene on it in virtue
of its own nature. And alien pleasures have been stated to
do much the same as pain ; they destroy the activity, only
not to the same degree.

Now since activities differ in respect of goodness and
25 badness, and some are worthy to be chosen, others to
be avoided, and others neutral, so, too, are the pleasures ;
for to each activity there is a proper pleasure. The
pleasure proper to a worthy activity is good and that
proper to an unworthy activity bad ; just as the appetites for noble objects are laudable, those for base objects
30 culpable. But the pleasures involved in activities are
more proper to them than the desires ; for the latter
are separated both in time and in nature, while the
former are close to the activities, and so hard to distinguish from them that it admits of dispute whether the
activity is not the same as the pleasure. (Still, pleasure
does not seem to *be* thought or perception—that would be
35 strange ; but because they are not found apart they
appear to some people the same.) As activities are different,
then, so are the corresponding pleasures. Now sight is
1176^{a} superior to touch in purity, and hearing and smell to taste ;
the pleasures, therefore, are similarly superior, and those of
thought superior to these, and within each of the two kinds
some are superior to others.

Each animal is thought to have a proper pleasure, as it has a proper function; viz. that which corresponds to its activity. If we survey them species by species, too, this will be evident; horse, dog, and man have different pleasures, as Heraclitus says 'asses would prefer sweepings to gold';[1] for food is pleasanter than gold to asses. So the pleasures of creatures different in kind differ in kind, and it is plausible to suppose that those of a single species do not differ. But they vary to no small extent, in the case of men at least; the same things delight some people and pain others, and are painful and odious to some, and pleasant to and liked by others. This happens, too, in the case of sweet things; the same things do not seem sweet to a man in a fever and a healthy man—nor hot to a weak man and one in good condition. The same happens in other cases. But in all such matters that which appears to the good man is thought to be really so. If this is correct, as it seems to be, and virtue and the good man as such are the measure of each thing, those also will be pleasures which appear so to him, and those things pleasant which he enjoys. If the things he finds tiresome seem pleasant to some one, that is nothing surprising; for men may be ruined and spoilt in many ways; but the things are not pleasant, but only pleasant to these people and to people in this condition. Those which are admittedly disgraceful plainly should not be said to be pleasures, except to a perverted taste; but of those that are thought to be good what kind of pleasure or what pleasure should be said to be that proper to man? Is it not plain from the corresponding activities? The pleasures follow these. Whether, then, the perfect and supremely happy man has one or more activities, the pleasures that perfect these will be said in the strict sense to be pleasures proper to man, and the rest will be so in a secondary and fractional way, as are the activities.

6   Now that we have spoken of the virtues, the forms of friendship, and the varieties of pleasure, what remains is to discuss in outline the nature of happiness, since this is what

---

[1] Fr. 9 Diels.

we state the end of human nature to be. Our discussion
will be the more concise if we first sum up what we have
said already. We said,[1] then, that it is not a disposition;
for if it were it might belong to some one who was asleep
throughout his life, living the life of a plant, or, again, to
35 some one who was suffering the greatest misfortunes. If
1176ᵇ these implications are unacceptable, and we must rather
class happiness as an activity, as we have said before,[2]
and if some activities are necessary, and desirable for the
sake of something else, while others are so in themselves,
evidently happiness must be placed among those desirable
in themselves, not among those desirable for the sake of
5 something else; for happiness does not lack anything, but
is self-sufficient. Now those activities are desirable in
themselves from which nothing is sought beyond the
activity. And of this nature virtuous actions are thought
to be; for to do noble and good deeds is a thing desirable
for its own sake.

Pleasant amusements also are thought to be of this
nature; we choose them not for the sake of other
10 things; for we are injured rather than benefited by them,
since we are led to neglect our bodies and our property. But most of the people who are deemed happy
take refuge in such pastimes, which is the reason why those
who are ready-witted at them are highly esteemed at
the courts of tyrants; they make themselves pleasant
15 companions in the tyrants' favourite pursuits, and that
is the sort of man they want. Now these things are
thought to be of the nature of happiness because people in
despotic positions spend their leisure in them, but perhaps
such people prove nothing; for virtue and reason, from
which good activities flow, do not depend on despotic
position; nor, if these people, who have never tasted pure
20 and generous pleasure, take refuge in the bodily pleasures,
should these for that reason be thought more desirable;
for boys, too, think the things that are valued among
themselves are the best. It is to be expected, then, that,
as different things seem valuable to boys and to men, so they

[1] 1095ᵇ 31–1096ᵃ 2, 1098ᵇ 31–1099ᵃ 7.   [2] 1098ᵃ 5–7.

should to bad men and to good. Now, as we have often maintained,[1] those things are both valuable and pleasant 15 which are such to the good man; and to each man the activity in accordance with his own disposition is most desirable, and, therefore, to the good man that which is in accordance with virtue. Happiness, therefore, does not lie in amusement; it would, indeed, be strange if the end were amusement, and one were to take trouble and suffer hardship all one's life in order to amuse oneself. For, in a word, 30 everything that we choose we choose for the sake of something else—except happiness, which is an end. Now to exert oneself and work for the sake of amusement seems silly and utterly childish. But to amuse oneself in order that one may exert oneself, as Anacharsis[2] puts it, seems right; for amusement is a sort of relaxation, and we need relaxation because we cannot work continuously. Relaxation, 35 then, is not an end; for it is taken for the sake of activity.

The happy life is thought to be virtuous; now a virtuous 1177^a life requires exertion, and does not consist in amusement. And we say that serious things are better than laughable things and those connected with amusement, and that the activity of the better of any two things—whether it be two elements of our being or two men—is the more serious; but the activity of the better is *ipso facto* superior and 5 more of the nature of happiness. And any chance person —even a slave—can enjoy the bodily pleasures no less than the best man; but no one assigns to a slave a share in happiness—unless he assigns to him also a share in human life. For happiness does not lie in such occupations, but, as 10 we have said before,[3] in virtuous activities.

7 If happiness is activity in accordance with virtue, it is reasonable that it should be in accordance with the highest virtue; and this will be that of the best thing in us. Whether it be reason or something else that is this element which is thought to be our natural ruler and guide and to take

---

[1] 1099ª 13, 1113ª 22-33, 1166ª 12, 1170ª 14-16, 1176ª 15-22.
[2] A Scythian prince who was believed to have travelled in Greece, and to have been the author of many aphorisms.
[3] 1098ª 16, 1176ª 35-^b9.

15 thought of things noble and divine, whether it be itself also divine or only the most divine element in us, the activity of this in accordance with its proper virtue will be perfect happiness. That this activity is contemplative we have already said.[1]

Now this would seem to be in agreement both with what we said before[2] and with the truth. For, firstly, this 20 activity is the best (since not only is reason the best thing in us, but the objects of reason are the best of knowable objects); and, secondly, it is the most continuous, since we can contemplate truth more continuously than we can *do* anything. And we think happiness has pleasure mingled with it, but the activity of philosophic wisdom is admittedly 25 the pleasantest of virtuous activities; at all events the pursuit of it is thought to offer pleasures marvellous for their purity and their enduringness, and it is to be expected that those who know will pass their time more pleasantly than those who inquire. And the self-sufficiency that is spoken of must belong most to the contemplative activity. For while a philosopher, as well as a just man or one possessing any 30 other virtue, needs the necessaries of life, when they are sufficiently equipped with things of that sort the just man needs people towards whom and with whom he shall act justly, and the temperate man, the brave man, and each of the others is in the same case, but the philosopher, even when by himself, can contemplate truth, and the better the wiser he is; he can perhaps do so better if he has fellow-
1177ᵇ workers, but still he is the most self-sufficient. And this activity alone would seem to be loved for its own sake; for nothing arises from it apart from the contemplating, while from practical activities we gain more or less apart from the action. And happiness is thought to depend on 5 leisure; for we are busy that we may have leisure, and make war that we may live in peace. Now the activity of the practical virtues is exhibited in political or military affairs, but the actions concerned with these seem

---

[1] This has not been said, but cf. 1095ᵇ 14-1096ᵃ 5, 1141ᵃ 18-ᵇ 3, 1143ᵇ 33-1144ᵃ 6, 1145ᵃ 6-11.

[2] 1097ᵃ 25-ᵇ 21, 1099ᵃ 7-21, 1173ᵇ 15-19, 1174ᵇ 20-23, 1175ᵇ 36-1176ᵃ 3.

to be unleisurely. Warlike actions are completely so (for
no one chooses to be at war, or provokes war, for the
sake of being at war; any one would seem absolutely 10
murderous if he were to make enemies of his friends in
order to bring about battle and slaughter); but the action
of the statesman is also unleisurely, and—apart from the
political action itself—aims at despotic power and honours,
or at all events happiness, for him and his fellow citizens—
a happiness different from political action, and evidently 15
sought as being different. So if among virtuous actions
political and military actions are distinguished by nobility
and greatness, and these are unleisurely and aim at an end
and are not desirable for their own sake, but the activity of
reason, which is contemplative, seems both to be superior
in serious worth and to aim at no end beyond itself, and to 20
have its pleasure proper to itself (and this augments the
activity), and the self-sufficiency, leisureliness, unweariedness
(so far as this is possible for man), and all the other attributes ascribed to the supremely happy man are evidently
those connected with this activity, it follows that this will
be the complete happiness of man, if it be allowed a complete term of life (for none of the attributes of happiness is 25
*in*complete).

But such a life would be too high for man; for it is not
in so far as he is man that he will live so, but in so far as
something divine is present in him; and by so much as this
is superior to our composite nature is its activity superior to
that which is the exercise of the other kind of virtue. If
reason is divine, then, in comparison with man, the life accord- 30
ing to it is divine in comparison with human life. But we
must not follow those who advise us, being men, to think of
human things,[1] and, being mortal, of mortal things,[2] but
must, so far as we can, make ourselves immortal, and
strain every nerve to live in accordance with the best thing
in us; for even if it be small in bulk, much more does it in 1178^a
power and worth surpass everything. This would seem, too, to
be each man himself, since it is the authoritative and better

[1] Eur. fr. 1040 Nauck².
[2] Pind. *Isthm.* 5. 16 Schroeder; Soph. (*Tereus*) fr. 531 Nauck²;
Antiphanes fr. 289 Kock.

part of him. It would be strange, then, if he were to choose
not the life of his self but that of something else. And what
5 we said before [1] will apply now ; that which is proper to each
thing is by nature best and most pleasant for each thing ;
for man, therefore, the life according to reason is best and
pleasantest, since reason more than anything else *is* man.
This life therefore is also the happiest.

But in a secondary degree the life in accordance with the 8
other kind of virtue is happy ; for the activities in accordance
10 with this befit our human estate.   Just and brave acts, and
other virtuous acts, we do in relation to each other, observing
our respective duties with regard to contracts and services
and all manner of actions and with regard to passions ; and
all of these seem to be typically human.   Some of them seem
15 even to arise from the body, and virtue of character to be in
many ways bound up with the passions.   Practical wisdom,
too, is linked to virtue of character, and this to practical
wisdom, since the principles of practical wisdom are in accordance with the moral virtues and rightness in morals is in
accordance with practical wisdom.   Being connected with
the passions also, the moral virtues must belong to our com-
20 posite nature ; and the virtues of our composite nature are
human ; so, therefore, are the life and the happiness which
correspond to these.   The excellence of the reason is a thing
apart ; we must be content to say this much about it, for to
describe it precisely is a task greater than our purpose
requires.   It would seem, however, also to need external
25 equipment but little, or less than moral virtue does.   Grant
that both need the necessaries, and do so equally, even if
the statesman's work is the more concerned with the body
and things of that sort ; for there will be little difference
there ; but in what they need for the exercise of their
activities there will be much difference.   The liberal man
will need money for the doing of his liberal deeds, and the
30 just man too will need it for the returning of services (for
wishes are hard to discern, and even people who are not
just pretend to wish to act justly) ; and the brave man will

[1] 1169^b 33, 1176^b 26.

need power if he is to accomplish any of the acts that correspond to his virtue, and the temperate man will need opportunity; for how else is either he or any of the others to be recognized? It is debated, too, whether the will or the deed is more essential to virtue, which is assumed to involve 35 both; it is surely clear that its perfection involves both; but 1178^b for deeds many things are needed, and more, the greater and nobler the deeds are. But the man who is contemplating the truth needs no such thing, at least with a view to the exercise of his activity; indeed they are, one may say, even hindrances, at all events to his contemplation; but in so far 5 as he is a man and lives with a number of people, he chooses to do virtuous acts; he will therefore need such aids to living a human life.

But that perfect happiness is a contemplative activity will appear from the following consideration as well. We assume the gods to be above all other beings blessed and happy; but what sort of actions must we assign to them? Acts of justice? Will not the gods seem absurd if they make 10 contracts and return deposits, and so on? Acts of a brave man, then, confronting[1] dangers and running risks because it is noble to do so? Or liberal acts? To whom will they give? It will be strange if they are really to have money or anything of the kind. And what would their temperate 15 acts be? Is not such praise tasteless, since they have no bad appetites? If we were to run through them all, the circumstances of action would be found trivial and unworthy of gods. Still, every one supposes that they *live* and therefore that they are active; we cannot suppose them to sleep like Endymion. Now if you take away from a living being 20 action, and still more production, what is left but contemplation? Therefore the activity of God, which surpasses all others in blessedness, must be contemplative; and of human activities, therefore, that which is most akin to this must be most of the nature of happiness.

This is indicated, too, by the fact that the other animals have no share in happiness, being completely deprived of such activity. For while the whole life of the gods is 25

---

[1] Reading ἀνδρείου ὑπομένοντος in l. 12 as suggested by Bywater.

blessed, and that of men too in so far as some likeness of such activity belongs to them, none of the other animals is happy, since they in no way share in contemplation. Happiness extends, then, just so far as contemplation does, and those to whom contemplation more fully belongs are
30 more truly happy, not as a mere concomitant but in virtue of the contemplation; for this is in itself precious. Happiness, therefore, must be some form of contemplation.

But, being a man, one will also need external prosperity; for our nature is not self-sufficient for the purpose of con-
35 templation, but our body also must be healthy and must
1179ᵃ have food and other attention. Still, we must not think that the man who is to be happy will need many things or great things, merely because he cannot be supremely happy without external goods; for self-sufficiency and action do not involve excess, and we can do noble acts without ruling
5 earth and sea; for even with moderate advantages one can act virtuously (this is manifest enough; for private persons are thought to do worthy acts no less than despots—indeed even more); and it is enough that we should have so much as that; for the life of the man who is active in accordance with virtue will be happy. Solon, too, was perhaps sketching
10 well the happy man when he described him [1] as moderately furnished with externals but as having done (as Solon thought) the noblest acts, and lived temperately; for one can with but moderate possessions do what one ought. Anaxagoras also seems to have supposed the happy man not to be rich nor a despot, when he said [2] that he would not be surprised if the happy man were to seem to most
15 people a strange person; for they judge by externals, since these are all they perceive. The opinions of the wise seem, then, to harmonize with our arguments. But while even such things carry some conviction, the truth in practical matters is discerned from the facts of life; for these are the decisive
20 factor. We must therefore survey what we have already said, bringing it to the test of the facts of life, and if it harmonizes with the facts we must accept it, but if it clashes with them we must suppose it to be mere theory. Now he

---

[1] Hdt. i. 30,   [2] Diels, *Vors.* 46 A 30.

who exercises his reason and cultivates it seems to be both
in the best state of mind and most dear to the gods. For
if the gods have any care for human affairs, as they are
thought to have, it would be reasonable both that they 25
should delight in that which was best and most akin to
them (i. e. reason) and that they should reward those who
love and honour this most, as caring for the things that are
dear to them and acting both rightly and nobly. And that
all these attributes belong most of all to the philosopher is
manifest. He, therefore, is the dearest to the gods. And he 30
who is that will presumably be also the happiest; so that in
this way too the philosopher will more than any other be
happy.

9   If these matters and the virtues, and also friendship and
pleasure, have been dealt with sufficiently in outline, are we
to suppose that our programme has reached its end?
Surely, as the saying goes, where there are things to be 35
done the end is not to survey and recognize the various
things, but rather to do them; with regard to virtue, then, **1179ᵇ**
it is not enough to know, but we must try to have and use
it, or try any other way there may be of becoming good.
Now if arguments were in themselves enough to make men
good, they would justly, as Theognis says,[1] have won very 5
great rewards, and such rewards should have been provided;
but as things are, while they seem to have power to encourage and stimulate the generous-minded among our
youth, and to make a character which is gently born, and
a true lover of what is noble, ready to be possessed by
virtue, they are not able to encourage the many to nobility 10
and goodness. For these do not by nature obey the sense of
shame, but only fear, and do not abstain from bad acts
because of their baseness but through fear of punishment;
living by passion they pursue their own pleasures and the
means to them, and avoid the opposite pains, and have not 15
even a conception of what is noble and truly pleasant, since
they have never tasted it. What argument would remould
such people? It is hard, if not impossible, to remove by

---

[1] Theog. 432–434.

argument the traits that have long since been incorporated in the character; and perhaps we must be content if, when all the influences by which we are thought to become good are present, we get some tincture of virtue.

20   Now some think that we are made good by nature, others by habituation, others by teaching. Nature's part evidently does not depend on us,[1] but as a result of some divine causes is present in those who are truly fortunate; while argument and teaching, we may suspect, are not powerful with all men, but the soul of the student must first have been cultivated

25 by means of habits for noble joy and noble hatred, like earth which is to nourish the seed. For he who lives as passion directs will not hear argument that dissuades him, nor understand it if he does; and how can we persuade one in such a state to change his ways? And in general passion seems to yield not to argument but to force. The character, then, must somehow be there already with a kin-

30 ship to virtue, loving what is noble and hating what is base.

But it is difficult to get from youth up a right training for virtue if one has not been brought up under right laws; for to live temperately and hardily is not pleasant to most people, especially when they are young. For this reason

35 their nurture and occupations should be fixed by law; for they will not be painful when they have become customary.

1180^a But it is surely not enough that when they are young they should get the right nurture and attention; since they must, even when they are grown up, practise and be habituated to them, we shall need laws for this as well, and generally speaking to cover the whole of life; for most people obey necessity rather than argument, and punishments rather than the sense of what is noble.

5   This is why some think[2] that legislators ought to stimulate men to virtue and urge them forward by the motive of the noble, on the assumption that those who have been well advanced by the formation of habits will attend to such influences; and that punishments and penalties should be imposed on those who disobey and are of inferior nature,

---

[1] Omitting ὑπάρχει in l. 22, with Richards.
[2] Pl. *Laws* 722 D ff.

while the incurably bad should be completely banished.[1]
A good man (they think), since he lives with his mind
fixed on what is noble, will submit to argument, while a bad ᵗᵒ
man, whose desire is for pleasure, is corrected by pain like
a beast of burden. This is, too, why they say the pains
inflicted should be those that are most opposed to the
pleasures such men love.

However that may be, if (as we have said)[2] the man who
is to be good must be well trained and habituated, and go ₁₅
on to spend his time in worthy occupations and neither
willingly nor unwillingly do bad actions, and if this can be
brought about if men live in accordance with a sort of
reason and right order, provided this has force,—if this be
so, the paternal command indeed has not the required force
or compulsive power (nor in general has the command of ₂₀
one man, unless he be a king or something similar), but the
law *has* compulsive power, while it is at the same time a rule
proceeding from a sort of practical wisdom and reason. And
while people hate *men* who oppose their impulses, even if
they oppose them rightly, the law in its ordaining of what
is good is not burdensome.

In the Spartan state alone, or almost alone, the legislator ₂₅
seems to have paid attention to questions of nurture and
occupations ; in most states such matters have been neglected,
and each man lives as he pleases, Cyclops-fashion, ' to his
own wife and children dealing law '.[3] Now it is best that
there should be a public and proper care for such matters ;
but if they are neglected by the community it would seem ₃₀
right for each man to help his children and friends towards
virtue, and that they should have the power, or at least the
will, to do this.[4]

It would seem from what has been said that he can do
this better if he makes himself capable of legislating. For
public control is plainly effected by laws, and good control
by good laws ; whether written or unwritten would seem to ₃₅
make no difference, nor whether they are laws providing for 1180^b

---

[1] Pl. *Prot.* 325 A.   [2] 1179^b 31–1180^a 5.
[3] *Od.* ix. 114 f.
[4] Placing καὶ δρᾶν αὐτὸ δύνασθαι after συμβάλλεσθαι in l. 32, as
Bywater suggests.

the education of individuals or of groups—any more than it
does in the case of music or gymnastics and other such
pursuits. For as in cities laws and prevailing types of
character have force, so in households do the injunctions
5 and the habits of the father, and these have even more
because of the tie of blood and the benefits he confers; for
the children start with a natural affection and disposition to
obey. Further, private education has an advantage over
public, as private medical treatment has; for while in
general rest and abstinence from food are good for a man
10 in a fever, for a particular man they may not be; and a
boxer presumably does not prescribe the same style of
fighting to all his pupils. It would seem, then, that the
detail is worked out with more precision if the control is
private; for each person is more likely to get what suits
his case.

But the details can be best looked after, one by one, by
a doctor or gymnastic instructor or any one else who has
the general knowledge of what is good for every one or for
15 people of a certain kind (for the sciences both are said to
be, and are, concerned with what is universal); not but
what some particular detail may perhaps be well looked
after by an unscientific person, if he has studied accurately
in the light of experience what happens in each case, just
as some people seem to be their own best doctors, though
20 they could give no help to any one else. None the less, it
will perhaps be agreed that if a man does wish to become
master of an art or science he must go to the universal, and
come to know it as well as possible; for, as we have said, it
is with this that the sciences are concerned.

And surely he who wants to make men, whether many or
few, better by his care must try to become capable of legis-
25 lating, if it is through laws that we can become good. For
to get any one whatever—any one who is put before us—
into the right condition is not for the first chance comer;
if any one can do it, it is the man who knows, just as in
medicine and all other matters which give scope for care
and prudence.

Must we not, then, next examine whence or how one can

learn how to legislate? Is it, as in all other cases, from
statesmen? Certainly it was thought to be a part of 30
statesmanship.[1] Or is a difference apparent between statesmanship and the other sciences and arts? In the others
the same people are found offering to teach the arts and
practising them, e.g. doctors or painters; but while the 35
sophists profess to teach politics, it is practised not by any 1181[a]
of them but by the politicians, who would seem to do so by
dint of a certain skill and experience rather than of thought;
for they are not found either writing or speaking about such
matters (though it were a nobler occupation perhaps than
composing speeches for the law-courts and the assembly),
nor again are they found to have made statesmen of their 5
own sons or any other of their friends. But it was to be
expected that they should if they could; for there is nothing
better than such a skill that they could have left to their
cities, or could prefer to have for themselves, or, therefore,
for those dearest to them. Still, experience seems to contribute not a little; else they could not have become 10
politicians by familiarity with politics; and so it seems
that those who aim at knowing about the art of politics
need experience as well.

But those of the sophists who profess the art seem to be
very far from teaching it. For, to put the matter generally,
they do not even know what kind of thing it is nor what
kinds of things it is about; otherwise they would not have
classed it as identical with rhetoric or even inferior to it,[2]
nor have thought it easy to legislate by collecting the laws 15
that are thought well of;[3] they say it is possible to select
the best laws, as though even the selection did not demand
intelligence and as though right judgement were not the
greatest thing, as in matters of music. For while people
experienced in any department judge rightly the works
produced in it, and understand by what means or how 20
they are achieved, and what harmonizes with what, the
inexperienced must be content if they do not fail to see
whether the work has been well or ill made—as in the case

---

[1] 1141[b] 24.　　　　　　　　[2] Isoc. *Antid.* § 80.
[3] Ib. §§ 82, 83.

of painting. Now laws are as it were the 'works' of the
1181^b political art; how then can one learn from them to be a
legislator, or judge which are best? Even medical men do
not seem to be made by a study of text-books. Yet people
try, at any rate, to state not only the treatments, but also
how particular classes of people can be cured and should
5 be treated—distinguishing the various habits of body; but
while this seems useful to experienced people, to the inexperienced it is valueless. Surely, then, while collections of
laws, and of constitutions also, may be serviceable to those
who can study them and judge what is good or bad and
what enactments suit what circumstances, those who go
10 through such collections without a practised faculty will
not have right judgement (unless it be as a spontaneous
gift of nature), though they may perhaps become more
intelligent in such matters.

Now our predecessors have left the subject of legislation
to us unexamined; it is perhaps best, therefore, that we
should ourselves study it, and in general study the question
of the constitution, in order to complete to the best of our
15 ability our philosophy of human nature. First, then, if
anything has been said well in detail by earlier thinkers, let
us try to review it; then in the light of the constitutions
we have collected let us study what sorts of influence
preserve and destroy states, and what sorts preserve or
destroy the particular kinds of constitution, and to what
causes it is due that some are well and others ill administered.
20 When these have been studied we shall perhaps be more
likely to see with a comprehensive view, which constitution
is best, and how each must be ordered, and what laws
and customs it must use, if it is to be at its best.[1] Let us
make a beginning of our discussion.

[1] 1181^b 12–23 is a programme for the *Politics*, agreeing to a large
extent with the existing contents of that work.

INDEX

94ᵃ–99ᵇ = 1094ᵃ–1099ᵇ, 0ᵃ–81ᵇ = 1100ᵃ–1181ᵇ

Abstraction 42ᵃ 18.

Action, dist. making 40ᵃ 2ᵃ 17, ᵇ 4, 6; actions always particular 10ᵇ 6, cf. 41ᵇ 16; begetter of actions 13ᵇ 18; the faculties that control action and truth 39ᵃ 18; starting-points of a. 44ᵃ 35; in actions the final cause is the first principle 51ᵃ 16, cf. 39ᵃ 31; the circumstances of action, unworthy of the gods 78ᵇ 17.

Actualization, activity 4ᵃ 29, 68ᵃ 6–15; dist. products 94ᵃ 4; dist. state of mind, &c. 98ᵃ 6, ᵇ 33, 3ᵇ 21, 22, 22ᵇ 1, 52ᵇ 33, 76ᵇ 1, cf. 57ᵇ 6; of soul 98ᵃ 7, cf. ᵇ 15; the best activities 99ᵃ 29; virtuous activities 0ᵇ 10, 13, 13ᵇ 5, 77ᵃ 10, ᵇ 7, cf. 78ᵃ 10; activities give life its character 0ᵇ 33; activity, dist. potentiality 3ᵃ 27, cf. 70ᵃ 17; the end of every a. conformity to the state of character 15ᵇ 20; dist. process 53ᵃ 16; unimpeded a. 53ᵇ 10; a. of immobility 54ᵇ 27; a. comes into being, is not present from the beginning 69ᵇ 29; perfect a. 74ᵇ 16; activities differing in goodness and badness 75ᵇ 24; activities necessary and activities *per se* desirable 76ᵇ 2; activity of reason 77ᵇ 19; of God 78ᵇ 21.

Advantageous, expedient, &c. dist. noble, pleasant 4ᵇ 31, 68ᵃ 12; conj. good 26ᵇ 19, 27ᵃ 5, 40ᵃ 27; apparently a., dist. noble 69ᵃ 6; to be ignorant of the a. 10ᵇ 31, 41ᵇ 5; the common advantage 29ᵇ 15, 60ᵃ 14; a. to another 30ᵃ 5; one's own advantage 41ᵇ 5, 60ᵇ 2; things just by virtue of expediency 34ᵇ 35; to pursue utility 56ᵃ 27; present advantage 60ᵃ 22.

Aeschylus 11ᵃ 10.

Agamemnon 61ᵃ 14.

Agathon 39ᵇ 9, 40ᵃ 19.

Age, old 0ᵃ 7, 23, 21ᵇ 13.

Alcmaeon 10ᵃ 28.

Alope (Carcinus) 50ᵇ 10.

Ambition, ambitious 7ᵇ 24–8ᵃ 4, 17ᵇ 24, 25ᵇ 1–25, 59ᵃ 13.

Amusement, jest 8ᵃ 13, 23, 27ᵇ 34, 28ᵃ 14, 20, ᵇ 4, 8, 50ᵇ 17, 76ᵇ 9, 28–77ᵃ 11.

Anacharsis 76ᵇ 33.

Analysis 12ᵇ 23.

Anaxagoras 41ᵇ 3, 79ᵃ 13.

Anaxandrides 52ᵃ 22.

Anger, passion, rage 3ᵇ 18, 5ᵃ 8, ᵇ 22, 8ᵃ 4, 11ᵇ 11, 13, 16ᵇ 23–17ᵃ 4, 25ᵇ 26, 30, 26ᵃ 22, 30ᵃ 31, 35ᵇ 29, 38ᵃ 9, 47ᵃ 15, 49ᵃ 3, 26, ᵇ 20, 24; acts done in 11ᵃ 25–ᵇ 2, ᵇ 18, 35ᵇ 21; such acts not done of malice aforethought 35ᵇ 26; to restrain, digest 26ᵃ 16, 21, 24; states relative to 26ᵇ 10; incontinence with respect to 45ᵇ 20, 47ᵇ 34, 48ᵃ 11, ᵇ 13.

Antiphanes alluded to 77ᵇ 32?

Aphrodite 49ᵇ 15.

Appetite, lust 3ᵇ 18, 5ᵇ 21, 11ᵇ 11–17, 17ᵃ 1, 19ᵃ 4, ᵇ 5–12, 48ᵃ 21, 49ᵃ 25–ᵇ 31; acts due to 11ᵃ 25–ᵇ 2; a. and anger 11ᵃ 25, ᵇ 11, 47ᵃ 15; common and peculiar appetites 18ᵇ 8–16, 49ᵇ 5; natural appetite 18ᵇ 15, 19; strong and bad appetites 46ᵃ 2, 10, 78ᵇ 16; good appetites 46ᵃ 13; weak appetites ib. 15; for noble and base objects 48ᵃ 22, 75ᵇ 28; differences of bodily appetites 49ᵇ 26.

Appetitive element 2ᵇ 30, 19ᵇ 14, 15.

Argives 17ᵃ 26.

Aristippus alluded to 72ᵃ 27?

Aristocracy 31ᵃ 29, 60ᵃ 32, ᵇ 10, 32, 61ᵃ 23.

Aristotle, references to other works 8ᵇ 7 (*Rhet.* ii. 6, 9, 10?), 30ᵇ 28

(*Pol.* 1288^a 32–^{b} 2 ?)), 35^a 15
(*Pol.* ?), 39^b 27 (*An. Post.* 71^a 1),
ib. 32 (ib. ^{b} 9–23), 74^b 3 (*Phys.*
vi–viii).

Art 97^a 17, 33^a 14, 39^b 16, 40^a 7–
23, 30, 41^a 10; def. 40^a 20;
syn. inquiry 94^a 1; synon.
science ib. 7; dist. science
12^b 7, 40^b 2, 34; synon. precept
4^a 7; conj. virtue 3^a 32, ^{b} 8,
5^a 9, 22; dist. virtue 5^a 26–^{b} 5,
cf. 6^b 14; dist. practical wisdom
40^b 3, 22; dist. nature 99^b 23,
6^b 14, cf. 3^a 32, 75^a 24; dist.
chance 5^a 22, 40^a 18; conj. work
6^b 8; excellence in 40^b 22, 41^a
12; product of 52^b 19, 53^a 23;
no a. of any activity 53^a 25;
advances of the arts 98^a 24.
Association for exchange 32^b 31;
associations in the household
60^a 24–61^a 8; friendship of a.
61^b 14. Cf. *Society.*
Athenians 24^b 17.
Athlete 11^b 24, 16^b 13.

Barbarians 45^a 31, 49^a 11.
Bashful man 8^a 34.
Bias 30^a 1.
Black Sea 48^b 22.
Boaster, boastfulness 8^a 21, 22,
15^a 29, 27^a 13, 20–^{b} 32.
Bodily 28^b 14, 51^b 23, 73^b 9;
pleasures 4^b 5, 17^b 29 (cf. 33),
18^a 2, 48^a 5, 49^b 26, 51^a 12, ^{b} 35,
52^a 5 (cf. 47^b 25, 27), 53^a 32,
^{b} 33, 54^a 8, 10, 26, 29, 68^b 17,
76^b 20, 77^a 7; pains 50^a 24;
goods 54^a 15.
Body, opp. soul 1^b 33, 61^a 35;
opp. mind 17^b 30; vices of 14^a
23, 28.
Boor, boorishness 4^a 24, 8^a 26,
28^a 9, ^{b} 2, 51^b 13.
Brasidas 34^b 23.
Brave 2^b 28, 3^b 17, 4^b 8, 8^b 19, 25,
15^a 11–17^b 22, 29^b 19, 37^a 20,
44^b 5, 67^a 20, 77^a 32, 78^a 10, 32,
^{b} 12.
Brute, opp. man 50^a 8, 54^a 33;
wild beasts, lower animals,
brutes 16^b 25, 32, 41^a 27, 44^b 8,
52^b 20, 53^a 28, 31; a. b. has no
vice or virtue 45^a 25, cf. 39^a 20,
49^b 31.
Brutish 18^b 4, 49^a 6–20, ^{b} 29;
b. pleasures 18^a 25; b. states

45^a 25, 48^b 19, 24; the b. type
45^a 30; b. cowardice 49^a 8, cf. 6.
Brutishness, dist. vice, incontinence 45^a 17, 49^a 1, 50^a 1.
Buffoon, buffoonery 8^a 24, 25, 28^a
4–^{b} 1.

Calculative faculty 39^a 12, 14.
Calypso 9^a 31.
Cannibalism 48^b 22.
Carcinus 50^b 10.
Category 96^a 29, 32.
Celts 15^b 28.
Cercyon 50^b 10.
Chance, fortune 99^b 10–0^a 9, 0^b 22,
12^a 27, 20^b 17, 53^b 22; conj. art
5^a 23, 40^a 18; dist. nature,
necessity, reason 12^a 32; goods
of f. 53^b 18.
Character 95^a 7, 11^b 6, 21^a 26, ^{b} 6,
27^b 23, 39^a 1, 55^b 10, 65^b 6–19,
72^a 22, ^{b} 15, 78^a 16, 17, 80^b 5;
facts about 27^a 16; movements
of 28^a 11; each type of, present
by nature 44^b 4 (cf. 79^b 29);
essential element of 63^a 23;
incorporated in the 79^b 17; love
of characters 64^a 12.
Child 97^b 10, 99^b 3, 0^a 20, 10^a 6,
13^b 19, 19^b 6, 48^a 31, ^{b} 23, 49^a
14, ^{b} 10, 52^b 19, 53^a 28, 31, 58^b
15–22, 60^a 1, ^{b} 25, 61^b 18, 62^a
28, 64^a 5, 68^a 3, 80^a 31; conj.
chattel 34^b 10, 14; intellect of
a c. 74^a 2.
Choice, purpose, pursuit (προαίρεσις) 11^b 5–13^a 14, 39^a 3–^{b} 11;
conj. action 94^a 1, 97^a 21; conj.
knowledge 95^a 14; opp. capacity
27^b 14; opp. passion 34^a 20;
conj. calculation 49^b 34; c. and
motive 17^a 5; mistaken purpose
10^b 31; right c. 44^a 20, 45^a 4;
good p. 52^a 17; according to c.,
by c. 13^b 5, 34^a 2, 35^b 25, 36^a 31,
38^a 21; the virtues are modes of
c. or imply c. 6^a 3, 63^a 23, cf.
64^b 1, 78^a 35; state of character
concerned with c. 6^b 36, 39^a 23;
object of c. 12^a 14 (cf. 17), 13^a
4–10, ^{b} 4, 39^b 6; to stand by
one's c. 50^b 30, 51^a 30–34.
Citizen, citizenship 97^b 10, 99^b 31,
2^a 9, 3^b 3, 30^b 29, 60^a 2, 5, 65^a
31, 77^b 14; courage of citizen-
soldiers 16^a 17.
City, state 3^b 3, 23^a 2, 67^a 26, 30,

80^a 27, 81^a 7, ^{b} 18; dist. monarch 15^a 32; dist. household 62^a 19, 80^b 4; conj. systematic whole 68^b 31; state and individual 94^a 27–^{b} 11, 41^b 23–42^a 11, 79^a 33–81^b 23; to wrong the c. and not oneself 38^a 11; wisdom concerned with the c. 41^b 25; proper size of the c. 70^b 30.

Cleverness 44^a 23–^{b} 15, 52^a 11.

Comedy 28^a 22.

Community. v. *Society*.

Companions, comrades, friendship of 57^b 23, 61^a 25, ^{b} 12, 35, 62^a 10, 71^a 14.

Compulsion, actions due to 9^b 35.

Confidence 5^b 22, 7^a 33, 15^a 7. 17^a 29.

Constitution, form of government 3^b 6, 42^a 10, 60 ^{b} 20, 21, 61^a 10, 63^b 5, 81^b 7–20; the ancient constitutions 13^a 8; a share in the constitution 30^b 32; one c. the best everywhere 35^a 5; kinds of c. and deviation-forms 60^a 31; the name applied to the c. based on property qualification ib. 34; collections of constitutions 81^b 7, 17.

Contemplation, theoretical knowledge 3^b 26, 22^b 17, 74^b 21, 78^b 5–28.

Contemplative, conj. artistic 80^b 21; the c. life 95^b 19, 96^a 4; c. intellect 39^a 27; c. activity 77^a 18, 28, ^{b} 19, 78^b 7, 22.

Continence, continent 2^b 14, 28^b 34, 45^a 18, ^{b} 8–14, 46^a 10–17, ^{b} 10–18, 47^b 22, 48^a 11, 68^b 34; c. and endurance 50^a 9–^{b} 28; what sort of choice the continent man stands by 51^a 29–^{b} 22; c. intermediate between incontinence and insensibility 51^b 23–32; temperance called c. by virtue of likeness to it 51^b 32–52^a 6; c. above the average of human nature 52^a 25–27.

Contracts 64^b 13.

Corrective justice (ἐπανορθωτικόν) 32^a 18. Cf. *Rectificatory*.

Courage 4^a 18, ^{b} 1, 7^a 33, 8^b 32, 9^a 2, 9, 15^a 6–17^b 22; of citizen soldier 16^a 7–^{b} 3; of experience 16^b 3–23; of passion ib. 23–17^a 9; of hope 17^a 9–22; of ignorance ib. 22–27. Cf. *Brave*.

Coward, cowardice 3^b 17, 4^a 21, ^{b} 8, 7^b 4, 8^b 19, 25, 9^a 3, 10, 15^a 20, 23, ^{b} 34–16^a 14, 16^a 20, ^{b} 16, 19^a 21, 28, 30^a 18, 31, 38^a 17, 66^b 10.

Cretans 2^a 10.

Cyclops-fashion 80^a 28.

Death 15^a 11–^{b} 5, 16^b 20, 22, 17^b 7, 11, 28^b 13.

Debt 62^b 28, 65^b 3.

Deliberation 12^a 19–13^a 12, 39^a 12, ^{b} 7, 40^a 26, 41^b 9; excellence in 42^a 32–^{b} 33; def. of excellence in 42^b 32.

Delos 99^a 25.

Democracy, democrats 31^a 27, 60^b 17, 20, 60^a 6, ^{b} 9.

Demodocus 51^a 8.

Demonstration, scientific proof 94^b 27, 40^a 33, 41^a 2, 43^b 10, 13, 47^a 20; intuitive reason presupposed by demonstrations 43^b 1.

Desiderative reason 39^b 4.

Desire 94^a 21, 95^a 10, 7^b 29, 16^a 28, 19^b 7, 8, 25^b 7, 38^b 11, 39^a 18–^{b} 5, 49^b 4, 59^b 20, 66^b 33, 75^b 30; conj. sensation, reason 39^a 18; deliberate d. 13^a 11, 39^a 23; ratiocinative d. 39^b 5; right d. 39^a 24; desiring element 2^b 30.

Deviation-forms 60^a 30, 31, 36, 61^a 30.

Diomede 16^a 22, 36^b 10.

Disease 96^a 33, 14^a 26, 15^a 11, 17, ^{b} 1, 48^b 25, 49^a 9, ^{b} 29, 50^b 14, 33.

Distribution 31^a 25, ^{b} 8, 30; justice in 30^b 31, 31^b 10.

Distributive justice 31^a 10–^{b} 24, ^{b} 27, 32^b 24.

Doctor, physician 97^a 12, 2^a 21, 5^b 15, 12^b 13, 14^a 16, 27^b 20, 33^a 17, 37^a 17, 48^b 8, 64^b 24, 74^b 26, 80^b 14, 18.

Drunkenness 10^b 26, 13^b 31, 32, 14^a 27, 17^a 14, 47^a 14, ^{b} 7, 12, 51^a 4, 52^a 15, 54^b 10.

Education 4^b 13, 61^a 17, 72^a 20, 79^b 24; public, private e. 30^b 26, 80^b 8.

Effeminacy 45^a 35, 50^b 3.

Emotion. v. *Passion*.

Empedocles 47^a 20, ^{b} 12, 55^b 7.

End, opp. means 11^{b}26, 12^{b}12, 33, 13^{b}3, 45^{a}5; dist. actions 14^{b}21; conj. activities 53^{a}10; some ends are activities, others products 94^{a}4; final e. 97^{a}28; good e. 40^{a}29; supervenient e. 74^{b}33; the e. of action relative to the occasion 10^{a}13; to assume the e. 12^{b}15, 14^{b}24; ignorance of the e. 14^{b}4; the aiming at the e. ib. 6; the e. of every activity conformity to the state of character 15^{b}20; each thing defined by its e. ib. 22; the end of courage 17^{b}1; to reach the e. ib. 16; the e. = what is best 44^{a}32, cf. 94^{a}22; architect of the e. 52^{b}2.

Endurance 45^{a}36, ^{b}8, 15, 46^{b}12, 47^{b}22, 50^{a}14, 33, ^{b}1.

Endymion 78^{b}20.

Enjoyment, life of 95^{b}17.

Envious, envy 5^{b}22, 7^{a}11, 8^{b}1, 4, 15^{a}23.

Epicharmus 67^{b}25.

Equal, fair, opp. the more, the less 6^{a}27-34, 8^{b}15 (cf. 30), 53^{b}6; = the just 29^{a}34, 30^{b}9-33, 31^{a}11-24.

Equality 31^{a}21, 33^{b}4, 18, 58^{b}1, 28, 62^{a}35, ^{b}2; of ratios 31^{a}31; opp. proportion 32^{b}33; proportionate, opp. quantitative e. 58^{b}30; in ruling and being ruled 34^{b}15; friendship is e. 57^{b}36, 68^{b}8, cf. 59^{b}1.

Equity, honesty 21^{b}24, 37^{a}31-38^{a}3, 43^{a}20, 31.

Eudoxus 1^{b}27, 72^{b}9; alluded to 94^{a}2 ?, 72^{a}27.

Euripides 10^{a}28, 36^{a}11, 42^{a}2, 55^{b}2; cited or alluded to 11^{a}12, 29^{b}28, 54^{b}28, 67^{a}33, 68^{b}7, 69^{b}7, 77^{b}32.

Evenus 52^{a}31.

Evil, of the nature of the infinite 6^{b}29; destroys itself 26^{b}12.

Exchange 33^{a}2, 19-28, ^{b}11-26; voluntary e. 32^{b}13; associations for ib. 32.

Experience 15^{b}4, 16^{b}3, 9, 42^{b}15-19, 43^{b}14, 58^{a}14, 80^{b}18, 81^{a}10, 20; conj. time 3^{a}16, 42^{a}16; dist. thought 81^{a}2.

Experienced people 41^{b}18, 81^{a}19, ^{b}5; conj. older people 43^{b}11.

Eye of the soul 44^{a}30, cf. 43^{b}14.

Fact, dist. reason 95^{b}6, cf. 98^{b}1; dist. argument 68^{a}35, 72^{a}35, ^{b}6, 79^{a}21.

Faculty, capacity, power, opp. things prized, things praised 1^{b}12; syn. part 2^{b}5; dist. activity 3^{a}26, 53^{b}25, 68^{a}7; defined by reference to activity 70^{a}17; dist. passion, state of character 5^{b}20-6^{a}12; dist. state of character 27^{b}14, 29^{a}12, 44^{a}29; syn. disposition 43^{a}28; opp. purpose 27^{b}14; happiness not a f. 1^{b}12; f. of soul 2^{a}34.

Father 2^{b}32 (cf. 3^{a}3), 35^{a}29, 48^{b}1, 49^{b}8, 13, 58^{b}12, 16, 60^{a}6, ^{b}24-28, 61^{a}19, 63^{b}19, 22, 65^{a}1-26; justice of 34^{a}9; friendship of 61^{a}15.

Fear 5^{b}22, 10^{a}4, 16^{a}31, 21^{b}28, 28^{b}11, 12, 35^{b}5, 79^{b}11; def. 15^{a}9; and confidence 7^{a}33, 15^{a}7, 17^{a}29.

Fearless, fearlessness 7^{b}1, 15^{a}16, 19, ^{b}24, 17^{a}19.

Feeling. v. Passion.

Flatterer 8^{a}29, 21^{b}7, 25^{a}2, 27^{a}10, 59^{a}15, 73^{b}32.

Fortune, good, prosperity 98^{b}26, 99^{b}8, 24^{a}14, ^{b}19, 53^{b}22, 24, 55^{a}8, 69^{b}14, 71^{a}21-^{b}28, 79^{b}23; goods of f. 29^{b}3.

Friend 26^{b}21, 49^{b}29; conj. fellow-citizen 97^{b}10; dist. flatterer 73^{b}32; what is done through friends is done by ourselves 12^{b}28.

Friendliness, friendly 8^{a}27, 28, cf. 26^{b}11-27^{a}12.

Friendly feeling, love (φιλία, φίλησις) 5^{b}22, 55^{b}27, 56^{a}6, 57^{b}28, 58^{b}27, 66^{b}32, 67^{b}30, 68^{a}19.

Friendship 26^{b}20, 22, 55^{a}3-72^{a}15; why discussed 55^{a}3-31; a virtue or implies virtue 55^{a}3; problems about 55^{a}32-^{b}16; whether between likes or unlikes 55^{a}32-^{b}9, cf. 56^{b}20, 34, 57^{b}3, 65^{b}17; three forms of f. between equals (58^{b}1-11), 55^{b}17-56^{a}10; what it is 55^{b}27-56^{a}5; f. of utility and pleasure 56^{a}10-^{b}6; of goodness 56^{b}7-32; the latter perfect, the former friendships only by re-

semblance to it ib. 7-24, 33-57
^{b} 5, cf. 57^b 28-59^a 36 ; activity
of f. shown in living together
57^b 5-24, cf. 65^b 30, 71^b 32 ; f.
between unequals 58^b 11-28 ;
it has three corresponding
forms 62^a 34 ; relation between
f. and equality 58^b 29-59^b 23 ;
f. like justice holds together all
communities, especially the
political 59^b 25-60^a 30 ; political
f. differs with the form of
government 60^a 31-61^b 10 ;
analogy between f. in the state
and in the household 60^b 22-
61^b 10 ; f. of kinship, of companionship, of association 61^b
11-16 ; forms of f. of kinsmen
ib. 16-62^b 33 ; f. of companions
61^b 12, 35, 62^a 10, 32, cf. 57^b
22-24, 61^a 25, 71^b 14 ; of fellow
citizens, clansmen, voyagers,
soldiers 61^b 13, cf. 59^b 26, 61^a
10, 63^b 34, 67^b 2, 71^a 17 ;
between men and gods 62^a 5 ;
sources of disagreement in f.
between equals 62^a 34-63^a 23 ;
between unequals 63^a 24-^{b} 27 ;
between dissimilars 63^b 32-
64^b 21 ; species of f. of utility—
legal and moral 62^b 21-63^a 23 ;
the claims of different classes
of friend 64^b 22-65^a-35 ; when
f. should be broken off 65^a 36-
^{b} 36 ; f. and self-love 66^a 1-
^{b} 29, cf. 68^a 28-69^b 2 ; one's
friend another self 66^a 31, cf.
69^b 6, 70^b 6 ; f. and goodwill
66^b 30-67^a 21, cf. 55^b 32-56^a 5,
58^a 7 ; f. and unanimity 67^a 22-
^{b} 16, cf. 55^a 24 ; why benefactors
love beneficiaries more than
vice versa 67^b 17-68^a 27 ; the
happy man needs friends 69^b 3-
70^b 19 ; f. the greatest of external goods 69^b 10 ; how many
friends one should have 70^b 20-
71^a 20 ; whether one needs
friends more in prosperity or in
adversity 71^a 21-^{b} 28, cf. 69^b 3-
16 ; for friends it is most
desirable to live together 71^b
29-72^a 14, cf. 56^a 27, ^{b} 4, 57^b 5-
24, 58^a 23 ; every man dear to
every man 55^a 21 ; natural f.
63^b 24 ; childish f. 65^b 26.

Function. v. *Work*.

Gain, opp. loss 32^b 18 ; and
honour 63^b 3.

Geometer 98^a 29, 42^a 12, 75^a 32.

Geometry 43^a 3.

Glaucus 36^b 10.

God 96^a 24, 1^b 30, 45^a 26, 59^a 5,
66^a 22, 78^b 21 ; gods 1^b 19, 23,
22^b 20, 23^a 10, ^{b} 18, 34^b 28, 37^a
28, 45^a 23, 58^b 35, 59^a 7, 60^a 24,
62^a 5, 64^b 5, 78^b 8-26, 79^a 25,
30 ; gift of the gods 99^b 11 ;
G. enjoys one simple pleasure
54^b 26.

Good, has as many senses as
being 96^a 23 ; dist. pleasant,
useful 55^b 19, 73^b 33 ; Idea of
95^a 27, 96^a 11-97^a 13 ; the g.
95^b 14, 25, 98^a 20, 1^b 30, 72^a 28,
^{b} 9, 25, 31, 33, 73^a 29, 74^a 9, cf.
97^b 27 ; the g., def. 94^a 3, 97^a
18, 72^b 14 ; column of goods 96
^{b} 6 ; chief g. 94^a 22, 97^a 28,
^{b} 22, 98^b 32, 52^b 12-26, 53^b 7-
26 ; final g., &c. 97^b 8, 14^b 7,
44^b 7 ; human g., goods 94^b 7,
98^a 16, 2^a 14, 40^b 21, 41^b 8 ;
g., goods achievable by action
97^a 23, 41^b 12, 95^a 16, 97^a 1, cf.
96^b 34 ; goods in themselves
and things useful 96^b 14 ; g.
absolutely, relatively 52^b 26, cf.
97^a 1, 29^b 3, 55^b 21, 56^a 14, ^{b} 13 ;
goods external, of soul, of body
98^b 13, cf. 53^b 17 ; external
goods 23^b 20, 29^b 2, 69^b 10 ;
bodily goods 54^b 15 ; apparent
g. 13^a 16, 14^a 32, 55^b 26 ; goods
that are objects of competition
69^a 21, cf. 68^b 19 ; g. divided
into activity and state 52^b 33 ;
another's g. 30^a 3, 34^b 5 ;
natural g. 73^a 4.

Good temper, good-tempered 3^a
8, ^{b} 19, 8^a 6, 9^b 17, 25^b 26-26^a 2,
26^a 29, ^{b} 1, 29^b 22.

Goodwill 55^b 33, 66^b 30-67^a 21.

Graces 33^a 3.

Gymnastics, exercise, &c. 96^a 34,
4^a 15, 6^b 4, 12^b 5, 17^b 2, 38^a 31,
43^b 27, 80^b 3.

Habit 95^b 4, 3^a 17, 26, 48^b 17-34,
54^a 33, 80^a 8 (cf. 79^b 25), ^{b} 5,
81^b 22 ; opp. nature, teaching
79^b 21 ; easier to change than
nature 52^a 30.

Habituation 98ᵇ 4, 99ᵇ 9, 19ᵃ 27, 51ᵃ 19, 52ᵃ 29.

Happiness 95ᵃ 18–2ᵃ 17, 44ᵃ 5, 52ᵇ 6, 76ᵃ 31–79ᵃ 32 ; def. of 95ᵃ 20–99ᵇ 8, cf. 53ᵇ 9–25, 69ᵇ 28, 77ᵃ 12–79ᵃ 32 ; how acquired 99ᵇ 10–0ᵃ 9 ; should no man be called happy while he lives? 0ᵃ 10–1ᵃ 21 ; can h. be affected after death ? 0ᵃ 27, 1ᵃ 22–ᵇ 9 ; not praised but prized 1ᵇ 10–2ᵃ 4 ; human h. 2ᵃ 15 ; h. and its components 29ᵇ 18 ; the happy man needs friends 69ᵇ 3–70ᵇ 19 ; h. not a feeling 73ᵃ 15 ; not to be found in amusement 76ᵇ 9–77ᵃ 10 ; but in intellectual activity 77ᵃ 10–78ᵃ 8, cf. 78ᵇ 3–32 ; and secondarily in moral activity 78ᵃ 9–ᵇ 3 ; must be moderately supplied with external goods 78ᵇ 33–79ᵃ 22 ; the wise man happiest because dearest to God 79ᵃ 22–32 ; no slave can be happy 77ᵃ 8 ; nor any lower animal 78ᵇ 27 ; perfect h. 77ᵃ 17, ᵇ 24, 78ᵇ 7.

Hector 16ᵃ 22, 33, 45ᵃ 20.

Helen 9ᵇ 9.

Heraclitus 5ᵃ 8, 46ᵇ 30, 55ᵇ 4, 76ᵃ 6.

Hermes, temple of, 16ᵇ 19.

Heroic virtue 45ᵃ 20.

Hesiod 95ᵇ 9 ; cited or alluded to 32ᵇ 27, 53ᵇ 27, 55ᵃ 35, 64ᵃ 27.

Homer 13ᵃ 8, 16ᵃ 21, ᵇ 27, 18ᵇ 11, 36ᵇ 9, 41ᵃ 14, 45ᵃ 20, 49ᵇ 17, 60ᵇ 26, 61ᵃ 14 ; cited or alluded to 9ᵃ 31, ᵇ 9, 16ᵃ 33, ᵇ 36, 18ᵃ 22, 22ᵃ 27, 24ᵇ 15, 55ᵃ 15, 34, 80ᵃ 28.

Honour (τιμή) 95ᵃ 23, ᵇ 23, 27, 96ᵇ 23, 97ᵇ 2, 7ᵇ 22–27, 16ᵃ 28, 23ᵇ 20–24ᵃ 26, 24ᵇ 25, 25ᵇ 7–21, 27ᵇ 12, 30ᵇ 2, 31, 34ᵇ 7, 47ᵇ 30, 48ᵃ 26, 30, 59ᵃ 18–22, 63ᵇ 3–16, 64ᵇ 4, 65ᵃ 24, 27, 68ᵇ 16 ; greatest of external goods 23ᵇ 20 ; incontinent with respect to 45ᵇ 20, 47ᵇ 34, 48ᵇ 14.

Honour (τὸ καλόν), the end of virtue 15ᵇ 12 (cf. 22ᵇ 6), 68ᵃ 33. Cf. *Noble*.

House, household 97ᵃ 20, 33ᵃ 7, 23, ᵇ 23–27, 52ᵇ 15, 60ᵇ 24, 75ᵃ 25 ; dist. city 80ᵇ 4 ; earlier than city 62ᵃ 18 ; household management, economics 94ᵃ 9, ᵇ 3, 40ᵇ 10, 41ᵇ 32, 42ᵃ 9 ; household justice 34ᵇ 17, 38ᵇ 8.

Humble, humility, 7ᵇ 23, 23ᵇ 10, 24, 25ᵃ 17, 19, 33.

Hypothesis 51ᵃ 17.

Ideas (Platonic) 96ᵃ 13–97ᵃ 13.

Ignorance 45ᵇ 29, 47ᵇ 6 ; acts done owing to 10ᵃ 1, ᵇ 18–11ᵃ 21, 13ᵇ 24, 36ᵃ 7, 44ᵃ 16, 45ᵇ 27 ; acts done in 10ᵇ 25, 35ᵃ 24, 36ᵃ 6 ; i. of the universal 10ᵇ 32 ; of the end 14ᵇ 4.

Immortality 11ᵇ 23, 77ᵇ 33.

Impetuosity 50ᵇ 19, cf. 26.

Incontinence, incontinent 95ᵃ 9, 2ᵇ 14, 21, 11ᵇ 13, 19ᵇ 31, 36ᵃ 32, ᵇ 2, 6, 42ᵇ 18, 45ᵃ 16–52ᵃ 36, 66ᵇ 8, 68ᵇ 34 ; opinions about it 45ᵇ 8–20 ; problems about it ib. 21–46ᵇ 5 ; in what sense compatible with knowledge 46ᵇ 8–47ᵇ 19 ; who is incontinent without qualification ? 47ᵇ 19–49ᵃ 20, cf. 46ᵇ 3, 19 ; incontinent in respect of anger, honour, gain 47ᵇ 33, 48ᵃ 11, ᵇ 13, cf. 45ᵇ 19, 49ᵃ 25 ; i. in anger less disgraceful than in appetite 49ᵃ 24–ᵇ 26 ; i. and brutishness 49ᵇ 27–50ᵃ 8 ; i. and softness 50ᵃ 9–ᵇ 28 ; i. and self-indulgence 50ᵇ 29–51ᵃ 28, cf. 2ᵇ 26–28, 45ᵃ 17, 33–ᵇ 2, 52ᵃ 4–6 ; what sort of choice the incontinent man abandons 51ᵃ 29–ᵇ 22 ; continence intermediate between i. and insensibility 51ᵇ 23–32 ; incompatible with practical wisdom 52ᵃ 6–15 ; the incontinent man, half-wicked ib. 15–24 ; i. is below the average of human nature ib. 25–27 ; which form of i. is the more incurable ib. 27–33, cf. 50ᵇ 19, 52ᵃ 18.

Indignation, righteous 8ᵃ 35, ᵇ 3.

Induction 98ᵇ 3, 39ᵇ 27–31.

Inirascible, inirascibility 8ᵃ 8, 26ᵃ 3.

Injustice, unjust 14ᵃ 5, 13, 29ᵃ 3–30ᵇ 19, 34ᵃ 32, 50ᵃ 6, 51ᵃ 10, 52ᵃ 17 ; meanings of 29ᵃ 3 ; u. acts and u. character 34ᵃ 17–23, 32, 35ᵃ 8–36ᵃ 9, cf. 38ᵃ 24 ; can one willingly be treated unjustly? 36ᵃ 10–ᵇ 13 ; can one treat oneself unjustly ? 36ᵇ 15–25, cf. 34ᵇ 12, 36ᵇ 1, 38ᵃ 4–28, ᵇ 5–13 ; is it the distributor or the receiver that is u. ? 36ᵇ 25–37ᵃ 4, cf. 36ᵇ 15 ; acting unjustly worse than being unjustly treated 38ᵃ 28–ᵇ 5, cf. 34ᵃ 12.

Insensibility, insensible 4ᵃ 24, 7ᵇ 8, 8ᵇ 21, 9ᵃ 4, 19ᵃ 7.

Intellectual virtue 3ᵃ 5, 14, 15, 38ᵇ 18–45ᵃ 11 ; the practical and i. 39ᵃ 29 ; i. faculties 39ᵇ 12 ; the i. element is the man himself 66ᵃ 17.

Involuntary 13ᵇ 15, 32ᵇ 31, 35ᵃ 17, 33, ᵇ 2, 36ᵃ 16–21 ; i. actions due to compulsion 9ᵇ 35–10ᵇ 17 ; or to ignorance 10ᵇ 18–11ᵃ 21 ; actions due to anger or appetite not i. 11ᵃ 24–ᵇ 3 ; i. transactions 31ᵃ 3, ᵇ 26 ; some i. acts excusable 36ᵃ 5.

Irascible, irascibility 3ᵇ 19, 8ᵃ 7, 25ᵇ 29, 26ᵃ 13, 19.

Irrational element in soul 2ᵃ 28, ᵇ 13, 29, 38ᵇ 9, 39ᵃ 4, 68ᵇ 20 ; passions 11ᵇ 1 ; creatures ib. 13 ; parts 17ᵇ 24, 72ᵇ 10.

Isocrates alluded to 81ᵃ 14.

Judge 32ᵃ 7–32.

Judgement 43ᵃ 23–ᵇ 9; def. 43ᵃ 19.

Just, justice 3ᵇ 1, 15, 5ᵃ 18–ᵇ 10, 8ᵇ 7, 20ᵃ 20, 27ᵃ 34, 29ᵃ 3–38ᵇ 14, 44ᵇ 5, 61ᵃ 11–ᵇ 10, 68ᵇ 35, 73ᵃ 18, ᵇ 30, 77ᵃ 29, 78ᵃ 10, 30 ; senses of 29ᵃ 3–31, cf. 30ᵇ 6 ; universal justice 29ᵃ 32–30ᵃ 13, cf. ᵇ 8, 19 ; particular j. 30ᵃ 14–ᵇ 5 ; its kinds 30ᵇ 30 ; distributive 31ᵃ 10–ᵇ 24 ; rectificatory 31ᵇ 25–32ᵇ 20 ; reciprocity 32ᵇ 21–33ᵇ 28 ; j., what sort of mean 33ᵇ 30–34ᵃ 13 ; political j. 34ᵃ 25–35ᵃ 8 ; natural and legal 34ᵇ 18, cf. 36ᵇ 32, 37ᵇ 12 (= natural and human 35ᵃ 3 ; = unwritten and legal 62ᵇ 21) ; household j. 34ᵇ 8–18, cf. 38ᵇ 7 ; not easy to be just 37ᵃ 5–26 ; justice and equity 37ᵃ 31–38ᵃ 3 ; doing just acts, dist. being just 44ᵃ 13 ; j. and friendship 55ᵃ 22–28, 58ᵇ 29, 59ᵇ 25–60ᵃ 8, 61ᵇ 6, 62ᵇ 21 ; the truest j. a friendly quality 55ᵃ 28 ; j. another's good 30ᵃ 3,

34ᵇ 5 ; just actions 33ᵇ 30, 35ᵃ 9, 12, 20.

King 13ᵃ 8, 50ᵇ 14, 59ᵃ 1, 60ᵇ 3–11, 61ᵃ 11–19, 80ᵃ 20.

Knowledge, scientific knowledge, science 39ᵇ 16–36, 41ᵇ 3 ; conj. art 94ᵃ 27 (cf. 18), 97ᵃ 4 ; dist. art 12ᵇ 7 ; conj. capacity, faculty 94ᵃ 26, 29ᵃ 13, 80ᵇ 32 ; dist. art, practical wisdom, philosophic wisdom, intuitive reason 39ᵇ 16 ; dist. practical wisdom 40ᵇ 2, 42ᵃ 24 ; dist. intuitive reason 40ᵇ 31 ; combined with intuitive reason, = philosophic wisdom 41ᵃ 19 ; dist. perception 42ᵃ 27 ; dist. excellence in deliberation 42ᵃ 34, ᵇ 9 ; dist. understanding 43ᵃ 1 ; dist. opinion, true opinion 45ᵇ 36, 46ᵇ 24 ; exact sciences 12ᵇ 1 ; wisdom the most finished form of knowledge 41ᵃ 16 ; the particular sciences 43ᵃ 3 ; proper, dist. perceptual knowledge 47ᵇ 15 ; bad kinds of k. 53ᵇ 8 ; one s. of things answering to one idea 96ᵃ 30 ; one s. of contraries 29ᵃ 13 ; Socrates thought courage was k. 16ᵇ 5, cf. 44ᵇ 29 ; object of scientific knowledge 39ᵇ 23, 25, 40ᵇ 34 ; no correctness nor error of k. 42ᵇ 10 ; having, dist. using knowledge 46ᵇ 32, cf. 43ᵃ 11 ; acting against k. 47ᵃ 2, cf. 45ᵇ 23–46ᵃ 4 ; the sciences concerned with the universal 80ᵇ 15, 23.

Law 29ᵇ 19, 30ᵇ 24, 32ᵃ 5, ᵇ 16, 34ᵃ 30, 31, ᵇ 14, 37ᵇ 13–38ᵃ 11, 80ᵃ 24 ; laws 2ᵃ 10, 13ᵇ 34, 16ᵃ 19, 29ᵇ 14, 37ᵃ 11, 44ᵃ 15, 52ᵇ 21, 42, 64ᵇ 13, 79ᵇ 32, 34, 80ᵃ 3, 34, ᵇ 25, 81ᵃ 17, 23, ᵇ 7, 22 ; a l. to oneself 28ᵃ 32 ; contrary to l. 30ᵃ 24 ; by l., opp. by nature 33ᵃ 30, cf. 94ᵇ 16 ; l. universal and therefore defective 37ᵇ 13, 24 ; opp. decree 37ᵇ 27–29 ; to share in l. or agreement 61ᵇ 7 ; l. a rule proceeding from practical wisdom and reason 80ᵃ 21.

Lawgiver, legislator 2ᵃ 11, 3ᵇ 3, 13ᵇ 23, 28ᵃ 30, 37ᵇ 18–23, 55ᵃ

23, 60^a 13, 80^a 25, 33, ^{b} 24, 29, 81^b 1.

Legislation, legislative 29^b 13, 41^b 25, 32, 81^b 13.

Leisure 77^b 4.

Lesbian moulding 37^b 30.

Liberal, liberality, generosity 99^a 19, 3^a 6, 7^b 9, 18, 21, 8^b 22, 32, 15^a 20, 19^b 22–22^a 17, 25^b 3, 51^b 7, 58^a 21 ; liberality, dist. magnificence 22^a 20–^{b} 18.

Life 98^a 1, 13, 0^b 33, 70^a 23, 29 ; in sense of activity 98^a 6 ; by nature good 70^b 2 ; l. an activity 75^a 12.

Loan 31^a 3, 64^b 32, 67^b 21, 30.

Loss, opp. gain 32^a 12, ^{b} 12, 18.

Love (ἔρως) 16^a 13, 58^a 11, 71^a 11, ^{b} 31.

Love (φιλία, φίλησις). v. *Friendly feeling.*

Lover, opp. beloved 57^a 6, 8, 59^b 15, 17, 64^a 3.

Magnificence, magnificent 7^b 17, 22^a 18–23^a 19, 25^b 3.

Making, dist. acting 40^a 2, ^{b} 4, 6 ; state of capacity to make 40^a 4–22. Cf. *Production, Productive.*

Man, born for citizenship 97^b 11, cf. 69^b 18 ; and for marriage 62^a 17 ; function of 97^b 25 ; m. a moving principle of actions 12^b 31, 13^b 16 ; other things more divine 41^a 34.

Margites 41^a 14.

Mathematical property 2^b 33 ; m. investigations 12^b 22.

Mathematician 94^b 26, 31^b 13, 42^a 12, 17.

Mathematics 51^a 17.

Mean, the 4^a 24, 6^a 26–8^b 13, 33^b 32.

Mean, meanness 7^b 10, 13, 8^b 22, 19^b 27, 28, 21^a 11–20, ^{b} 13–17, 22^a 5–14, 30^a 19.

Medicine, art of 94^a 8, 96^a 33, 97^a 17, 19, 2^a 21, 4^a 9, 12^b 4, 38^a 31, ^{b} 31, 41^a 32, 43^a 3, ^{b} 27, 33, 44^a 4, 45^a 8, 80^b 8, 27.

Megara 23^a 24.

Merope 11^a 12.

Method of ethics 94^b 11–95^a 11, 95^a 28–^{b} 13, 98^a 20–^{b} 12, 3^b 34–4^a 5, 45^b 2–7, 46^b 6–8, 65^a 12–14, 72^b 36–73^a 2, 79^a 33–81^b 23.

Milesians 51^a 9.

Milo 6^b 3.

Misadventure 1^a 10, 28 ; def. 35^b 17.

Mistake 35^b 18 ; def., ib. 12.

Mock-modest, mock-modesty, irony, understatement 8^a 22, 24^b 30, 27^a 22, ^{b} 22, 30.

Monarchy 60^a 32–^{b} 10, ^{b} 24, 27.

Money 9^a 27, 19^b 26, 27^b 13, 33^a 20–31, ^{b} 11–28, 37^a 4, 64^a 1, 28, 32, 78^b 15.

Money-making 96^a 5, 53^a 18, 63^b 8.

Moral state 39^a 34, 45^a 16 ; m. part, opp. part which forms opinions 44^b 15 ; m. virtue and vice 52^b 5 ; m. friendship 62^b 23, 31.

Mother 48^b 26, 59^a 28, 61^b 27, 65^a 25, 66^a 5, 9.

Music 80^b 2, 81^a 19.

Musician 5^a 21, 70^a 10, 77^b 30, 31, 75^a 13.

Natural amount 18^b 18 ; n. justice 34^b 18 : n. virtue 44^b 3, 51^a 18 ; n. friendship 63^b 24 ; process to a n. state 52^b 13.

Nature 3^a 19–25, 14^b 14, 16, 40^a 15 ; dist. art 99^b 21, 6^b 15 ; dist. necessity, chance, reason 12^a 25, 32 ; opp. habit 48^b 30, 52^a 30, 79^b 30, cf. 3^a 20 ; by n., opp. by convention, law, enactment 94^b 16, 33^a 30, 35^a 10 ; opp. incidentally 54^b 17 ; opp. by habit, teaching 79^b 23 ; prior in n. 96^a 21 ; that which is by n. is unchangeable 34^b 25 ; n. a cause 43^b 9, 48^b 31, cf. 14^a 24, 26 ; n., conj. state 52^b 36, 53^b 29, cf. 52^b 27 ; n. in settled state, opp. being replenished 53^b 2.

Necessity, opp. nature, chance, reason 12^a 32 ; opp. argument 80^a 4.

Neoptolemus 46^a 19, 51^b 18.

Niggardliness, niggardly 7^b 20, 22^a 30, ^{b} 8, 23^a 27.

Niobe 48^a 33.

Nobility, intrinsic 36^b 22.

Noble, dist. advantageous, pleasant 4^b 32. Cf. *Honour* (τὸ καλόν).

Nutrition, life of 98^a 1.

Nutritive faculty 2^a 33, ^{b} 11, 44^a 10.

Obsequious 8ᵃ 28, 26ᵇ 12, 27ᵃ 8, 71ᵃ 17, 18.

Odysseus 46ᵃ 21, 51ᵇ 20.

Oligarchy 31ᵃ 28, 60ᵇ 12, 35, 61ᵃ 3.

Olympic games 99ᵃ 3, 47ᵇ 35.

Opinion, dist. choice 11ᵇ 11, 30–12ᵃ 13; dist. excellence in deliberation 42ᵃ 33, ᵇ 9–12; dist. judgement 43ᵃ 2; dist. knowledge 45ᵇ 36, 46ᵇ 24; is about the variable 40ᵇ 27; but also about eternal things 11ᵇ 31; o. not inquiry but assertion 42ᵇ 13; error possible in 39ᵇ 17; its correctness truth 42ᵇ 11; faculty of forming opinions 40ᵇ 26, 44ᵇ 15; o. about a sensible object 47ᵇ 9; opinions of the wise 79ᵃ 17.

Paederasty 48ᵇ 29.

Pain upsets and destroys the nature 19ᵃ 23, cf. 29; freedom from 52ᵇ 16, 53ᵃ 28, 71ᵇ 8, 73ᵇ 16. Cf. *Pleasure*.

Painters 80ᵇ 34.

Painting 18ᵃ 4, 75ᵃ 24, 80ᵃ 3.

Parental friendship 61ᵇ 17.

Parents 97ᵇ 9, 1cᵃ 6, 20ᵇ 14, 48ᵃ 31, 58ᵇ 15–22, 60ᵃ 1, 61ᵃ 21, 61ᵇ 18–62ᵃ 4, 63ᵇ 17, 64ᵇ 5, 65ᵃ 16, 24.

Passion, feeling, emotion (πάθος), dist. faculty, state of character 5ᵇ 20–6ᵃ 12; opp. state of character 28ᵇ 11, 15, cf. 55ᵇ 10; conj. the irrational part of the soul 68ᵇ 20; following one's passions, &c. 95ᵃ 4, 8, 28ᵇ 17, 56ᵃ 32, 79ᵇ 13, 27; means in the passions 8ᵃ 31; the irrational passions 11ᵇ 1; necessary or natural passions 35ᵇ 21; passions neither natural nor human 36ᵃ 8; friendliness implies no passion 26ᵇ 23.

Paternal rule 60ᵇ 26; p. injunctions 80ᵃ 19, ᵇ 5.

Perceptible object 47ᵇ 10, cf. 9ᵇ 22, 74ᵇ 14–34; p. process 52ᵃ 13, 53ᵃ 13.

Perception, sensation, sense 49ᵃ 35, 70ᵇ 10, 74ᵇ 14–29; the senses 3ᵃ 29, 18ᵇ 1, 61ᵇ 26, 75ᵃ 27; conj. induction, habituation 98ᵇ 3; conj. reason, desire 39ᵃ 18,

cf. 70ᵃ 17; = reason 43ᵇ 5; life of 98ᵃ 2; p. decides 9ᵇ 23, 26ᵇ 4; particulars are matters of p. 13ᵃ 1, 47ᵃ 26; qualities peculiar to one sense 42ᵃ 27; living by the senses 49ᵃ 10; power of p. 70ᵃ 16; p. that one perceives 70ᵃ 31, cf. 71ᵇ 34; facts of p. 72ᵃ 36.

Perceptual knowledge 47ᵇ 17.

Pericles 40ᵇ 8.

Persia, Persian 34ᵇ 26, 60ᵇ 27, 31.

Phalaris 48ᵇ 24, 49ᵃ 14.

Phidias 41ᵃ 10.

Philoctetes of Sophocles 46ᵃ 20, 51ᵇ 18; Philoctetes of Theodectes 50ᵇ 9.

Philosophers 96ᵃ 15.

Philosophy 96ᵇ 31, 64ᵇ 3, 77ᵃ 25; of human nature 81ᵇ 15.

Philoxenus alluded to 18ᵃ 32.

Phoenissae 67ᵃ 33.

Pindar alluded to 77ᵇ 32 ?

Pittacus 67ᵃ 32; alluded to 13ᵇ 31.

Pity 5ᵇ 23, 9ᵇ 32, 11ᵃ 1.

Plato 95ᵃ 32, 4ᵇ 12, 72ᵇ 28; alluded to 97ᵃ 27, 98ᵇ 12, 11ᵃ 24, 30ᵃ 3, 33ᵃ 14, 45ᵇ 23 ?, 64ᵃ 24, 73ᵃ 15, 29, ᵇ 9, 12 ?, 80ᵃ 6, 9.

Platonists alluded to 95ᵃ 26, 96ᵃ 17–97ᵃ 14.

Pleasant, conj. noble, advantageous 4ᵇ 32, 5ᵃ 1; conj. good 55ᵇ 21, 56ᵇ 23; by nature, opp. incidentally 54ᵇ 16; the activity of philosophic wisdom the pleasantest 77ᵃ 23.

Pleasantness, opp. truth 8ᵃ 13, 28ᵇ 7.

Pleasure 96ᵇ 18, 24, 1ᵇ 28, 4ᵃ 23, 34, ᵇ 4–5ᵃ 8, 5ᵃ 16, 7ᵇ 4, 8ᵇ 2, 9ᵇ 8, 13ᵃ 34, 17ᵇ 25, 18ᵃ 17, 23, ᵇ 5–27, 19ᵃ 5–24, 52ᵇ 1–54ᵃ 31, 72ᵃ 19–76ᵃ 29; bodily pleasures 4ᵇ 6, 49ᵇ 26, 51ᵇ 35, 52ᵃ 5, 53ᵇ 34–54ᵇ 15; opp. pleasures of soul 17ᵇ 28; pleasures of touch and taste 50ᵃ 9; necessary and unnecessary pleasures, ib. 16; noble pleasures 48ᵃ 22, cf. 51ᵇ 19; painless p. 52ᵇ 36, 73ᵇ 16; pure and liberal, opp. bodily pleasures 76ᵇ 20; pleasures of social life 26ᵇ 30, cf. 28ᵇ 8; the virtuous life has its p. in itself 99ᵃ 7–31, cf. 77ᵃ 22–27; pleasures are peculiar to individuals 18ᵇ

21; to pursue the present p. 46ᵇ 23; the causes of p. 47ᵇ 24; opinions about p. 52ᵇ 8-24; it does not follow that p. is not good or the chief good ib. 25-53ᵃ 35; p. a good 53ᵇ 1-54ᵃ 7; but excess of bodily p. blameworthy 54ᵃ 8-21; why bodily p. is thought preferable ib. 22-ᵇ 31; love based on p. 56ᵃ 12-ᵇ 6, 57ᵃ 1; why p. should be discussed 72ᵃ 19-27; opinions about it ib. 27-74ᵃ 12; Eudoxus 72ᵇ 9-28; Plato ib. 28-35; opponents of p. refuted ib. 35-73ᵇ 31; Eudoxus refuted 73ᵇ 31-74ᵃ 9; what is pleasure? 74ᵃ 13-76ᵃ 29; not a movement or coming into being 74ᵃ 13-ᵇ 14; but what completes activity as a supervenient end 74ᵇ 14-75ᵃ 3; why no one is continuously pleased 75ᵃ 3-10; all men desire p. ib. 10-21 (and all animals too 4ᵇ 34, cf. 57ᵇ 16, 72ᵃ 15, ᵇ 10, 73ᵃ 2); different kinds of p. ib. 21-ᵇ 24, cf. 73ᵇ 13-31, 74ᵃ 1; as of activity 75ᵇ 24-76ᵃ 3; p. neither thought nor perception 75ᵇ 34; each animal has its proper p. 76ᵃ 3-9; man has those which perfect the activity of the perfect man ib. 10-29.

Poets 20ᵇ 14, 68ᵃ 1.

Political science, politics 94ᵃ 27, ᵇ 11, 15, 95ᵃ 2, 16, ᵇ 5, 99ᵇ 29, 2ᵃ 12, 21, 5ᵃ 12, 30ᵇ 28, 41ᵃ 20, 29, ᵇ 23-32, 45ᵃ 10, 77ᵇ 15, 80ᵇ 31, 35, 81ᵃ 11; student of politics, &c. 2ᵃ 18, 23, 12ᵇ 14, 42ᵃ 2, 52ᵇ 1, 77ᵇ 12, 78ᵃ 27, 80ᵇ 30; the true student of politics 2ᵃ 8; works of the political art 81ᵃ 23; p. life 95ᵇ 18; p. power 99ᵇ 1; p. society 29ᵇ 19, 60ᵃ 11, 21-29; p. justice 34ᵃ 26, 29, ᵇ 13-18; p. friendship 61ᵃ 10-ᵇ 10, ᵇ 13, 63ᵇ 34, 67ᵇ 2, 71ᵃ 17; man a p. creature 69ᵇ 18, cf. 97ᵇ 11, 62ᵃ 18; p. actions 77ᵇ 10.

Polity 60ᵃ 34.

Polyclitus 41ᵃ 11.

Poverty 15ᵃ 10, 17, 16ᵃ 13, 55ᵃ 11.

Practical intellect 39ᵃ 27, 36; the p. and intellectual part ib. 29;

p. virtues 77ᵇ 6; intuitive reason involved in practical reasonings 43ᵇ 2.

Praise 1ᵇ 19, 9ᵇ 31, 10ᵃ 23, 33, 20ᵃ 16, 27ᵇ 18, 78ᵇ 16.

Priam 0ᵃ 8, 1ᵃ 8, 45ᵃ 21.

Pride, proud (μεγαλοψυχία, μεγαλόψυχος) 7ᵇ 22, 26, 23ᵃ 34-25ᵃ 16, 25ᵃ 33, 34, ᵇ 3.

Principles, first, arguments from and to 95ᵃ 31; the fact the first principle 98ᵇ 2, cf. 42ᵃ 19; first p. of inference not themselves inferred 39ᵇ 30, cf. 40ᵇ 34, 51ᵃ 15; grasped by intuitive reason 41ᵃ 8; the wise man must know p. as well as conclusions ib. 17.

Prodigal, prodigality 7ᵇ 10, 12, 8ᵇ 22, 32, 19ᵇ 27-20ᵃ 3, 20ᵇ 25, 21ᵃ 8-ᵇ 10, 22ᵃ 15, 51ᵇ 7.

Production, opinions concerned with 47ᵃ 28. Cf. *Making*.

Productive intellect 39ᵃ 28, ᵇ 1. Cf. *Making*.

Proportion 31ᵇ 11-32, 34ᵃ 8, 12, 36ᵃ 3; def. 31ᵃ 31; arithmetical 6ᵃ 36, 32ᵃ 2, 30; geometrical 31ᵇ 12; discrete, dist. continuous 31ᵃ 32, ᵇ 15; proportionate return 33ᵃ 6; proportional equality ib. 10, 34ᵃ 5, 27; bring into figure of proportion 33ᵇ 1.

Prosperity. v. *Fortune*.

Protagoras 64ᵃ 24.

Proverbs 29ᵇ 29, 46ᵃ 34, 54ᵇ 26, 59ᵇ 31, 68ᵇ 6.

Punishment 4ᵇ 16, 9ᵇ 35, 26ᵃ 28, 80ᵃ 9.

Pythagoreans 96ᵇ 5, 6ᵇ 30, 32ᵇ 22.

Rash, rashness 4ᵃ 22, 7ᵇ 3, 8ᵇ 19-9ᵃ 9, 15ᵇ 29-16ᵃ 7, 51ᵇ 7.

Ratiocinative desire 39ᵇ 5.

Rational principle, r. ground, reasoning, argument, rule, rule of life (λόγος) 98ᵃ 14, 2ᵇ 14-3ᵃ 2, 7ᵃ 1, 12ᵃ 16, 17ᵃ 21, 19ᵇ 11-18, 34ᵃ 35, 39ᵃ 24, 40ᵃ 10-ᵇ 33, 42ᵃ 26, ᵇ 3, 12, 43ᵇ 1, 44ᵇ 30, 45ᵇ 14, 49ᵃ 26, 32, ᵇ 1, 3, 50ᵇ 28, 51ᵃ 1, 17, 29-34, ᵇ 10, 26, 52ᵃ 13, 69ᵃ 1, 80ᵃ 12, 21; according to a rational principle, &c. 95ᵃ 10, 98ᵃ 7, 19ᵇ 15, 69ᵃ 5; to have a r.p., &c. 98ᵃ 3, 2ᵃ 28, 3ᵃ 2, 38ᵇ 9, 22,

39ᵃ 4-15 ; obedient to r.p., opp. possessing it and thinking 98ᵃ 5, cf. 2ᵇ 31 ; to share in a r.p. 2ᵇ 14, 25, 30 ; opposed to the r.p., &c. 2ᵇ 17, 24, 48ᵃ 29, 51ᵇ 35, 52ᵃ 3 ; as the rule directs 15ᵇ 12, 19, 17ᵃ 8, 25ᵇ 35 ; right rule 3ᵇ 33, 38ᵇ 34, 44ᵇ 27, 47ᵇ 3 ; according to the r.r. 3ᵇ 32, 38ᵇ 25, 44ᵇ 23, 26, 51ᵃ 22 ; as the r.r. prescribes 14ᵇ 29, 19ᵃ 20, 38ᵇ 20, 29 ; contrary to the r.r. 38ᵃ 10, 47ᵇ 31, 51ᵃ 12, 21 ; r.r. = practical wisdom 44ᵇ 28 ; reasoning with a view to an end 39ᵃ 32 ; true, false course of reasoning 40ᵃ 10, 22 ; Socrates thought the virtues were rules 44ᵇ 29 ; to be incontinent under the influence of a rule 47ᵇ 1 ; the activity concerned with argument 75ᵇ 6, cf. 4.

Ready wit, ready-witted 8ᵃ 24, 27ᵇ 33-28ᵃ 33, 56ᵃ 13, 57ᵃ 6, 58ᵃ 31, 76ᵇ 14.

Reason, intuitive reason 96ᵃ 25, ᵇ29, 97ᵇ 2, 12ᵃ 33, 39ᵃ 18, 33, ᵇ 17 41ᵃ 19, ᵇ 3, 76ᵃ 18 ; = faculty for knowing first principles 40ᵇ 31-41ᵃ 8, 42ᵃ 25, 26 ; concerned with first and last terms 43ᵃ 35-ᵇ 7 ; dist. argument 43ᵇ 1, 5 ; desiderative r. 39ᵇ 4 ; r. involved in practical reasonings 43ᵇ 2 ; practical r. 44ᵇ 9, 12, 50ᵃ 5, 68ᵇ 35, 69ᵃ 17, 18, 80ᵃ 22 ; = contemplative r. 77ᵃ 13, 20, ᵇ 19, 30, 78ᵃ 22, 79ᵃ 27 ; years of r. 43ᵃ 27, cf. ᵇ 9 ; to acquire r. 44ᵇ 12 ; r. is the man himself 69ᵃ 2, 78ᵃ 4, cf. 7 ; life according to r. 77ᵇ 30, 78ᵃ 7, 80ᵃ 18 ; to be active with one's r. 79ᵃ 23.

Reciprocity 32ᵇ 21-33ᵇ 6.

Rectificatory justice (διορθωτικόν) 31ᵃ 1, ᵇ 25, 32ᵇ 24. Cf. *Corrective.*

Repentance 10ᵇ 19, 22, 11ᵃ 20, 50ᵃ 21, ᵇ 30, 66ᵃ 29, ᵇ 24.

Replenishment 18ᵇ 18, 73ᵇ 8-20.

Rhadamanthus 32ᵇ 25.

Sardanapallus 95ᵇ 22.

Satyrus 48ᵃ 34.

Science, scientific knowledge. v. *Knowledge.*

Sculptor 97ᵇ 25, 41ᵃ 10.

Scythians 12ᵃ 28, 50ᵇ 14.

Self-consciousness 70ᵃ 31, 71ᵇ 34.

Self-indulgence, 7ᵇ 6, 9ᵃ 4, 16, 14ᵃ 28, 17ᵇ 27, 18ᵃ 24, ᵇ 1, 28, 19ᵃ 21, 30ᵃ 30, 47ᵇ 28, 48ᵇ 12, 49ᵃ 5, 22, ᵇ 30, 50ᵃ 10, 51ᵇ 31 ; the name applied to childish faults 19ᵃ 33 ; human s. 49ᵃ 20.

Self-indulgent, 3ᵇ 19, 4ᵃ 23, ᵇ 6, 8ᵇ 21, 14ᵃ 5, 12, 20, 17ᵇ 32-18ᵇ 7, 18ᵇ 24, 19ᵃ 1-33, ᵇ 31, 21ᵇ 8, 30ᵃ 26, 45ᵇ 16, 46ᵇ 20, 48ᵃ 6, 13, 17, 49ᵇ 31, 50ᵃ 21, ᵇ 29, 52ᵃ 4, 53ᵃ 34, 54ᵃ 10, ᵇ 15 ; the lover of amusement thought to be s. 50ᵇ 16.

Self-love 68ᵃ 28-69ᵇ 2.

Self-sufficiency 97ᵇ 7, 8, 14, 34ᵃ 27, 77ᵃ 27, ᵇ 21, 79ᵃ 3.

Senses. v. *Perception.*

Sexual intercourse, &c. 18ᵃ 31, 47ᵃ 15, ᵇ 27, 48ᵃ 29, 49ᵃ 14, 52ᵇ 17, 54ᵃ 18.

Shame 8ᵃ 32, 16ᵃ 28, 31, 28ᵇ 10-33, 79ᵇ 11.

Shameless, shamelessness 4ᵃ 24, 7ᵃ 11, ᵇ 8, 8ᵃ 35, ᵇ 21, 14ᵃ 10, 28ᵇ 31.

Sicyonians 17ᵃ 27.

Simonides 21ᵃ 7 ; cited oᵇ 21.

Slave 45ᵇ 24, 60ᵇ 28, 29, 61ᵃ 35-ᵇ 5, 77ᵃ 7, 8.

Society, community, political 29ᵇ 19, 60ᵃ 9, 28. Cf. *Association.*

Socrates (Σωκράτης) 27ᵇ 25, 44ᵇ 18, 28, 45ᵇ 23, 25, 47ᵇ 15 ; (ὁ Σωκράτης) 16ᵇ 4.

Soft, softness 16ᵃ 14, 45ᵃ 35, ᵇ 9, 47ᵇ 23, 48ᵃ 12, 50ᵃ 14, 31-ᵇ 17.

Solitary life 97ᵇ 9, 99ᵇ 4, 57ᵇ 21, 69ᵇ 16, 70ᵃ 5.

Solon oᵃ 11, 15, 79ᵃ 9.

Sophists 64ᵃ 31, 80ᵇ 35, 81ᵃ 12.

Sophocles 46ᵃ 19, 51ᵇ 18 ; alluded to 77ᵇ 32 ?

Soul, activity of 98ᵃ 7-18, ᵇ 15, 99ᵇ 26, 2ᵃ 5, 17 ; goods of 98ᵇ 14, 19 ; state of 4ᵇ 19, 38ᵇ 32 ; pleasures of 17ᵇ 28 ; part of 38ᵇ 9, 39ᵃ 4, 9, 43ᵇ 16, 44ᵇ 9, 45ᵃ 3 ; eye of 44ᵇ 30, cf. 96ᵇ 29 ; divided into rational and irrational, and the latter into nutritive and desiderative 2ᵃ 23-3ᵃ 3, cf. 98ᵃ 4, 19ᵇ 14, 38ᵇ 8, 39ᵃ 3, 68ᵇ 21 ; rational divided into scientific and calculative 39ᵃ 6-17, cf.

INDEX

43[b] 16, 44[a] 2 ; or opinionative 40[b] 26, 44[b] 14 ; moral (= desiderative) 44[b] 15 ; better part (= scientific) 45[a] 7, 77[a] 4 ; best, authoritative, divine part (= reason) 68[b] 30, 77[a] 13, [b] 30, 78[a] 1 ; a single s. 68[b] 7.

Sparta, Spartan 2[a] 11, 12[a] 29, 17[a] 27, 24[b] 16, 27[b] 28, 45[a] 28, 67[a] 31, 80[a] 25.

Speusippus 96[b] 7, 53[b] 5 ; alluded to 4[b] 24 ?, 72[a] 28.

Spite, spiteful 7[a] 10, 8[b] 1, 5.

State. v. *City*.

State of soul, of character, of mind (ἕξις) 4[b] 19, 14[a] 20, [b] 2, 31, 15[b] 21, 17[a] 20, 23[b] 1, 26[b] 21, 29[a] 14-18, 41[b] 24, 43[b] 26, 47[a] 12, 74[b] 32, 81[b] 10 ; dist. activity 98[b] 33, 3[b] 21, 23, 52[b] 33, 57[b] 6, cf. 14[a] 30-15[a] 3 ; dist. passion, faculty 5[b] 20-6[a] 12 ; dist. feeling 28[b] 11, 57[b] 29, 32 ; conj. process 54[a] 13 ; laudable states 3[a] 9 ; s. concerned with choice 6[b] 36, 39[a] 22 ; s. is determined by its activities and its objects 22[b] 1 ; middle s. 26[b] 5-21, 28[a] 17 ; best s. 39[a] 16 ; moral s. ib. 34 ; s. of capacity to make 40[a] 4-22 ; to act ib. 4, [b] 5, 20 ; reasoned s. of capacity 40[b] 20, 28 ; true s. of capacity ib. 20 ; natural s. 44[b] 8, 52[b] 34, 53[a] 14 ; s. in accordance with practical wisdom 44[b] 25 ; s. of most people 50[a] 15, cf. 52[a] 26.

Statesman. v. *Political*.

Suicide 16[a] 12, 38[a] 6, 10, 66[b] 13.

Syllogism 39[b] 28-30, 42[b] 23, 46[a] 24 ; syllogisms about acts to be done 44[a] 31, cf. 46[b] 35-47[b] 19.

Tact 28[a] 17, 33.

Tastelessness 7[b] 19, 22[a] 31.

Teaching 3[a] 15, 39[b] 26 ; opp. nature, habit 79[b] 21, 23.

Temperance, temperate 2[b] 27, 3[a] 6, 8, [b] 1, 19, 4[a] 19-[b] 6, 5[a] 18-[b] 10, 7[b] 5, 8[b] 20, 9[a] 3, 19, 19[b] 17, 24, 23[b] 5, 25[b] 13, 29[b] 21, 40[b] 11, 45[b] 14, 15, 46[a] 11, 12, 47[b] 28, 48[a] 6, 14, [b] 12, 49[a] 22, [b] 30, 31, 50[a] 11, 23, 51[a] 19, [b] 31, 34, 52[a] 1, [b] 1, 5, 53[b] 27-35, 68[b] 26, 77[a] 31, 78[a] 33, [b] 15 ; discussed 17[b] 23-19[b] 16.

Thales 41[b] 4.

Theatre 75[b] 12.

Theodectes 50[b] 9.

Theognis 70[a] 12, 79[b] 6 ; cited 29[b] 29, 72[a] 13.

Thetis 24[b] 15.

Timocracy 60[a] 36, [b] 17, 18, 61[a] 3, 28.

Trojan cycle 0[a] 8.

Troy 39[b] 7.

Truthful, truthfulness 8[a] 20, 24[b] 30, 27[a] 24-[b] 9, [b] 32.

Tyranny 60[b] 1-12, 28, 61[a] 32, [b] 9.

Unambitious, unambitiousness 7[b] 29-8[a] 1, 25[b] 10, 22.

Unanimity 55[a] 24, 67[a] 22-[b] 16.

Understanding 3[b] 5, 42[b] 34-43[a] 18, 43[a] 26, 34, [b] 7, 61[b] 26, 81[a] 18 ; goodness of 42[b] 34, 43[a] 10.

Universal, ignorance of the 10[b] 32 ; scientific knowledge = judgement about universals 40[b] 31, cf. 80[b] 15, 22 ; u. premiss 47[a] 3 ; u. opinion ib. 25, 32 ; u. term 47[b] 14 ; the u. good 96[a] 11, 28.

Unjust. v. *Injustice*.

Usurers 21[b] 34.

Utility, friendship of 57[a] 2, 59[b] 13, (cf. 56[a] 14), 62[b] 6, 22.

Vain, vanity 7[b] 23, 23[b] 9, 25, 25[a] 18, 27, 33.

Vegetative principle 2[a] 32, [b] 29.

Vices of the body 14[a] 22 ; vice destructive of the originating cause of action 40[b] 19.

Virtue, def. 6[b] 36, cf. 39[a] 22 ; = laudable state 3[a] 9 ; = best state 39[a] 16 ; best and most complete v. 98[a] 17 ; complete, perfect v. 0[a] 4, 2[a] 6, 24[a] 7, 28, 29[b] 26 ; justice = exercise of complete v. 29[b] 31 ; v. entire 30[a] 9, 44[a] 5 ; v. entire, dist. justice 30[a] 13 ; human v., excellence 2[a] 14, [b] 3, 12, 6[a] 22 ; moral v. 4[b] 9, 39[a] 22, 44[a] 7, 52[b] 5 ; v. of character 72[a] 22, [b] 15, 78[a] 16 ; moral virtues 3[a] 5, 78[a] 18 ; virtues of character 39[a] 1 ; practical virtues 77[b] 6 ; virtues of the composite nature 78[a] 20 ; intellectual virtues 3[a] 5, 39[a] 1 ; rational virtues 8[b] 9 ; natural v., dist. strict v. 44[b] 3, 36, cf. 3[a] 23 ; v. either natural or produced by habit 51[a] 18 ; superhuman. v.

45ᵃ 19 ; exercise of the virtues 13ᵇ 5, 77ᵇ 8 ; activities of v. 73ᵃ 14 ; honour the end of v. 15ᵇ 13 ; the friendship based on v. 64ᵇ 1; v. divided into moral and intellectual 2ᵃ 5–3ᵃ 10, cf. 3ᵃ 14, 38ᵇ 35 ; how produced 3ᵃ 14–ᵇ 25, cf. 5ᵃ 17–ᵇ 18, 9ᵃ 20–ᵇ 26, 79ᵇ 20, 80ᵇ 25 ; the actions that produce v. like those in which it results 4ᵃ 27–ᵇ 3 ; v. indicated by pleasure accompanying actions 4ᵇ 3–5ᵃ 13, cf. 99ᵃ 17, 72ᵃ 21 ; v. concerned with pleasures and pains 4ᵇ 8, cf. 52ᵇ 4 ; what virtue is 5ᵇ 19–7ᵃ 27 ; list of moral virtues 7ᵃ 28–8ᵇ 10 ; moral virtues described in detail 15ᵃ 4–38ᵇ 14 ; intellectual virtues 38ᵇ 18–45ᵃ 11 ; moral v., how related to practical wisdom 44ᵃ 6–9, 20, ᵇ 14, 78ᵃ 16–19 ; v. and continence 45ᵃ 17, 33–ᵇ 2, 50ᵇ 29–51ᵃ 28, 51ᵇ 32–52ᵃ 6 ; the best v. that of contemplation 77ᵃ 13, 18, 28.

Voluntary and involuntary 9ᵇ 30–11ᵇ 3, 14ᵇ 30, 32ᵇ 3c, 35ᵃ 20–ᵇ 9, 36ᵃ 16–ᵇ 14 ; the v., dist. choice 11ᵇ 7 ; v. actions the occasion of shame 28ᵇ 28 ; v. transactions 31ᵃ 2–5 ; v. exchange 32ᵇ 13 ; v. contracts 64ᵇ 13.

Vulgar, vulgarity 7ᵇ 19, 22ᵃ 31, 23ᵃ 19.

War 96ᵃ 32, 15ᵃ 35, 17ᵇ 14, 60ᵃ 17, 77ᵇ 10.

Weak, weakness 46ᵃ 15, 50ᵇ 19, 76ᵃ 14.

Wealth, riches 94ᵃ 9, ᵇ 19, 95ᵃ 23, 25, 96ᵃ 6, 97ᵃ 27, 99ᵇ 1, 20ᵃ 5, 6, 23ᵃ 7, 25, 24ᵃ 14, 17, 31ᵃ 28, 47ᵇ 30, 61ᵃ 2 ; def. 19ᵇ 26.

Wife 97ᵇ 10, 15ᵃ 22, 34ᵇ 16, 58ᵇ 13, 17, 60ᵇ 33, 61ᵃ 23, 62ᵃ 16–33.

Wisdom, philosophic wisdom (σοφία) 98ᵇ 24, 3ᵃ 5, 39ᵇ 17, 41ᵃ 2–ᵇ 8, 43ᵇ 19, 33–44ᵃ 6, 45ᵃ 7, 77ᵃ 24 ; def. 41ᵃ 19, ᵇ 2.

Wisdom, practical (φρόνησις) 98ᵇ 24, 3ᵃ 6, 39ᵇ 16, 40ᵇ 35, 41ᵃ 5, 7, 21, 42ᵇ 33, 43ᵇ 7–15, 24, 45ᵇ 17, 46ᵃ 4, 52ᵃ 6, 12, ᵇ 15, 53ᵃ 21, 27, 72ᵇ 30, 78ᵃ 16, 19, 80ᵃ 22, ᵇ 28 ; discussed 40ᵃ 24–ᵇ 30, 41ᵇ 8–42ᵃ 30 ; its use, what 43ᵇ 18–45ᵃ 11 ; the virtues said to be forms of p.w. 44ᵇ 18–45ᵃ 2.

Wish 11ᵇ 11–30, 13ᵃ 15–ᵇ 2, 55ᵇ 29, 56ᵇ 31, 78ᵃ 30 ; contrary to wish 36ᵇ 5, 7, 24.

Woman 48ᵇ 32, 60ᵇ 34, 61ᵃ 1, 62ᵃ 23, 71ᵃ 10.

Work, work of art, handiwork, product, function (ἔργον), dist. activity 94ᵃ 5 ; conj. activity 97ᵇ 29, 1ᵇ 16 ; dist. possession 22ᵇ 15–23ᵃ 18 ; w. of man 97ᵇ 24–33, 98ᵃ 7, 13, 6ᵃ 23, cf. 44ᵃ 6 ; of man, of woman 62ᵃ 22 ; of eye 97ᵇ 30, 6ᵃ 18 ; of the shoemaker 33ᵃ 9, cf. 13, 33, ᵇ 5 ; of the intellectual element 39ᵃ 28, cf. ᵇ 12 ; of the practically wise man 41ᵇ 10 ; virtue of a thing, related to its proper work 39ᵃ 17 ; the w. reveals in actuality what a thing is in potentiality 68ᵃ 9 ; product of art 52ᵇ 19, 53ᵃ 23 ; men love their own handiwork 67ᵇ 34.

Xenophantus 50ᵇ 12.

Young, youth 95ᵃ 3, 6, 18ᵇ 11, 28ᵇ 16, 19, 42ᵃ 12, 15, 54ᵇ 10, 11, 55ᵃ 12, 56ᵃ 26–ᵇ 6, 58ᵃ 5, 20, ᵇ 13, 79ᵇ 8, 31, 34, 80ᵇ 1.

Zeus 24ᵇ 16, 60ᵇ 26, 65ᵃ 15.